Extreme
Rifle Accuracy

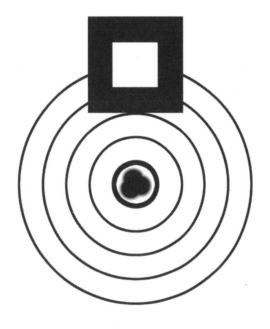

by
Mike Ratigan

Published by:

Indian Creek Publishing

a division of

M & M Engineering
1116 Bel-Mar Circle
Woodward, Oklahoma 73801 USA

Cover Art Design & Photography: Mike Ratigan,

Ratigan photo by Ed Adams
Art and Software Consultant - Margie Barron

Manufactured in the United States of America by;

Central Plains Book Manufacturing

Library of Congress Cataloging-in-Publication Data is available

First Edition

Paper Back	ISBN-13	978-0-9792528-0-8
	ISBN-10	0-9792528-0-6
Hard Back	ISBN-13	978-0-9792528-1-5
	ISBN-10	0-9792528-1-4

Acknowledgements

I would like to thank the following people for their help with this undertaking.

Butch Fjoser, Friend, Inspiration and Editing

Jack Jackson MD,PhD, Primary Editor, Content Editor
Don Powell, Strategy and Content Consultant, Editing
Dr. Tim Oltersdorf, editing
Skip Gordon, History and Content
Margie Barron, Editing, Design and Software Consultant
My Children Lacey and Dani.
Don Powell, Beau Murlin,
Jim Bird, Pat Byrne, Scott Smallwood,
Paul Ferrell, Content Editing
Larry Engelbrecht, Range and Bench Etiquette
Larry Kuse, Glenn Newick
George Kelbly Sr.,
Jim Borden,Skip Otto,
Jackie Schmidt, Lou Murdica,
Walt Berger, Turk Takano
Tony & Faye Boyer,
Tommy Deeze, Bob White
Billy Richards

Kelbly's Inc.

Some photos provided by

Roland Paolucci (Smiley Hensley, and WBC Match Report),
Hobie Bond, Todd Tyler,
Faye Boyer, Glenn Newick, Stan Buchtel,
Stuart and Annie Elliott,
Dan Dowling, Turk Takano, Don Geraci
Don & Carole Powell
Farley's

Forward

Benchrest Shooting has never grown to include as many participants as most of the other shooting sports. Some say this is due to the technical nature of the sport. Others point to the influence benchrest has had on not only the other shooting disciplines but also on general shooting and hunting accuracy. Even the major firearms manufacturer's have mimicked benchrest practices such as glass bedding, barrel fluting, lighter triggers, opposite side bolts and loading ports.

Books devoted to benchrest shooting have been few and far between. Generally every 15 to 20 years someone comes along putting pen to paper and bringing the devotees up to speed, so to speak, with things as they are today in this rapidly evolving sport. The author of this treatise has taken the reader from some basic principles of the sport through many if the nuances and more recent practices such as tuning for competition, wind flag variations and how to properly use the flags and the strategies of benchrest competition. Anyone serious about their bench shooting can gain great insight into ways to improve what they have been doing by reading and putting into practice principles put forth in this work.

To world class BR competitors Mike Ratigan needs no introduction. To the many others who will read this book be aware that the author writes using personal experience and not merely information gleaned from research. I have competed many times with Mike at National Championships, the Firearms Industry Super Shoot and even at the World Championships. We have both shared the pride and position of the gold medal winning team in 1999 and competed for the top two spots individually at the same World Championships. The author knows from whence he writes and wise practitioners of benchrest will extract from this work all that they can use to improve their own competitive skills.

Bob White

IBS Past President (many times over)
Two Time US World Team Member
Owner of 8 Hall of Fame Points

About the Author

Super Shoot Champion, National Champion & World Champion

In 1998 at the NBRSA Nationals a young man was shooting some really small groups in practice. I checked out the groups and was impressed. As I watched this fellow shoot, I could see he had some good bench technique. As a shooter always looking for good bullets, I asked Mike whose bullets he was shooting, he told me they were his own bullets. I asked him if he would sell me two thousand and he just smiled and said he did not sell bullets. This was my first meeting with Mike Ratigan. As the year progressed, I learned Mike and I both qualified for the US World Benchrest Team.

The following year as we prepared for the 5th World Benchrest Championships (WBC5) in Italy, I got to know Mike and we became good friends. He was on a mission to learn everything he could about benchrest. At the World Benchrest Championships in Italy, Mike and I shared a room and it was great to talk benchrest non-stop for two weeks. I tried to learn all I could from a young shooter and tried to pass along all I had learned from Faye Boyer, Tony Boyer and Smiley Hensley, plus information that I had picked up from many other great shooters over the years.

How did Mike do at WBC5? He was also on the Gold Medal winning Team. He won individual Gold Medals in Light Varmint 200, Light Varmint Grand and the 2 Gun. Four Gold Medals at his first World Benchrest Championship. Yet he was still wanting to learn more about shooting benchrest.

Mike has qualified for, and competed in, three World Benchrest Championships and won four Gold Medals in Italy in1999 and at WBC7 a team Bronze in Umea, Sweden in 2003. In 2005 at WBC8 in the USA, Mike was on the Bronze Medal Team, and finished third winning a Bronze medal in the Heavy Varmint 200. At these team shoots Mike is always a team player and a leader. Thanks Mike!

At the National Level, Mike was the Heavy Varmint 200 yard National Champion in 1998. In 2002 he won the Heavy Varmint Grand and 3 Gun National Championship. Mike has five Hall of Fame Points and will get more. He is one of only 26 to have won the big one, The Super Shoot, in 2004. In his local region, Mike is the competition the local shooters know that they have to beat.

Mike is the Vice President for the World Benchrest Shooting Federation, which is the governing body for the World Competition.

Mike Ratigan is a leader, he works hard at everything he does. I have enjoyed this book and am sure you will enjoy and learn from this great book. Benchrest, a sport that leads to great friendships

Don Powell

Super Shoot Champion
Five Time US World Team Member
US Benchrest Hall of Fame Member & friend

Autobiography

I was born and raised in Omaha, NE., now living in a small town in Northwest Oklahoma called Woodward. Before discovering the little known sport of benchrest I spent ten years involved in drag racing. My racing fueled my passion for physics, I spent hours learning about why things are the way they are. The property's of air became a particular interest, and this ultimately had it's place in the shooting sports.

I purchased my first Benchrest rifle in 1992, from Jack Dever of Oklahoma City. While at Jacks to pick up my rifle he rummaged around in the corner of his shop and pulled out this thing on a tripod and said, "you're going to need some of these." "What is that?" I asked,

Jack quickly explained that what it was was a wind flag. After a short pause of about 10 seconds, I nodded in agreement, air has mass and is in motion and would effect a bullet in it's brief flight to the target. I was well aware of the physics of air with my previous background in Top Alcohol class drag racing.

After a couple years shooting my benchrest gear, I began to wonder how my shooting ability compared to others. I attended my first registered tournament in 1994 at a range in central Oklahoma, Okie Shooters, also known as, "Benchrest Hell." (more about this later) I would say that my shooting skill or gun handling is about average. My adopted home state is a great place to learn to shoot in the wind because... we have LOTS of WIND. Within three hours of my home is the range at Okie Shooters, which is referred to by all who have ever shot there as "Benchrest Hell", and is my favorite place to shoot. The only shooters who think there is a tougher place to shoot have never been to Luther, or at the very least have never shot there.

Lacey Renee age 16 December 2005

Dani Lynn at age 9 in December 2005

I'm single-handedly raising my two girls since the passing of their mother in late August 2001. This has greatly reduced my practice time, but is great fun just the same. I am not sure which activity is tougher! There is no written strategy info for making these kids bigger. Let's go for a ride and learn about some of the things only a handful of shooters know… they live and breathe this information every day.

Mike Ratigan

Dani Lynn "My daddy has spent lots of time on this, I hope you like it!"

Table of Contents

Places to Shoot

Portland Australia

Raton
New Mexico

Canberra, Capitol
City of Australia

Canastota, NY

Mooreland Okla.

Introduction

The occasional shooter, varmint hunter and target shooters of all disciplines will benefit from the information contained in these pages. I'll attempt to fill in the gaps in the material as it applies to Benchrest shooting and bring to light some of the more up to date techniques and information concerning extreme rifle accuracy.

I learned to shoot from many great shooters. The major contributors are Rex Reneau, my mentor during the first four years, Don Powell, Tony and Faye Boyer from 1998 till the present. We've spent thousands of hours talking on the phone discussing strategy and every aspect of the sport. Thanks in part to Jack Dever, JT Powell, Dennis Wagner, Red Cornelison, Larry Scharnhorst, Jerry Johnson (deceased), Ron Hoehn, Skip Otto (deceased), Ed Adams, Wayne Campbell, Jack Neary, Allen Arnette, and many others. Special thanks to Okie Shooters Range, which I feel is partly responsible for my shooting ability. It's extremely tough to shoot.

This book has been both a labor, of love and a learning experience. I'll address many questions you might have concerning rifle accuracy and dispel many common misconceptions about the sport, it's equipment, and its competitors.

Benchrest is regarded as 100, 200 and 300 yard group shooting with a centerfire rifle, the term has been used of late to describe many rifle disciplines. Such as Hunter Class for score, Rimfire for group & score, 1000 yards for group & score, and Varmint for Score. Although I have shot a few score matches for fun, the majority of my shooting experience has been group shooting at 100-300 yards in sanctioned or registered tournaments.

No book can adequately describe the excitement, challenge, and sense of fellowship and camaraderie of this little known sport called Benchrest. I will share my experience and enjoyment from over a decade of competitive shooting and attempt to convey what this game and sport is all about. There are no secrets, even amongst the most accomplished shooters. This will become apparent by examining this writing.

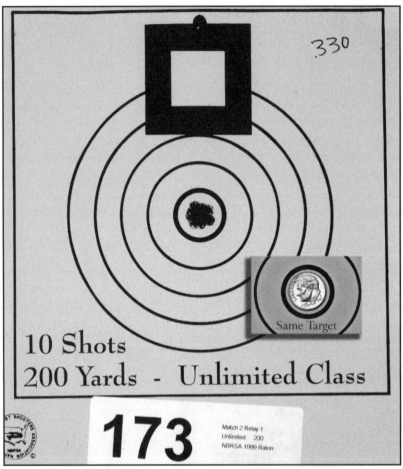

.330

10 Shots
200 Yards - Unlimited Class

Same Target

173 Match 2 Relay 1
Unlimited   200
NBRSA 1999 Raton

Figure 1. 10 shot target at 200 yards.
Shot at the 1999 NBRSA Nationals at Raton, NM.

Everyone, from the casual shooter to the most sophisticated reloader, will find tips and techniques in this book to improve their understanding and enjoyment of extreme rifle accuracy. Many shooters are only a short step away from competition. Many already shoot from a bench, whether they are concrete or wood, permanent or portable.

I have talked to many shooters who think they know something about accuracy. I sure did when I started competing. I quickly learned the extent of my knowledge was the correct spelling of "accuracy." For most shooters interested in rifle accuracy, to be introduced to the world of Benchrest shooting is comparable to looking through a looking glass into a magical wonderland.

The vast majority of accuracy minded shooters have never seen a Benchrest match, or talked with someone who shoots competitively. But nonetheless they are seeking to improve their rifle's accuracy. The methods and tools used in Benchrest are commonly used to improve the accuracy of varmint and hunting rifles.

Many shooters strive to improve their equipment and themselves, but unless shooting in side by side competition with others who have equally good equipment and skills, there's little chance of knowing whether your equipment or ability is up to the challenge.

If you're in search of rifle accuracy, step into the wonderful world of Benchrest. You will quickly learn there are many fascinating things which seem to defy logic. What follows is my interpretation of extreme rifle accuracy and the endless pursuit of it. To really find out about this little known sport of Benchrest, I urge you to visit a match in your area, talk to the shooters, look over the equipment and observe the methods and groups being shot.

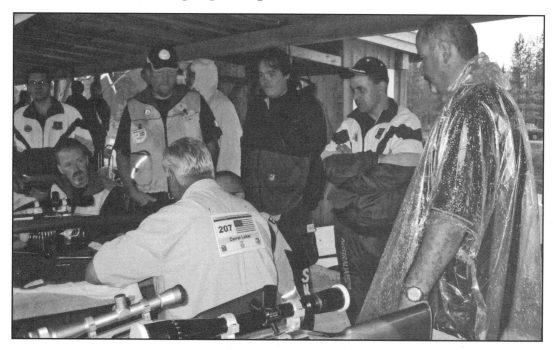

Figure 2. Time to visit about conditions during a target change.

Before and after the matches you'll find many shooters engaged in the free exchange of knowledge, ranging from components to strategy. Feel free to introduce yourself and jump right in. If you introduce yourself before the match starts you will be overwhelmed by shooters encouraging you to step up and give the sport a try. There's usually enough extra equipment to accommodate several shooters. Visitors who have never been exposed are often amazed by what they witness during a tournament and come away with a thirst for more knowledge, that's where the problems start...

How I got Started

My interest in accurate rifles started at an early age, shooting rimfire rifles at a South Omaha ROTC indoor range near my high school. Since then I have owned many rifles in different calibers, none of which ever performed to the level I thought should be possible from a centerfire rifle.

After reading a small article about a little known cartridge, the 6PPC, and what it was designed to do, I knew I needed one. This led me to a Prestigious firearms dealer in central Oklahoma. Of the millions of dollars of high end rifles, they did not have a rifle chambered in 6PPC or know where to find one.

By coincidence, I traveled to Oklahoma City with a friend to the home of a local gun witch doctor named Jack Dever. The moment I entered Jack's workshop, (converted garage) I knew by gazing at the tiny groups hanging on the wall of Jack's shop, I found what I had been looking for. Jack, a retired technical writer for the aircraft industry, was building custom guns for hunters, silhouette pistol, and Benchrest shooters. Jack introduced me to my first bench gun, a used Remington 6PPC. I knew instantly I'd found what I'd been looking for.

I now know I should have gone to a class on watching paint dry or water evaporating instead. I bought the rifle; Jack gave me some instructions, a couple tools, and sent me on my way.

Figure 3. Jack Dever at Mooreland Oklahoma

My traveling companion went home empty handed; looking back, I think it was some sort of conspiracy. I spent many afternoons in Jack's den trading stories and hypothesizing about techniques, tools and strategy.

Ever since, I have been a student of the holy grail of extreme rifle accuracy... Benchrest Shooting. I have spent the better part of the last fifteen years trying to learn why and how we do the things we do. I have experienced much joy, excitement and frustration along the way.

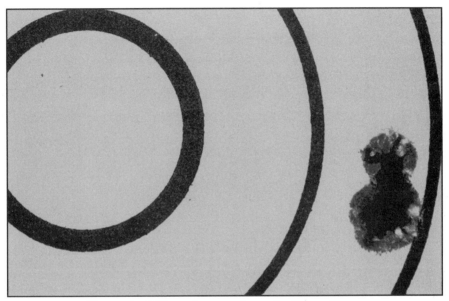

Figure 4. 200 yard group from the Super Shoot.

I will share some of my successes and failures, like trying to explain the feeling of frustration when shooting your first four shots into one small hole at 200 yards, then seeing the rifle move up just as the trigger breaks, the last shot hitting just above the first four. The group still measured .277 at 200 yards, but what could have been, eh? That one shot added about .200 (two tenths of an inch) to my group which cost me the small group trophy, a beautiful set of brass drink coasters. It would have been smaller than any world record group for any varmint rifle class at 200 yards! What a feeling!

It was 1989 when Glenn Newick released his book "The Ultimate in Rifle Accuracy". Since its release, we have made a few advancements in equipment and components, but none as dramatic as the refinement of what to do and when, and how to make better use of our wind flags.

My goal is to help explain the principles required for success in arguably the most difficult of the shooting sports on the planet ... Benchrest Shooting.

There is hardly a Benchrest shooter alive who doesn't like to spread this disease to anyone who gets close. To see the thrilled look on the face of someone trying a 1.5 ounce trigger for the first time. Nothing is better than the look of disbelief after letting them shoot a group with a real Bench Gun. Most first time Bench Gun shooters will comment "I can't believe a rifle can shoot like that!", or "That's the smallest group I have ever shot!"

Anyone who shoots at targets can understand the joy of a small group, or hitting the mark. It has never been easier to find a rifle that will often out perform the shooter, or better than can be believed.

While practicing at home, I ran into a local friend and owner of a Ruger 6PPC. I encouraged him to give my competition rifle a try. He was stunned into silence. He couldn't believe the trigger, the scope power... "All the bullets touched!" You could see the wheels turning.

The Challenge

In the late 1990's I began writing a teaching outline. Primarily to help myself (bad memory) and other competitors refine our skills. Many friends encouraged me to elaborate on my teaching outline "to fill in the blanks," so to speak, so the information would be understandable just by reading. New, old and prospective shooters will gain an insight into the difficult and Wonderful World of Benchrest Shooting!

Never in our history have shooters spent so much time learning and talking strategy of what to do and when. When working properly, our equipment has been refined almost past our ability to evaluate it. If you have a good rifle and make equipment improvements, it can be hard to find someone who shoots good enough AND has the flag reading skill to evaluate the changes, especially any improvements.

It is unusual for a new shooter to acquire a new rifle and have instant and continued success. Why? Because top shooters spend endless hours refining their equipment and their ability to figure out the fine details of our passion. With the advancements in equipment and techniques it's common to see grand aggregates (average of ten groups in minute of angle) in the low twos and high teens (approximately .240 - .180), and multi guns in the low twos or under that magical 1/4 inch.

A yardage aggregate is the average of 5 groups converted to minute of angle or MOA. At 100 yards the targets are added together then divided by 5. At 200 yards the five targets are added together then divided by 5, then divided by two in order to get to MOA. Five groups at 300 yards would be divided by 5, then divided by

3 to convert to MOA. A grand aggregate is two yardages added together then divided by two.

How much smaller can we shoot? Well, that is anyone's guess, but the aggregates must stop shrinking sometime. It is unreasonable to assume we could regularly shoot zero aggregates knowing all of the things which must be addressed and controlled, not to mention those pesky wind conditions.

Most of the Top Guns in Benchrest use the methods and concepts addressed in this book. This information can help you become a consistent performer on the firing line come tournament time or just for fun. Consistent application of the methods and concepts discussed here can help the social or casual shooter who participates only for the fun, as well as the competitor aspiring to become a champion. The best shooters in this exciting sport are lifelong students of this all consuming pastime.

These pages contain my attempt to help give you an insight into rifle accuracy and competitive target shooting. For those who already compete, you will get a glimpse into my psyche. A well known comedian once said...

"You better be sure, once you get inside my head there is no turning back."

I have included a few stories about things I have witnessed and done which I thought you might find interesting and informative.

I hope you get as much enjoyment from this as I've had preparing it.

Mike Ratigan

Life member National Benchrest Shooters Association NBRSA
Life member International Benchrest Shooters IBS
United States Delegate to the World Benchrest Shooting Federation
United States World Benchrest Team Director
Vice President - World Benchrest Shooting Federation

Lifelong Student of Extreme Rifle Accuracy

Besides this book, I recommend four other works on the subject.
"The Ultimate in Rifle Accuracy" published in 1989 by Glenn Newick.
"The Benchrest Shooting Primer" by Precision Shooting, Inc., contains
    many previously published articles in Precision Shooting Magazine
    from 1982 to 1996 on many "how to" related topics.
"Precision Reloading & Shooting Handbook," by Sinclair International, and
"Rifle Accuracy Facts" by Harold Vaughn.

Dr. Manny Garcia

Dr. Carl

Levi Cordes & Larry Engelbrecht

Larry Baggett

Larry Scharnhorst

Butch Fjoser

Dennis Wagner

Mike Bryant

Jack Snyder

Bart Sauter

Safety

Every writing about shooting or reloading has warnings about safety. There is a good reason for this, one lapse in judgment while on the firing line or reloading can result in a life ending or changing accident. This sport and pastime has given me many fond memories. Please understand that the very nature of the sport makes it dangerous; caution and awareness are the name of the game. We use components which even by themselves are hazardous. Powder is flammable and primers are explosive. When combined with a case and bullet, you have everything needed to kill someone or yourself in an accident. All that is lacking is a bit of poor judgement.

I must re-repeat the;

Ten Commandments of Firearms Safety;

1. Treat every gun as you would the respect due a loaded gun.

2. Always be sure the barrel and action are clear of obstructions.

3. Always be sure of your target before you pull the trigger.

4. Never point your gun at anything you do not intend to shoot.

5. Never leave your gun unattended unless you unload it first.

6. Avoid alcohol both before and during shooting.

7. Never climb a tree or cross a fence with a loaded gun.

8. Never fire at a hard, flat surface or the surface of water.
   Always make sure you have a safe backstop.

9. Carry only empty guns, taken down or with the action open, into your camp, car or home.

10. Store guns and ammunition separately under lock and key.

DANGER

What is safe today might not be safe tomorrow. Handloading of ammunition is subject to a virtual host of different variables. Simple things cannot be controlled, such as a rise in temperature which can cause dangerously high pressures.

I cannot accept responsibility for mishaps that may occur as a result of following or attempting to follow, any advice in this book.

If you participate long enough you will be witness or know someone who has been affected by an accident. While at Raton in the late 90's, I heard a loud bang in the loading area while I was out on the firing line. A cigarette had melted through the side of a powder bottle which then started the powder burning until it ruptured the powder bottle. Jeez, I thought it was common sense:

"No smoking around gun powder!"

I have two memories of shooters so oblivious to their surroundings that they approached the firing line to shoot another practice group, sat down and chambered a round, and fired during a cease fire when the firing line was closed to change targets. In both cases other shooters and target crew were down range during the cease fire. It was luck that no one was hurt or killed. When you approach the firing line just pretend it is not open for firing unless you hear others shooting. If you're alone, be very cautious and aware of your surroundings. It costs nothing to look before you shoot.

Some ranges have downrange warning systems, but these are few and far between. Come tournament time, while at these ranges, most visiting participants are not familiar with the use of the downrange warning systems of the host range. Many times visiting shooters will not activate the down range warning systems before going down range to change targets or set flags. And they are not aware of what some of the indicators are, such as a red light, flags etc.

LOOK DOWN RANGE BEFORE SHOOTING! You might save a life some day.

Remove Your Bolt

I am really proud of the long standing Benchrest tradition of having your bolt out of the rifle at all times unless you're shooting. Never trust a safety on a trigger. If the rifle has a loaded round chambered with the bolt is closed the rifle is NOT safe and is ready to fire. A loaded rifle should never be considered safe because the trigger safety is on. If the trigger fails the rifle can fire.

With lighter weight of pull triggers a safety is much less effective, and about any shock to the trigger can disengage the sear (part holding the firing pin back) and when the safety is moved to the fire position the rifle can discharge. I encourage everyone to remove the bolt from any bolt action rifle when not behind the loaded rifle and ready to shoot. Without the bolt installed the rifle cannot fire.

Figure 1.
Scott Smallwood heading to the firing line at Raton, NM.
Notice the bolt is out of the action.

It's very common for first time spectators at benchrest tournament's to be very nervous at our disregard for where the rifle barrels are pointed. I've had several spectators comment about how unsafe it appears to have shooters around the benches during a ceasefire. But with our long standing safety requirements of having the bolt removed, it makes these rifles no more dangerous than a teenagers room.

My anxiety levels have been known to go through the roof when practicing at home. Often the other shooters are not afraid to go down range in front of their own loaded rifle, but hey the safety is on. They walk down range to look at their target while their own loaded rifle is pointed right at them. All that's needed now is a bit of bad luck or a friend or relative playing with the loaded rifle on the bench. Then you'll become a statistic. Please just remove your bolts.

Ear and Eye Protection

Your hearing is precious! Protect it like you would one of your children. Shooting without hearing protection WILL PERMANENTLY damage your hearing. When it's gone, it's gone. There is no way to restore your hearing. Along with this line of thinking, be conscious of others around the firing line without their hearing protection. It is bad manners to shoot without warning them about their lack of hearing protection. Children are another story; they need our help to protect their precious hearing.

Eye protection or safety glasses are always a great idea. Your eyes are filled with liquid and are easily damaged by very small particles. If you are one of the fortunate ones and don't wear glasses yet, clear and gray safety glasses are a good idea. They might save your sight some day! If you were to lose your sight, by not wearing glasses, you will spend the rest of your life wishing you had worn them.

Match Time Safety Rules

Come match time you're not allowed to have your bolt in your rifle until instructed by the range officer, which includes the loading area. Get in the habit of keeping your bolt out until instructed to on the firing line.

Another safety related rule states that you are not allowed to install loaded ammunition in the action or the loading ramp until after the "commence fire" command is given. In English this means we should never hear "commence fire bang".

The commands,   "Ready on the right,"
                 "Ready on the left,"
                 "Ready on the firing line,"
                 "Place bolts in rifles,"
                 "Commence fire."

If you have a loaded round on the loading ramp and close the bolt on the "place bolts in rifles" command, it could go off before the "commence fire" command and you WILL be disqualified. I don't understand why some feel the need to shoot in the first second of available time. My advice is to Wait until after the "commence fire" command to insert your bolt and then place ammunition into the action or breach of your rifle after that.

Find a Mentor

Want to improve your shooting skill? I strongly recommend you visit a good shooter in your area. They can do more in one weekend to improve your knowledge and understanding of extreme rifle accuracy quicker than anything else you can do. Be sure to bring a pen and paper. You will get information overload. Early on, when I first started my pursuit of competitive Benchrest, I spent many hours traveling, talking and theorizing with J.T. Powell from Meade, Kansas.

Shooters new to the accuracy game focus on equipment, but soon turn to questions about flag reading, strategy and what to do. A mentor will be able to evaluate your equipment and help with decisions of what equipment you might need. This alone can save you a small fortune. I went as fast as my feet would take me to the best shooter I could find in my area. I drove Rex Reneau out of his mind with questions about everything related to rifle accuracy and competitive shooting.

Rex Reneau, United States Benchrest Hall of Fame member,
at the World Benchrest Championships 2005

Extreme Rifle Accuracy

It's important, when selecting a willing mentor, that you choose someone who knows how to shoot. Your mentor does not need to be one of the big names in Benchrest. There are many shooters, with decades of experience, any of which would make a great source of information and knowledge. If you select a lesser experienced shooter for your mentor, you might learn some bad habits which will be hard, if not impossible, to correct later.

I love to hear stories about the history of our sport and have had the opportunity to get personally acquainted with many of the most experienced competitors in the game.

**Don Powell, United States Benchrest Hall of Fame member
at the World Benchrest Championships 2003 in Umea, Sweden.**

I was first acquainted with Don Powell at the 1998 NBRSA Nationals. I remember visiting with Ron Hoehn about my practice at the Nationals; I commented "Why can't I shoot like that during the tournament?" Ron asked "How good is it?" I invited Ron to look through my scope; I shot five groups in a row which were very small which would have averaged about .100, very small indeed. Ron asked where the groups were, I told him they were the groups from left to right on the practice target which all looked about like single bullet holes.

Don overheard my conversation with Ron and quickly inquired about the bullets I was shooting. I informed Don that I had in fact made the bullets. He followed me around like a puppy dog all week long wanting to buy bullets. We've been friends ever since.

Don and I shared accommodations during the 10 days of the World Benchrest Championships in Italy in 1999. We spent hours talking about strategy.

If only I would have purchased stock in the Telephone company, I'd be rich from all of the money I've spent talking about extreme rifle accuracy on the telephone.

The Benchrest Rifle

The most accurate rifles in the world, at any distance. Every accuracy record for group or score has been shot with a rifle modeled after a bench gun. They might be heavier or look different but all use the same technology, precisely fit barrels & chambers, close tolerance actions, triggers, quality optics and loading principles.

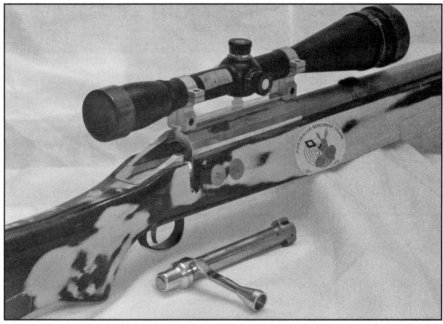

Figure 1.
My rifle, Panda action, right bolt, left port, left eject, no flutes, Sako extractor, .068 firing pin. Borden stock, Hart barrel, Jewell trigger, Sightron scope.

The modern bench gun, or as Skip Otto would say "Bullet Launcher," is made of expensive bits of stainless steel, aluminum, carbon, fiberglass, glue, and sometimes wood. They are assembled with attention to every detail. The rifles used in Benchrest competition are weight restricted to 10.5 pounds (ready to shoot, including scope and rings) for the Sporter and Light Varmint classes, and 13.5 pounds for the Heavy Varmint class. There's no weight limit in Unlimited class.

Many beginners seem to think a mediocre rifle will be good enough to get them started on their road, learning to shoot a rifle accurately. One of the most common questions by prospective newcomers is whether or not they can be competitive with a factory rifle. This group of shooters has read something about the sport and believes you can use a factory rifle to get started learning the game.

It's next to impossible to learn to cope with range conditions and learn how to shoot with a substandard rifle. Your rifle must be capable of placing every bullet in almost exactly the same spot EVERY time. Frankly speaking, almost no factory rifle, even when chambered in a Benchrest caliber, will be accurate enough.

It's a great time to shoot because of the relative ease to obtain good equipment and components. Twenty-five to thirty years ago it was more difficult to get a rifle capable of competitive accuracy. In the last fifteen or so years we have seen several new action, stock, barrel and bullet manufacturers who cater to this little known sport.

The job of the bench gun, or any rifle with a purpose to shoot accurately, is to get the bullet started on its way to the target the same way every time. Every modern improvement in rifle accuracy is a direct result of the sport of Benchrest. Factory rifles benefit from the methods and equipment developed for the sport: Stock, scope improvements, triggers, barrels, bullets, shooting techniques, loading techniques, tools, and action improvements, just to name a few. Rifles used in competition are one of the tools of the trade, so to speak.

The building of any new truly accurate rifle should be done by an experienced Benchrest gunsmith. Talk to shooters in your area for advice on choosing a gunsmith. Then talk to the gunsmith about your preferences and seek advice about the components that will be used in your new project.

The best advice for anyone considering the sport is to buy a 10.5 pound rifle chambered in 6PPC. You'll be able to shoot any NBRSA or IBS class. Almost 100% of the field today is using a 6PPC. Don't "buck the system" when you're new. There are many things you will need to learn. Use a 6PPC. Almost everyone in the game will be able to help you with bullets, powder, cases, dies, tuning advice... Building an odd caliber rifle will start you with a handicap even if it's got the right stuff.

Anyone considering building the benchrest rifle of their dreams, should look at current equipment lists published in the NBRSA news, as well as match reports, for a guide. Visit active competitors in your area. Talk to the person who will be building your rifle. They can save you a fortune when trying to decide on what equipment to use to assemble your new gem. Many benchrest gunsmiths are present and

Figure 2   Dual port Panda, right bolt, left port, right eject.

past competitors who know what is required to build a rifle capable of Benchrest accuracy. Gunsmiths who have never built a bench gun would not be your best choice. This endeavor requires some very specific knowledge. Included at the end of this chapter is the equipment list from the 8th World Benchrest Championships held in September, 2005 in the USA.

The Action

Is the logical starting spot or building block when building a new rifle. You might want to consider resale value when selecting an action. A factory action, such as the Remington, has the potential to perform at the same level after being worked on by a BR gunsmith with two distinct differences. First, they will be more difficult to operate, because of the cocking cam design and shorter bolt handle. Smooth operation of the action is important so as to not disturb the rifle in the bags when reloading. Secondly, the resale value is much less--about half the value of a custom action. This is one reason you don't see factory actions on the line today. Rifles built on custom actions usually maintain their value. By staying with a popular configuration, you can expect to get most of your money back come time to sell.

About half of the current actions on the line are made of aluminum most others are made of stainless steel. Popular aluminum actions are made by Kelbly's Inc., and Stiller's Precision, they are made with a steel thread insert and hard point for the cocking cam. Unlike many factory actions, the customs <u>almost</u> always have everything in line with and square/perpendicular with the bolt raceway.

The desire to shoot faster has spawned several new action configurations, which have been designed with the sole intention of making them faster to operate. Most Benchrest action makers offer ejector pins, microports for ejection, or have dropports. The Panda microport, as seen in figure 2, is just large enough to eject the fired case through an ejection port in the right side of the action.

Figure 3.
Viper drop port hole in action

Figure 4.
Case falls out hole in front of trigger

Jerry Hensler is credited with the dropport idea pictured in figures 3 & 4. The dropport has a hole machined into the bottom of the action which allows the fired case to fall out of a hole in the bottom of the stock in front of the trigger guard.

The only disadvantage of the microport and dropport are their inability to eject a loaded round. However, removing a loaded round during competition is rare. Now if we just had a better way to keep from fumbling the rounds going into the action.

The Bolt

The bolt's the heart of the action and where much of the time is spent building the action. Custom bolts have longer bolt handles--nice, considering most stocks on the firing line are wider in the pistol grip area. This gives the shooter something to grab onto. The bolt front on most of the actions is coned (angle cut as seen in figure 5A), the barrel has a matching angle, which eases the loading of the rifle. Most new actions come standard with a smaller firing pin than the old Remington standard .075 diameter. This eliminates primer piercing.

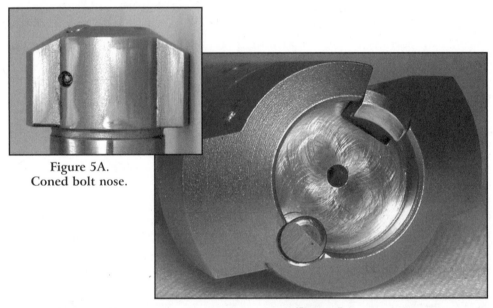

Figure 5A.
Coned bolt nose.

Figure 5.
My Panda bolt with left port, left eject, .068 firing pin.

Primer Piercing

Ever blow a primer? It's possible to blow a primer without having seriously over-pressured the action. I had no trouble until starting to shoot my 22 caliber. Contrary to popular belief, the firing pin does not usually punch a hole into the primer by traveling forward into the primer. The hole in the primer is caused by the pressure overcoming the firing pin spring pressure, thus pushing the firing pin back into the hole, leaving a hole in the primer.

There are three ways to stop piercing: Reduce your load, use a stronger firing pin spring, or reduce the pin diameter and hole size. Often the chamber pressure isn't too high, there's no resistance to opening the bolt, no primer flattening, cases are not getting tight, you just have a hole in the primer. A stronger firing pin spring is the least attractive fix. By increasing the spring rate, opening (cocking) the bolt becomes harder, and makes it harder to keep the gun still in the bags during the reloading process. Finally, reducing the firing pin hole size and pin size will eliminate primer piercing without making the action harder to operate. Now, you can shoot the load the rifle wants to shoot without knocking a hole in the primer.

Reducing the firing pin diameter makes it almost impossible for the primer to push the firing pin back into the firing pin hole. Reducing the pin and hole size from .075 to .068, is a reduction in the area of about 18% - - a huge change. Making the pin size any smaller isn't necessary, but if it makes you feel better, go for it.

If you pierce a primer you <u>should</u> stop shooting, take your bolt apart, and remove the small discs which now reside inside the bolt body. Some shooters keep a firing pin removal tool handy just incase. I prefer the smaller firing pin and lighter load. Piercing a primer can be distracting when it happens after your third shot on the record target during a match. If you don't remove the discs from the bolt body they can cause mechanical problems. They can become wedged between the firing pin hole and firing pin. They can also stop the firing pin from traveling far enough forward to strike the primer with enough force to light it. Just remove any pieces if you ever blow a primer.

Lug Contact
Custom actions will have nearly 100% lug contact which holds everything stable when firing. No movement of the bolt and action parts during firing is a great accuracy enhancer. Almost all modern BR actions are single shot, which makes the action more rigid and gives more bedding and gluing area underneath.

Trigger Hanger
Custom actions, designed to be glued into the stock, are fitted with a trigger hanger. This allows removal of the trigger from the bottom after removing the trigger guard. Important after gluing the action into the stock.

Two BR action makers, Kelbly's Inc., builder of the Panda Action, and Jerry Stiller, maker of the Viper Action, mill the scope base into the top of the action. These type bases almost never work loose. Current custom action manufacturers are Kelbly's, Allan Hall, Nesika, Stiller, Bat, Farley, and recently, Jim Borden.

The Trigger
Triggers manufactured by Jewell Triggers, Inc. have been the standard for many years. A Jewell trigger is designed to be adjusted from the bottom of the rifle after removing the trigger guard. The adjustments are for sear engagement, over-travel, and the weight of pull from about 1.5 to 4 ounces. Light aren't they? George Kelbly started working on a new trigger design in 2005. He's purchased a new water jet cutter to make some of the parts. The Kelbly triggers hit the market in early 2006 and look very promising. Jim Farley is also working on a new trigger idea. Jim is the maker of the Farley Action and Coaxial Front rests. Shilen also makes a trigger with a weight of pull light enough for benchrest.

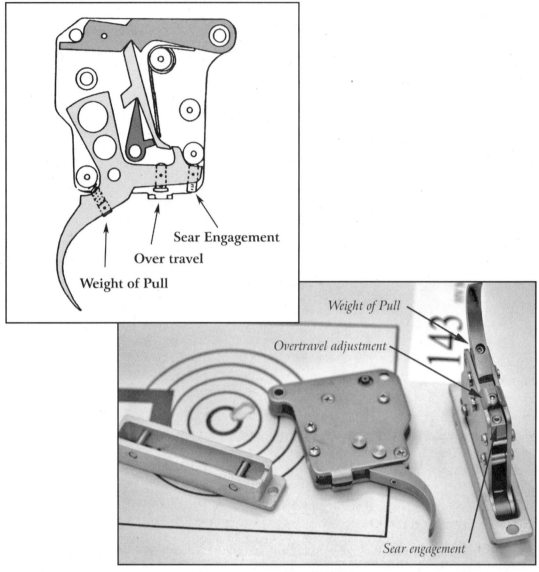

Figure 6.   Jewell triggers and Panda trigger hangers.

Figure 6 shows the Jewell trigger's adjustments. The adjusting screw in the front of the trigger (opposite the trigger shoe) is for the sear engagement. The middle adjustment is for the over-travel. The over-travel adjustment isn't something a Benchrest shooter would normally care about. I adjust my triggers so they don't hit the over-travel stop when pulling on the trigger. I don't want to hit a hard stop after the trigger breaks.

It's been said many times, DON'T OIL YOUR TRIGGER. These things are stainless and only work consistently when dry. Oil attracts dirt and dust and will eventually cause your trigger to fail to operate properly.

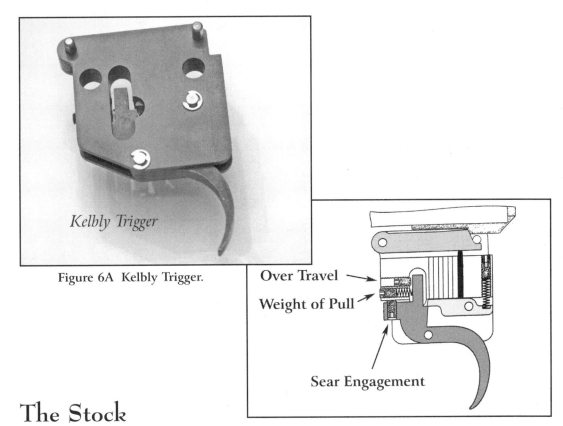

Figure 6A Kelbly Trigger.

The Stock

The purpose of the modern BR stock is to provide a strong, lightweight, stable, and vibration dampening platform that is straight when sliding back and forth in the bags. An important attribute of the stock is it's ability to track. Having the sides parallel, perpendicular, and in the same line as the butt stock. This indicates the stock is straight in the area of the pistol grip.

If the stock is bent at the pistol grip the front of the stock and butt stock are out of parallel. It's east to test, set the rifle in the front rest and rear bag. While on the sighter target, slide the rifle back in the bags. If the crosshair moves straight up and down on the target, your stocks front and rear lines are parallel. If not, you're in the majority of the population. You will see your crosshairs move up and down at an angle.

Glue In

There have been many changes since the late '60s in the stock, from moving away from wood, to fiberglass and carbon fiber, to the glue in. Gluing the action into the stock has dramatically decreased bedding problems and is much easier to be done properly without stressing the action. Laminated wood stocks have made a bit of a comeback in the last several years. The new wood stocks are of lightweight wood like balsa and redwood, some are wood and carbon fiber sandwiches. The main difference is these wood stocks are sealed in an attempt to try and attenuate the effects of atmospheric conditions (temperature and humidity).

Lower Center of Gravity

The modern design trend is to lower the center of gravity a bit more to increase the recoil stability, be reducing the butt stock taper to the minimum allowed by the rules. Bob Adamowicz was the first to design the lower stock, and many new stocks are basic copies of his design from 1986. Jim Borden approached Bob about making a mold and copying the stock design, Bob agreed. Jim had Lee Six make a mold and Jim began offering the popular design for sale. The early Adamowicz copies were hollow, later Jim began installing a foam and carbon sandwich inside. Unfortunately Jim no longer offers them for sale. Too much work.

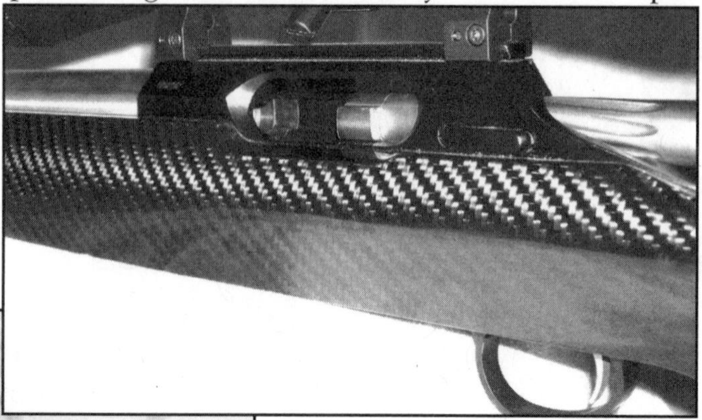

Figure 7. Bob Scoville stock.

The high density foam and carbon fiber sandwich inside a fiberglass shell was very good at minimizing vibration.

Bob Scoville makes a popular wood stock made of balsa, covered with carbon fiber, and sealed with a nice looking clear coat (figure 7.)

Figure 8. Several new style stocks.

Left to right in figure 8 are a Kelbly Six, Kelbly Klub, Cecil Tucker redwood stock, Borden Rimrock, and a Scoville balsa wood stock. Most new stocks are lighter in weight, which gives the builder more flexibility when choosing action, barrel, and scope combinations. With the newer heavier scopes, this is a necessity.

Years ago you'd never convince a hunter to give up their nice looking wood stock. But just as with many innovations in our sport, the lighter weight synthetic stocks are now commonplace on many new varmint and hunting rifles.

As mentioned, almost all bench guns have the action glued into the stock. This eliminates the common bedding problems of the good ole days. Several shooters have campaigned bench guns which are pillar bedded and bolted in rather than glued in. Mike Bryant and Ron Hoehn are two shooters from my area.

The Stock Weight System

Weight systems are gaining popularity. There are two basic types of weight systems. The most popular system enables you to add some weight to bring the rifle up to 10.5 pounds by adding a few ounces.

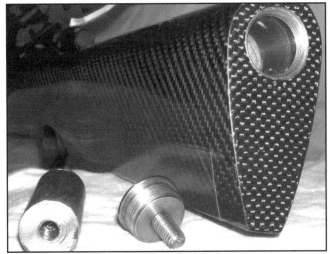

Figure 9.   Scoville with small 6oz to 8oz weight system.

The second and less popular, (the one I use) is the mother of all weight systems. My weight system allows you to add weight to get up to 10.5 pounds, but will also accept a weight big enough to get you up to 13.5 pounds without changing barrels. Making your gun weigh 13.5 pounds for the Heavy Varmint class is to every shooter's advantage. In today's competitive environment I suggest you take every possible advantage. The heavier rifle doesn't jump around as much under the recoil forces, making them easier to handle.

There are three ways to make a heavy varmint rifle. First, is to make a dedicated heavy gun. Second, you can take the barrel off your Sporter or Light gun, install a bigger heavier barrel, and add some weight to the back of the gun. Third is my way. Add three pounds to the rear of the rifle.

If my rifle displays competitive accuracy in the 10.5lb weight limit I don't like to change barrel, dies, bullets, powder, seating depth, or anything else to shoot another class.

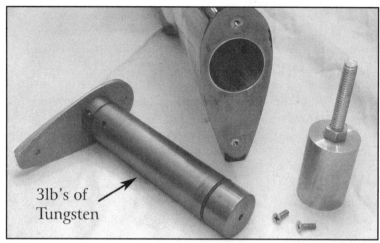

3lb's of Tungsten

Figure 10.
My weight system, 3 pound piece of tungsten, small weight to make 10.5.

When I've got a hot combination, I like to shoot it any time I wish. Changing rifle weights lets me stay with the same action, with the same familiar feeling. It's a bad thing to have your favorite rifle in the case because it doesn't meet class requirements. My barrels are all about the same weight. I can shoot any barrel any time, except the 22s of course. I believe making a heavy barrel, which can only be used in Heavy Varmint class, is a strategy mistake. A friend from Minnesota say's it best, Keep It Simple Stupid (KISS).

I install a small weight for the 10.5 pound classes and insert a 3 pound piece of tungsten (shown in figure 10) when shooting in Heavy Varmint or the 13.5 pound class. Years ago, it was thought this type system would not perform properly. I have been shooting this type of weight system since 1996. I have proven the fundamental principals to be sound. Take every advantage you're allowed. This sport is becoming too competitive to approach the firing line with any disadvantage.

In deciding on a weight system you must consider what surface will act as the recoil lug. I've made several weight systems where the weight was threaded and then screwed into the tube installed in the stock. This is a very clean looking weight system with one drawback. The front of the tube must be closed and then bedded to the stock. When the rifle starts to move to the rear under the shock loading of the recoil force, some part of the stock must push the weight to the rear. On the first couple weight systems I left the front of the tube open. After a couple shots with the large weight installed in the tube, the whole weight system started its trip into the back of the stock after breaking the glue bond. To correct this problem, I closed the hole and bedded the front of the tube to the stock.

In my latest system (figure 10) the weight is attached to the butt plate with a 1/4 - 20 screw. During the recoil force the butt plate pulls the weight to the rear. The front of the tube is bedded to the stock to reduce vibration and help ease the tension on the small screws holding the butt plate forward.

The Barrel

Harold Vauhn's work "Rifle Accuracy Facts," covers in great detail many physical properties of thread joint motion, muzzle blast, and thermal properties.

The job of the barrel is to contain the pressure of the expanding gas, guide and spin up the bullet, ultimately releasing it at the end of its travel. You would think at the point the bullet is released at the crown that its influence would be over--not so. Non-concentric wave shaping of the expanding gases of the burning powder can effectively push the bullet off axis if the crown is non concentric.

The crown should be concentric to the major bore diameter. One easy way to eliminate any concentricity problems is to cut the crown perpendicular to the bore centerline. The straight cut crown is pictured on the right in figure 11 and is common to many benchrest barrels. We're not afraid of damaging the crown in the floorboard of the truck or car.

Panda barrel tenon.

Figure 11. Some different crowns,
left to right. Recessed, 11 degree, ground, straight.

Benchrest barrels are the best in the world. Popular barrels used today are of two manufacturing types--button and cut rifling. In the USA, the popular manufacturers can be found by looking through the equipment lists from the match reports: Hart, Shilen, Krieger, Broughton, Douglas, Spencer, Turbo, Kostyshyn, MacLennon, and Bartlein just to name a few. The material of choice is 416 stainless steel, another modern technology that hunters were slow to warm up to thinking they would not last. Now stainless barrels are common and most all rebarreled varmint and hunting rifles will be fitted with a new stainless steel barrel.

With the advent of the stronger and lighter stocks, we are able to use bigger, more rigid barrels, which help pull the heat away from the bore. Thermal drift in these barrels is a rare thing. Occasionally you'll see one which will move its point of impact predictably as it's temperature increases. Many manufacturers of Benchrest barrels stress relieve them as part of the manufacturing process.

Every now and then you will find a barrel which requires several shots to settle down the impact point after cleaning. Some barrels even show temperament when sitting after a couple minutes without being fired. If you happen across one of these gems, exercise caution. If you stop shooting on the record for more than a minute or so, you must fire a shot on the sighter to put some heat in the barrel before continuing on the record. When you have this type of barrel and return to the sighter after pausing on the record, don't use you first shot as a sighter. You went down to put some heat in the barrel, knowing the shot would not be predictable. If you need a sighter shot, shoot another. Using your barrel warming shot as a sighter would be no better than just shooting it on the record. This type barrel is better left at home come match time, or relegated to prairie dog detail.

Using the proper exterior finish will speed the cooling process. Although a nice shiny barrel looks attractive, an 40-80 grit sanded finish increases the surface area speeding the cooling process.

Figure 12.   Sanded Finish

How long will a barrel last and shoot accurately? This is a commonly asked question. There is no good answer. I have had barrels covering all ends of the spectrum of competitive accuracy. I've had barrels which had competitive accuracy from as little as 300 rounds to as many as 7500. Unless you just get a barrel that will not perform, where you live and how bad your relative conditions are will determine its usable life. I retire barrels when they start to show the inability to shoot at a competitive accuracy level. Was that vague? Many barrels which have outlived their useful competitive life often find a second home on a varmint rifle.

Most competitors are no stranger to a barrel vise and action wrench for changing barrels. Just add a couple of C-clamps, an adjustable wrench, some bolt lube, and you are ready to change a barrel at the range.

Similar Rifles and Cooperation

Your rifles should be as similar as practical: stock, action, weight, scope, and everything. Switching rifles should be a smooth transition from one to another. You should not notice any difference. You complicate matters with more than one style

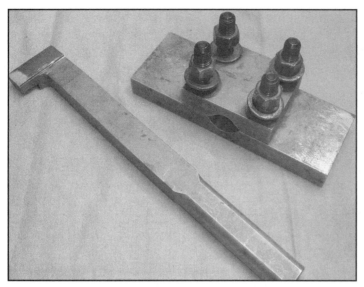

of rifle. You must remember how to operate each and what equipment peculiarities the rifle has. I recommend you stay with the same action and stock manufacturer.

Figure 13. Barrel tools from Sinclair International.

If you and your traveling companions use similar rifles and bench equipment you might consider sharing rests and rear bags. Tony & Faye Boyer and Wayne Campbell use similar stocks and share a front rest and rear bag at big matches during bench rotation.

Tony sets up the equipment on the bench and shoot his group. When finished with his group, he picks up his rifle and loading block and heads back to the loading area. Tony leaves the rest and bags on the bench. Faye then comes to the line and doesn't have to set up any of the equipment. She puts her gun in the rest and bag and is ready to shoot. When Faye is finished shooting her group she picks up her rifle and loading block and away she goes. Wayne shoots after Faye, removes the equipment from the bench and moves it to the next bench in the rotation. What a time saver. By cooperating they have plenty of time to watch the flags and visit while everyone else is setting up. This type of cooperation is no accident, and I am surprised more shooters don't follow their lead.

The Good, the Ugly and the Bad

Benchrest rifles come in many different shapes and sizes, different action manufacturers, stocks, barrels, new and used, but at the end of the day, some rifles are just better performers than others. Once in awhile a shooter will get their hands on a rifle or action which shoots pretty good with many barrels. Conversely, some rifles put up a fight from the beginning. No matter what barrel, bullet, powder, scope, trigger, stock, or any amount of inspection by a good Benchrest gunsmiths, they just won't shoot. My favorite rifle is one that shoots pretty well, no matter what style I use to shoot it, no matter what barrel I screw on it.

This is some of the best advice I can give you about your rifle. If you have a rifle that fights your every attempt to make it shoot--multiple barrels, scopes, powders, bullets--send it down the road. These rifles are just the tools of the trade. If it's no good, get rid of it. Life is too short to waste time on a great looking, bad shooting rifle.

Figure 14. Wayne Campbell just after winning the award for the most original use of primer from a spray can.

FACT: Pretty will not make a gun shoot!

New shooters have trouble with this fact. One very common theme among the best shooters in the game is to spend money on things which will effect the performance of their equipment. This is why my rifles are just plain UGLY. When you finally embrace this simple concept, one thing becomes instantly apparent. Who cares what the thing looks like? Give me one that shoots!

I would pay three times the cost of the ugly rifle which Pat Byrne brings to the line at the Super Shoot, rather than pay 80% of the cost of a brand new, unproven, shiny painted shooting stick.

"The grim truth is that a new custom rifle made of the best parts available has a much higher probability of being mediocre than it does of being competitive."

Wilbur Harris,   NBRSA SE Regional Director
Administrator of Benchrest.com

It's worth re-repeating. If you inquire about a rifle for sale from any well known shooter and they tell you it's no good and should be used as a varmint rifle, there's nothing you will do to make it shoot to Benchrest standards. Believe it.

This is often heard after a competitor wins and is then caught changing rifles saying...

My Other Rifle Shoots...
J U S T as Good!

8th World Benchrest Championships, North Lawrence Ohio USA
September 11 –17, 2005

Light Varmint Top 20 Equipment List

Shooter	Caliber	Action	Scope	Barrel	Gunsmith	Powder	Bullet
Paul Jung	6PPC	Veit	Leupold	Krieger	Gros	N133	Euber
Lester Bruno	6PPC	BAT	Leupold	Krieger	Ocock	T-322	Bruno
Char. Decanini	6PPC	Panda	Leupold	Krieger	Gros	N133	Gros
J. Raudaskoski	6PPC	Panda	Leupold	Shilen	Jalonen	N133	Barts
L. Scharnhorst	6PPC	Panda	Leupold	Hart	Rex	8208	GC
Bill Goad	6PPC	Panda	Leupold	Broughto	Green	T322	Barts
Billy Stevens	6PPC	BAT	Leupold	Hart	Stevnes	N133	Barts
Vlad Lobaev	6PPC	Hall	Leupold	Krieger	Lobayev	T322	Speedy
Allie Euber	6PPC	Farley	Leupold	Krieger	Lachapell	N133	Euber
Dave Holmes	6PPC	Panda	Leupold	Krieger	Holmes	N133	Hottenstein
Ed Adams	6PPC	Farley	Sightron	Hart	Adams	N133	Adams
Mike Ratigan	22-100	Panda	Sightron	Hart	Ratigan	N133	Ratigan
Jean-L. Espinet	6PPC	Farley	Leupold	Krieger	Scott	N133	Gentner
Paul Sullivan	6PPC	BAT	Leupold	Krieger	Scott	N133	Barts
Robert Persson	6PPC	Panda	Leupold	Krieger	Kelbly	N133	Barts
Vince Bottemly	6PPC	BAT	Leupold	Hart	Bottemly	N133	Fowler
Bill Gammon	6PPC	Panda	Leupold	Maclenna	Pierce	H322	Hottenstein
Russell Gall	6PPC	Panda	Leupold	Krieger	Gall	N133	Fowler
David Kerr	6PPC	Panda	Leupold	Shilen	Kerr	N133	Kerr
Jyrky Vuorjoki	6PPC	Panda	Leupold	Shilen	Otto	N133	Barts

Heavy Varmint Top 20 Equipment List

Shooter	Caliber	Action	Scope	Barrel	Gunsmith	Powder	Bullet
Jack Neary	6PPC	Panda	Leupold	Krieger	Kelbly	N133	AA
A. Komkov	6PPC	Farley	Leupold	Shilen	Lobayev	N133	Speedy
Jyrky Vuorjoki	6PPC	Panda	Leupold	Shilen	Otto	N133	Barts
J. Raudaskoski	6PPC	Panda	Leupold	Shilen	Jalonen	N133	Barts
Jean-L. Espinet	6PPC	Farley	Leupold	Krieger	Scott	N133	Gentner
Mike Ratigan	22-100	Panda	Sightron	Hart	Ratigan	N133	Ratigan
Dwight Scott	6PPC	BAT	Sightron	Shilen	Stevens	8208	Barts
Bill Goad	6PPC	Panda	Leupold	Broughtn	Green	T322	Barts
Steve Williams	6PPC	Panda	Leupold	Krieger	Kelbly	N133	Barts
Ed Adams	6PPC	Farley	Sightron	Hart	Adams	N133	Adams
Dale Boop	6PPC	Panda	Leupold	Krieger	Goodling	N133	Barts
Billy Stevens	6PPC	BAT	Leupold	Hart	Stevnes	N133	Barts
Robert Persson	6PPC	Panda	Leupold	Krieger	Kelbly	N133	Barts
L. Scharnhorst	6PPC	Panda	Leupold	Hart	Rex	8208	GC
Rex Reneau	6PPC	Farley	Sightron	Krieger	Reneau	N133	Bishop
Allie Euber	6PPC	Farley	Leupold	Krieger	Lachapelle	8208	Euber
Bill Gammon	6PPC	Panda	Leupold	Maclenn	Pierce	H322	Hottenstein
J. Pierre Troin	6PPC	Panda	Leupold	Hart	Gros	N133	Gros
K. Duckworth	6PPC	Stolle	Leupold	Krieger	Kelbly	N133	Fowler
Stuart Elliot	6PPC	Panda	B & L	Madd Co	Sori	N133	Conaway

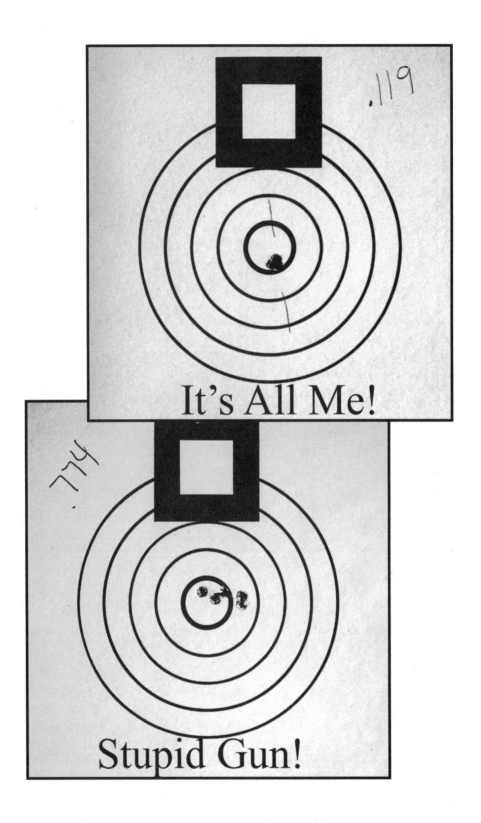

Scopes, the Weakest Link!

The rifle scope is one of the biggest contributors to modern accuracy. Since the introduction of the internally adjusted scope, and the addition of the locking ring for the parallax adjustment in the early 1970s very little has changed. With all of the advancements in our sport this is still the single weakest link in the chain. Let's face it -- these things are fragile. Our scopes need to be light enough to fit atop the weight restricted rifles and be solid enough to hold their impact point.

The purpose of the rifle scope is to track where the barrel is pointed--either the absolute or relative position. There are many things which can cause a scope to not properly track where the barrel is pointed. The scope should remain pointed in the same place after every shot in reference to where the barrel is pointed. I like to refer to our scopes as a "barrel pointing device." Adding cross hairs to the telescope adds a degree of complication to the job of the magnifying telescope.

Figure 1. Leupold 45 with leather caps over lenses

Today, more than ever, attention is being focused on why scopes move and how to stop the movement. In the competitive environment of Benchrest there is no place for a scope that will not hold its point of impact. We're developing methods to measure scope impact shifts under actual shooting conditions to help isolate problem scopes. But even when we return the scopes to the manufacturer, often they cannot isolate or correct the problems. Worse, some manufacturers who do testing for impact point shifts, often return the units saying "the scope was within the manufacturer's specifications for impact point shift."

There is no room for scope impact point shifts in the competitive arena known as Benchrest. During the 2004 Super Shoot only .050 (or 50 thousandths of an inch) would effect the finishing place from 34th to 144th, or 87th to 212th. No problem, right?

Quite frankly, some manufacturers seem disinterested in the unique problems in benchrest. Until our unique problems effect their bottom line, we will be ignored and looked at as a bunch of cry babies. Let's face reality for a moment. Our sport does not have the numbers required to force action to correct impact point shifts once and for all. Subsequently, several shooters in our sport are trying to solve the problems with the equipment we have available--often with drastic modifications. The other shooting sports cannot tell and don't care about impact point shifts of .125 (1/8) of an inch. Manufacturers become upset when they see one of their prized gems on the front cover of a magazine, after being modified to the extreme, in an attempt to eliminate impact point shifts. Enough with the ranting and raving--the saga continues. Even if the engineering departments could design the scope of our dreams in the needed weight range, the bean counters (accountants) would overrule.

Figure 1A. Cecil Tucker, at the 2005 World Championships, using one of his modified 45s.

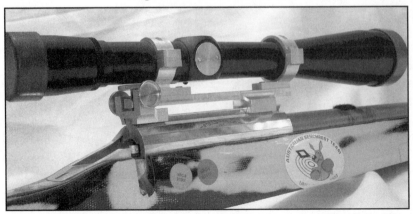

Figure 2. Gene Bukys first protype, Leupold 45 with no turrets, adjustable mount.

Reasons for Impact Point Shift

Many things will cause the scope's crosshairs to change relative to the barrel centerline. Some common things not directly related to the scope are barrel thread joint motion, and the scope mounts themselves. Many actions have separate scope mounts attached to the action with small screws. This attachment point can be the cause of movement. Gluing the mounts to the action can help stop base movement, but it's hard to tell when the glue fails. One sure way to eliminate base movement is to use an action which has the scope base milled atop the action.

The scopes themselves are often the cause of impact point shift problems. Scopes have many things which can move under the extreme shock loading forces of recoil. This shock load is many times the acceleration of gravity and would be akin to striking the scope with a hammer. During the recoil force, the scope's internal parts must not move. If they do move, they must return to exactly the same place they were before the shot was fired. Like that's gonna happen!

Rifle scopes contain several lens cells. These cells, which hold the lenses, can fail, resulting in movement of a lens causing impact point shifts. The most common reasons for scope impact point shifts are related in some way to the parts of the scope which are designed to move. These moving parts are the turrets, erector tube, the spring holding the erector tube against the turrets, erector tube clamping mechanism, rear lens cell, and parallax adjustment.

Many years ago the front lens cell was addressed, a locking ring was used to hold the cell during firing. The main focus of our efforts today is in the area of stopping the erector tube from moving. Scopes, as delivered from the factory, have no way to lock down the erector tube to stop sideways and front-to-back movement.

The erector tube is inside the main scope tube. The erector tube holds a lens cell and crosshairs. It can be held in the rear or the front of the main tube. In the Weaver scope, the erector tube is held at the front of the main tube. Most other manufacturers hold the erector tube at the rear. The end of the erector tube is normally held in place with a threaded nut. The erector tube extends past the adjustment turrets for windage and elevation. A spring is used to hold the erector tube against the turrets.

Cecil Tucker (Benchrest Gunsmith, bullet maker, and long time Benchrest competitor) has been modifying scopes for many years. Cecil's modifications increase the spring pressure by about 6-10 times. Cecil also installs some parts to eliminate the front-to-back movement of the erector tube. Sorry, I am not at liberty to tell anymore about the modification; however, Cecil does a top notch job and you find many scopes Cecil has worked on at any registered tournament.

In 1997, Leupold started working on the new Competition series scopes offered in 35, 40 and 45 power. The lenses with this new series are good. This scope weighs in at about 4.5 ounces heavier than the 36D model. One nice thing about this new series of scopes is the relocation of the parallax adjustment, from moving the front lens cell to an adjustment opposite the windage adjustment turret.

One very common problem with this scope model is that the rear eyepiece locking ring works loose. The thread on the rear eyepiece adjustment is very course compared to many. This reduces the ability to properly tighten the locking ring. You must get very aggressive with this locking ring. Hold the ring while tightening the eye piece against it. Stay vigilant about checking to make sure it's tight.

Figure 3. Leupold 36 with front Parallax adjustment and locking ring.

I can assure you that leaving the locking ring loose on the front lens of a 36 makes shooting 1.2 inch groups at 200 yards very easy.

At the Super Shoot in 2003, I remember shooting a very loose group for no apparent reason according to the flags, during the warm up target at 200 yards. I wasted no time getting the backup gun ready to shoot. I changed loads--both up and down on my primary rifle. During a quiet moment between relays, I sat calmly looking at my best rifle, wondering if some small detail was overlooked. Was something broken? Maybe a scope ring? In my finite (that's a small amount) of wisdom, I had the presence of mind to reach up and feel the locking ring and discovered it was loose. I felt like a married man which was just caught flirting with a 500 pound belly dancer. I did what anyone in that situation would do. I looked to see if anyone was watching. About the time I looked up, Tony Boyer was walking by. Oh great, of all people to catch me. I did what any self respecting Benchrest shooter would do. I asked Tony if the loose parallax locking ring would make 1.2 inch groups on the target. He simply said "Yep."

I rushed my first record group to have enough time to change rifles if needed. I shot another 1.1 inch group at 200 yards because I was stupid and rushed. Gun was okay, shooter was not. I stuck my head in the toilet and flushed three times. This exercise did not seem to wash out the stupid. The Competition series scopes would have eliminated this mistake with the side Parallax adjustment.

Sightron, a new comer to the BR scope scene, produces a 36 power scope that is about ½ ounce heavier than the older Leupold 36 and 36D series. The optics are not quite as clear as the Competition scopes from Leupold, but they hold their point of aim very well. Within the first year of the release of the 36 power from Sightron, several big name shooters were using them with success.

Figure 4. Sightron 36 with screws opposite turrets and scope caps

Ed Adams, from Albuquerque, NM, had one scope in particular which was moving between shots. After urging from Dr. Jack Jackson of Farmington, NM, and talking to the engineers from Sightron, Ed installed the first plastic screws opposite the turrets in one of the Sightrons. This simple installation settled down the impact point shifts of the scope. The screws apply more pressure directly to the erector tube opposite the turrets, helping hold the erector tube in place.

Soon after Ed started installing screws in the Sightron, others followed. At the World Benchrest Championships in Ohio in 2005, five of the twelve United States World Team Members brought Sightron scopes with them to the Championships. High praise!

NEW ≠ GOOD

NEW = JUST MADE

This is why I have 12 scopes and 3 rifles.

Several shooters are working towards removing the internal adjustments of several scope models. The idea is to hold the erector tube solid. An externally adjustable mount is used to change the point of aim. Part of the battle is locking up the adjustments and still having some way to repair them when finished. Several shooters are gluing the erector tube in place using epoxy. When epoxying the erector tube in place, you will not be able to repair the erector tube lens cell if needed.

Evolution, back to externally adjusted scopes.

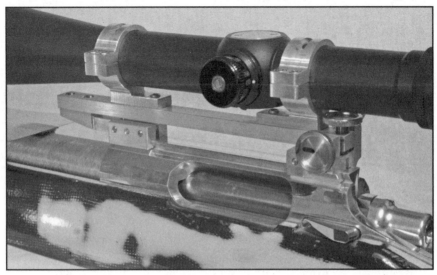

Figure 5. Gene Bukys second prototype mount for a dovetail mount, Panda, Viper.

Gene Bukys is working with Dwight Scott and Jerry Simison to remove all the moving parts from the newer Leupold Competition Series scopes. Gene has removed the turrets and locked down the erector tube where it does not move. This removes the windage and elevation adjustments and the ability for the erector tube to move front-to-rear. They are still perfecting a way to change the aiming point by an external mount as seen in figure 5. I have been helping with the research, development, and testing for several months. About the only other change I would make would be to dovetail the top beam. This would allow use of a standard dovetail mount ring and ease removal of scope without removing it from the rings.

Leupold was approached about making the modifications, but had shown little interest. It would be nice to get the manufacturer to do the modifications. Might be able to keep the warranty, a nice extra for a scope costing almost a thousand dollars. Gene has made several mounts which look very promising. When removing the turrets and adding the mount and rings, the total weight is about the same.

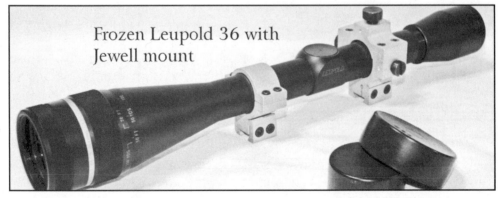

Frozen Leupold 36 with
Jewell mount

Figure 6. Leupold 36D with adjustments removed, by Jackie Schmidt

Figure 7.
Sightron w/screws, Ratigan

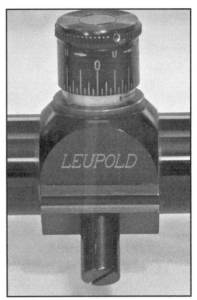

Figure 8.
Leupold 36 w/Tucker

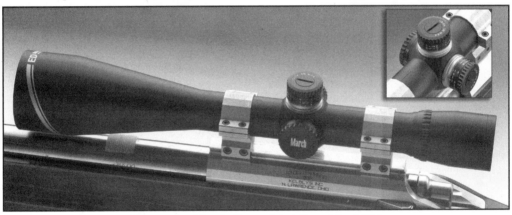

Figure 9. March Scope introduced in 2006

" From dream to reality" . Turk Takano' s dream of great optical resolution with improved, simple internal components, to help eliminate point of impact shifts. Dr. Yuzuru Nagayama, a friend of Turk 's from Japan wanted to see if such a scope could be built "just for fun. " Dr Nagayama invested the money to build three prototypes with no expectations of making a profit. A combination of dreams " It can be done" and the designers dream of "Doing it without interference from the accountants" brought this scope to life. The erector tube is of a ball joint or gimbal design, with a heavy spring, and no plastic internal parts. The desire was to have as few moving parts as possible. Turk was in constant contact with the design team, providing input derived from prototype testing throughout the development stages.

From prototype in 2005 to viable scope in 2006. The "March scope from Deon Kogaku Giken / Koto 's Precision in Japan looks promising. This newcomer to the Benchrest scope market offers optical quality of " ED" glass found in high end camera lenses. The first Production run was about 100 units. These were a sell out prior to shipment to the USA from Japan. Benchrest competitor and friend Lou Murdica, is primarily credited with making a personal and financial commitment to the initial introduction of the " March" scope to the US Market.

Scope Checker

How to properly identify scope movement between shots has been a problem. In July of 2001, Darrel Loker, from Tulsa, OK, invented a scope mount which would allow the mounting two scopes on a sporter rifle for the purpose of testing for point of impact shift. About the same time, Charlie Hood introduced his scope checker.

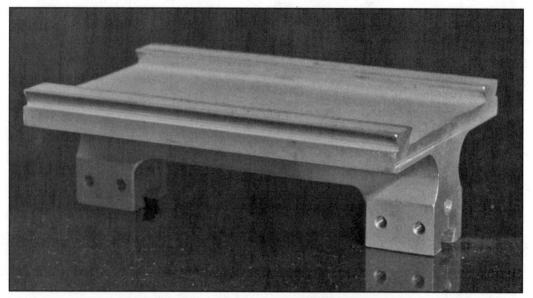

Figure 10. Picture of my scope checker from Darrel.

In theory, you put the two scopes atop a rifle, set the sights to the same spot on the target, shoot the rifle, and look to see if they still converge. If either scope has moved, you would see that the scopes no longer converge.

In reality, if you have a scope shooting .400 or bigger, bullet holes rarely touch. You would know something was wrong. The issue becomes more complicated when the scope in question is suspected to move a smaller amount. For the sake of this discussion, we expect movement of .050 to .075. Then we set up our two scopes, which are impossible to get to converge on the target, because the adjustment resolution is not fine enough to get them to aim at exactly the same place. These scopes have magnification ranging from 35 to 45 power and have adjustment increments of 1/8 to 1/4 inch per click adjustment. Herein lies the problem. To start the test, use one scope to aim with, then look through the other before shooting to find the crosshair slightly to one side and a little above or below. After firing and inspection, we're unsure if the relative position is the same.

Figure 11. Scopes mounted on Scope Checker

To make effective use of the scope checkers you will need to make up some finely divided graph paper with very small divisions. Make (or have someone make) some one inch squares with grid lines .050 to .100 apart. This grid is the actual size of the grid I use when evaluating scope movement.

We are not shooting groups when checking scopes, just using the rifle to shock load the scopes to check for movement. In the good ole days, a rail gun was used. With the relatively small recoil of most rail guns, results would often show no problems.

Put this grid out about 40 or 50 yards, aim with your test scope at whichever corner which puts the questionable scope inside the grid. Now you can more accurately gage how far apart the crosshairs are and make a note. Remember to set the parallax. The fact of the matter still remains--it is very hard to tell if your scope is 100, 99, 98, or maybe 95 percent. You will have to decide.

One final thought about the scope checker. Just proving a scope is okay today doesn't mean it won't fail tomorrow. These darn things just are

"THE WEAKEST LINK."

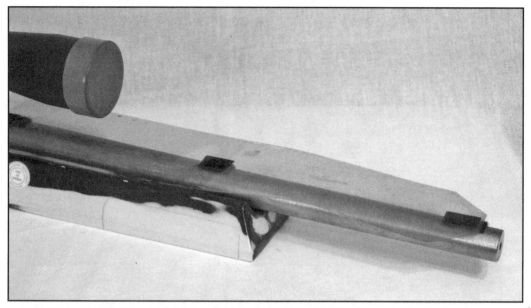

Figure 12. Mirage shield made of exposed x-ray film, attached with Velcro

Heat shields, also known as "mirage shields," are used to deflect the heat from the barrel around the air we will look through. Modern mirage shields are attached to the barrel with small pieces of Velcro. An exposed piece of x-ray film is a popular choice. Some shooters use a thin piece of aluminum, like a piece of a window shade. Half of a target taped to the barrel will work fine. Some scopes come with 3-4 inch tubes to screw on the front of the scope. Don't use them. They add weight to the front of the scope and are not long enough to deflect the heat of the barrel. Even worse, you can heat up the air inside the tube, creating the very problem you are trying to correct. Years ago a tube was screwed to the scope which extended to the end of the barrel. The air inside the tube would heat up and could cause the very problem we were trying to avoid. We have certainly evolved.

Walk the line observing the top shooters--big names you recognize. Very few use anything attached to a scope like the old mirage tubes or the factory tubes.

Miscellaneous Scope Stuff:

1) Cover the scope lenses when not looking through them, and certainly before cleaning your rifle. When a brush saturated with solvent exits the muzzle it makes a cloud of solvent, that can drift in the breeze and damage the lens coatings.
2) Never carry the rifle by the scope, it is fragile!
3) Keep your scope out of the direct sunlight when outside. This heats up air inside scope which can make scope hard to see through. I use a towel to cover mine. There are a couple of shooters who make scope covers which fit right over the scope to keep the sun and solvent off.

Parallax

Parallax is one of the most misunderstood things about a rifle scope. What is it and how does it effect our shooting? The effect of parallax and subsequent effect on our shooting and group size is misunderstood by more shooters than the reading of wind flags. You may be asking why I am bringing this up. I look through many scopes at about every match I attend and notice many are mal-adjusted.

Figure 1. Parallax adjustment on a Leupold 36D (left) and a Sightron 36 (right).

Parallax is defined as the apparent displacement of an object as seen from two different points (when the object or cross hair is not moving). What does this mean? Apparent displacement means nothing has changed but your point of view. In Benchrest, having a maladjusted parallax will increase aggregate scores because of aiming errors.

To help understand this effect I have included a couple photos of analog meter movements. These photos help illustrate parallax error. This meter has a needle, which is above the scale that have the numbers are printed on. There's a mirror behind the needle which is used to help align your eye properly to obtain a correct reading. The user will only get a true reading if he reads the meter where no reflection of the needle can be seen. Change your point of view until the reflection of the needle is hidden behind the needle.

Figure 2. Picture of meter, almost parallax free.

When you are looking at the meter properly, you will not see the reflection of the needle in the mirror as shown in the figure 2. In figure 3, you see the reflection of the needle left of the needle because of the misalignment.

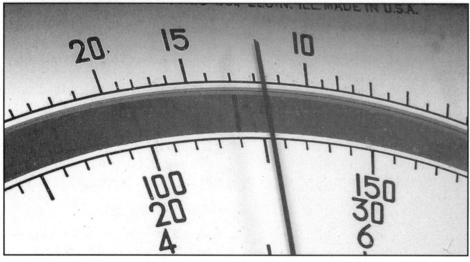

Figure 3. Reading meter from the side.

You'll also notice that the apparent meter reading is different in each photo, when in fact the needle has not moved. The difference was the camera misalignment, which appeared to have changed the meter reading.

In the shooting environment there are all the elements needed to have the effect of parallax. Parallax error can be seen by looking through the scope at the target and moving your eye up and down or side to side while maintaining a clear sight picture. The cross hairs should not appear to move on the target. If it does, you have your parallax mal-adjusted.

The goal for the user of the rifle scope is to set the rear eyepiece or ocular lens and the front objective lens in the same focal plane (focused on the cross hair). When you have the scope set this way, it's like putting down the needle onto the scale in the previous photos, thus, eliminating the effect of having your eye in the wrong place. If the needle and scale of the meter were at the same height, the reading would be the same no matter what angle you would look at the meter. By setting the ocular lens or eyepiece and objective lens in the same focal plane, you'll have the same net effect and small misalignments from your eye and centerline of the scope will not change your apparent aim point. Now--how to properly set up your scope!

Figure 4. New Leupold with the objective adjustment on the side.

Set Ocular Lens or Rear Eyepiece First

The focal plane of the ocular lens should be adjusted before putting the scope into service for the first time, and unless your prescription changes, you will not make any further adjustments. The rear eyepiece is set while looking through the scope at the sky, or even inside the house at a white wall.

Young eyes have the ability to accommodate for changes or force-focus things which are in different focal planes at different distances from the eye. This effect is called "Accommodation." Your eye accommodates by bending the lens of the eye. As we age, our eyes become less flexible, thus, are no longer able to accommodate for the differences in distance, which will require the use of glasses. Welcome to the wonderful world of trifocals!

Just as in an eye exam, we need to know how the focus is set at the first instant you look through the scope before your eye has had a chance to accommodate for any out of focus condition. When adjusting the ocular lens to focus on the crosshairs, make major adjustments of about a couple of complete turns at a time, (for all but the Competition series Leupold, which has a course thread), without looking through the scope. When looking through your scope after making adjustments, you need to know if the picture is better or worse at the first instant you see the crosshair before your eye has a chance to accommodate. Continue to turn the eyepiece out, while checking every so often for improvement, until the crosshairs start to become out of focus. If you go too far, just move the eyepiece back a bit.

Now, you should have a nice clear cross hair when looking at the sky or an interior wall. Lock down the locking ring good and tight. You are now ready to adjust the objective lens, or front lens or side parallax adjustment.

In order to properly adjust your scope's objective lens to reduce the parallax, sit down behind the gun and look through the scope while pointing at the target. Turn the parallax adjustment (sometimes labeled focus) until the sight picture becomes focused, then move head slightly up and down a bit while maintaining a full sight picture and observe the crosshairs for movement against the target. If the crosshairs move against the target, adjust the parallax adjustment until the crosshairs do not move while moving your eye up and down slightly.

Figure 5. Camera off center, inside ring not concentric with outside.

One simple thing the shooter can do, is to position the scope forward in the mounts so that you get a black fuzzy ring around the image on the rear eye piece. When you center the image, your eye will be centered behind the scope, where it should be and will negate any remaining parallax from a maladjusted lens. The fuzzy ring is hard to photograph but in figure 5 you can see that the camera is slightly off center, which illustrates the misalignment I am trying to describe.

Factory Settings

Most scopes with parallax adjustments, whether it be the front lenses or a side adjustment, have markings to aid in the adjustment of parallax setting. Very few parallax adjustable scopes will be set correctly by aligning the yardage settings printed on the scope. These factory suggested settings are just that, they are suggestions. It matters not if the indicators are lined up. As seen in the following photo of a 36 power scope which is set parallax free at 200 yards, you can see the factory markings are not lined up.

Figure 6.
Notice the factory markings are not lined up. If they were, the scope would not be parallax free which could cause aiming errors.

Even if you were to re-label your scope markings, you may still need to make very slight adjustments to compensate for temperature changes throughout the day -- especially at long range. I change parallax settings as the day progresses during a match. The mirage must not be too bad in order to tell if you have minor amounts of parallax. When the mirage gets heavy (target seems to be moving an inch or two) it's hard to see the rings on the target, you have other aiming problems and a minor parallax mal-adjustment won't hurt much as trying to figure out where to aim because the target seems to be moving.

Keep direct sunlight off the scope, it can heat up the tube which makes it longer. Heating up the scope tube moves the lenses farther apart changing the parallax setting.

Larry Engelbrecht on the firing line at Luther, early 2006.
Larry has been a fixture on the firing line for more than 50 years.

Don Creach at the 1997 Nationals at Phoenix, AZ.
NBRSA President from 1993-4 through 2004, friend, and great shooter.

Rest and Bag Setup

In order to shoot small groups consistently you <u>MUST</u> have a stable front rest and rear bag. If you find yourself re-aiming more than about ½ inch at 100 yards or an inch at 200 after shooting, reloading, and returning the gun to battery, you do not have a stable setup. I refer to an unstable rest setup as the "Jell-O gelatin syndrome." Many shooters have this affliction and don't know why.

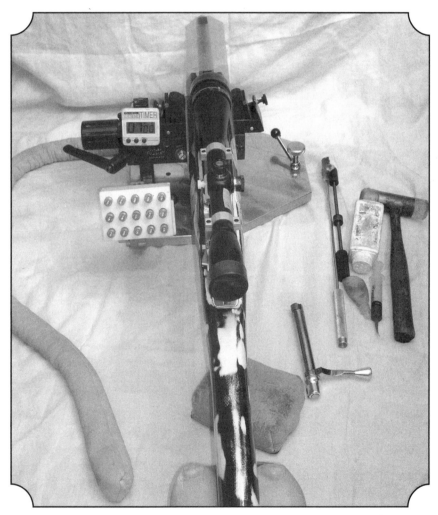

Figure 1. Stuff I take to the firing line.

I've tried to explain what constitutes a stable rest setup, at least for the purposes of shooting Benchrest with a varmint class gun. I have failed to get the thought conveyed correctly and have come to learn even when using the correct words it's very difficult, if not impossible, to properly convey the idea. Show and tell is almost a requirement. Don't pass up an opportunity to ask a successful shooter if you can look at their rest setup with their gun in the bags.

I was invited to help with the NBRSA Benchrest school at the NRA Whittington Center in Raton, NM, at the end of April, 2004. About half of the participants had some previous Benchrest experience. One of the topics was rest stability. With my past inability to properly explain what's required, we had everyone set their equipment up for critique. Speedy Gonzales (Benchrest Hall of Fame member) and I looked at every setup, critiquing them for stability. After inspecting the rest setups for the Jell-O gelatin syndrome, only two made the grading scale. I didn't say they were very good, just that they made the scale. We inspected more than 30 rest setups. Speedy and I used our setups to demonstrate what's required. Many of the rest setups were greatly improved by just substituting an extra rear bag and/or Otto bag stabilizer, which will be covered in detail later in this chapter. I brought both just for this purpose. The students made the usual comment, "I didn't realize it could be like that!"

Location on Bench

If you have a windage top, Farley or Seb front rest, set the rest in the middle of its travel for windage. The rest and bag should be set up on the bench so it's comfortable to use. Start your bench set up by placing the rear bag at the edge of the bench (left side for a right handed shooter). Set your front rest in line with the target and rear bag. Rotate the front rest so the rest top is perpendicular with the target line. Set the gun in the front rest and rear bag. Make small adjustments to the front rest to get on target. Use the scope to find the target keeping the rear bag on the edge of the bench. When adjusting the height of the front rest, use the course height adjustment first. Keep the fine adjustment about as low as you can, the rest is more stable with the fine adjustment as low as practical.

Figure 2.
Notice all of the muzzles are over the front of the bench.

The muzzle should extend forward of the firing line, which is assumed to be the front edge of the bench, or a line painted conspicuously on the bench. The muzzle should be forward of the front of the bench unless it's impossible (figure 2).

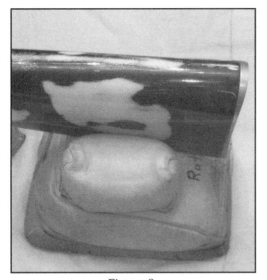

Figure 3.
Rear bag at bench edge, 1" beyond ears.

Figure 4
Use front edge of stock to square rest.

With the gun in the rest and bag, situate the position of the butt stock so that it extends beyond the ears of the rear bag about 1 inch, as seen in figure 3.

The photo in figure 3 shows the bag I use in competition. Notice the ears on my bag are leather. There are many bags on the market with cordura ears and I have used many of them. My attempts to use the cordura ears have lead to some instability, which seemed to be caused by the ears moving when the gun was fired. The best word to describe my feeling about the movement would be to say that they seem to be "alive." No matter how much better the breakaway friction was, they seemed to be alive. After every shot I had to re-aim the rifle more than usual. When using this type ear, the bag never seemed to find a home or settle down. However, many good shooters have success using bags with cordura ears.

Figure 4A.
Sinclair Rest, no longer produced.

Figure 4B.
Jon Loh rest.

Rest Rotation

Once you've found the target, square the front rest by sliding the gun back so the front edge of the stock is even with the front edge of the rest top, as in figure 4. Rotate the front rest until it's parallel with the front of the stock. Look though your scope and check to make sure you're on the correct target. If you're close, set the rest feet into bench by tapping them with a plastic or dead blow hammer. While looking though the scope, slide the gun back and forth and observe the crosshair traveling straight up and down on the target (if your rifle tracks straight). When returning the rifle to the firing position it should return to the aiming point with a minimum of re-aiming.

A stable rest setup will have very little or no vibration when touching the stop or when touching the gun or barrel. While dry firing, the crosshairs should not bounce very much on the target. You should also be able to operate the action or load the rifle without it moving all over the place.

Be careful that no part of your body should touch the rear bag. When sitting at the bench your chest should not touch the rear bag when you are in the shooting position. It would be no different than placing your head nice and firm against the stock. Many shooters squeeze the bag (bag squeezers) to aim their rifle--most with their hand. Women and larger men will have more of an issue keeping their chest away from the rear bag.

Watch Your Feet!

Be conscious of where the feet of your rest are on the bench. At the Super Shoot the benches have many divots in the bench tops, where thousands of people have tapped their rest into the concrete. Make sure your feet are planted solidly and not on the side of another hole. Not many things effect your group size more than the rest moving when you shoot. This is more of an issue with the rail guns because many of the bases are difficult (if not impossible) to see under.

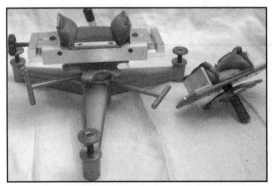

Figure 5.
Hart rest with Gebhardt or Hoehn windage top, standard Hart top to right.

Figure 5A.
Bob Dodd front rest

Figure 5B. Bald Eagle Rest

Figure 5C. Wichita Front Rest

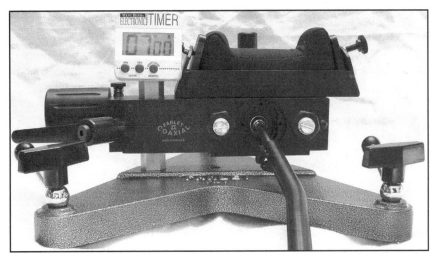

Figure 6. Farley Coaxial Rest

Farley Rest

With the introduction of the Farley rest there are new issues to consider, and with a couple easy changes, the operation can be improved. As mentioned above, the handle should be in the middle of its adjustment for windage or right and left on the initial setup.

Farley Modifications

Benchrest is extremely detail oriented. The front rest is no exception. I'm very discriminating about my personal rest, and have changed several things to eliminate potential problems. As delivered, the rifle forend stop is mounted on the bottom of the rest which is stationary. In the original configuration, the front stop slides against the front of the rifle stock from side to side and up and down. I have moved the front stop to the movable top portion of the rest (as seen in figure 10A, sorry for the page jumping). Moving the front stop allows the rifle and stop to move together when making adjustments in windage and elevation to the rest. When pinning my rifle to the front stop, I do not want the rifle to drag across the front stop while making changes in my hold for windage and/or elevation.

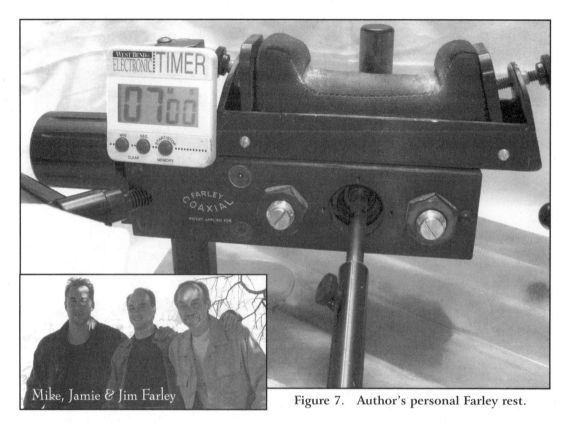

Mike, Jamie & Jim Farley

Figure 7. Author's personal Farley rest.

Boot Removal

In figure 7 it's easy to see a couple changes. A heavier base was added to my five year old rest. This added a bit more weight to prevent the rest from moving when pinning the rifle to the stop. Newer Farley rests come with a heavier base. You should notice the boot (as seen on the rest in figure 8), which covered the hole around the handle, has been removed. It has no purpose except to make the rest look better. Many shooters believe the boot is used to keep the dust out. This is ABSOLUTELY FALSE! There is a large opening underneath the top and everything falls into that slot, which is about ½ by 4.5 inches, as seen in figure 8.

Figure 8. Farley rest with top removed.

Figure 8A.
Boot as seen from inside

What the boot does do is introduce kinetic energy to the handle when in any position other than the center. It restricts overall travel. What this means is, that when you have the handle up to shoot 100 yards, the boot is trying to push the handle back down into the neutral position. The boot restricts the overall travel of the handle because of the internal size of the hole in the front of the boot facing the rest, which you cannot see. If you already own a Farley rest, remove the boot, then call me after you use it the next time to let me know how much more you liked the feel when moving the handle. The handle will not fight back.

Elevation Lock
I changed the elevation clamping knob the stock thumb wheel to one with more leverage. This is one area where more IS better. No shooter would dream of shooting on a rest leaving the elevation knob loose. I never felt able to apply enough locking force with the original knob. After changing the knob to an adjustable handle, another problem surfaced. When tightening the locking knob, the front plate on the rest, which holds the tensioners, would actually bend, decreasing the tension on the rest. This would normally be of no consequence, but the tensioners in my rest have a very high spring rate. Very little movement is a great change in applied force. To correct this problem I added the two bolts through the front plate located to the left of the tensioners, and between the elevation lock, as seen in figure 7. This addition holds the front plate in place. Now the force applied to the elevation lock does not change the tension of the main adjustments. Wow, that was a mouthful!

Farley Rest, How to Use
Proper use of the Farley front rest is important. In my opinion you <u>must</u> hold the handle when shooting the rifle. The weight of the handle is pulling down on the rest. The rifle is pushing down in the same direction. All that is needed is to add a bit more force, and the rest will move down. During recoil the shock loading of the rifle is severe, and can move the rest top if the handle is left hanging in mid air.

To test, raise the rest handle off of the bench top, stand over the rifle, and push down on the rifle above the rest. The rifle, rest and handle will go down. Have you ever had unexplained shots fall out the bottom (hitting low)?

Proper Height Setup
Now that we have decided to remove the boot and hold the handle when shooting, our next goal is to be comfortable. Keeping your hand grounded to the bench when shooting the record portion of the target is important. It's hard to hold your arm in mid air and hold the handle still, without influencing the rest by pulling or pushing on the handle.

Tilt the rest up in the front... way up. The base does not need to be level from the back to the front. Level the front bag from side to side. The bottom of the rifle forearm needs to be level from side to side. Tilting the rest up in the front will allow the handle to ride lower, without hitting the bottom side of the hole in the rest top.

Figure 9.   Dani showing proper location of handle on sighter.

Roll the bend in the handle to the right or clockwise (left and counter clockwise for left handed shooters), and touch the bench with the knob on the handle. Then set the height using the major height adjustment so the crosshairs are just barely below the sighter target. When moving to the record target, rotate the handle counter clockwise, which lifts the rest without raising the handle, and then add the extra height by lifting the knob (left handed shooters use the reverse). This will keep the end of the handle much lower when shooting the record target at 100 yards. This keeps your hand grounded on the bench instead of holding your hand in mid air trying to stay still. You can concentrate on the flags instead of holding your arm and hand still.

Loading Block or Loaded Round Storage

I use a holder which holds my loaded rounds just below and in front of my loading port, as seen in figure 10. Just reach up and grab one. One advantage of this type of holder became obvious at the 2005 NBRSA Nationals. I put my loaded rounds into the holder, and much to my surprise when looking at the holder I noticed a round with a fired primer. It is nice to find this out before trying to shoot it on the record. In figure 10, I have put empty cases in the holder for taking of the pictures. If you have one without a primer it is very easy to see. A fired primer in a sea of new primers really stands out.

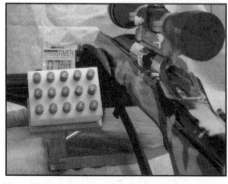

Figure 10.   Showing my loading block.

Figure 10A. My front stop, relocated

Front Stop Misconceptions

The front stop on your rest will be set once when you start to use your new rifle rest, and then forgotten about. Walk the line at any tournament and you will see that more than 95% of shooters use a front stop. The primary function of the front stop is to aid in positioning the rifle the same for each shot, which is important. The stop needs to be set so the front of the forearm extends about an inch in front of the front bag. Set the front stop far enough forward so that when the rifle recoils, the front edge of the stock stays forward of the front bag. This will help you return to your aiming point after reloading. Make sure the rifle doesn't recoil completely out of the bag. This can really slow the shooting process if you have to put the rifle back into the front bag after every shot.

Many new shooters comment about returning the rifle to the stop and then pulling back on the rifle so it doesn't touch the stop. I don't understand this at all. Unless your stop is spring loaded it will not effect the rifle on recoil. When you fire the rifle it will move away from the stop. A front stop which is not spring loaded will not influence the rifle. Pulling the rifle back away from the stop slows the shooting process. This introduces another inconsistent step to getting the rifle ready for the next shot. The idea is to have the rifle in the same place every time. If the stop were to have any influence at all on your setup, it would be when the shooter slams the rifle up to the stop after reloading, moving or scooting the rest forward on the bench.

I pin my rifle so hard from time to time that if the rest were light, the rest and rifle would end up in a pile in front of the bench after the first couple shots. Enough about the front stop.

Heavier the Better

Heavier is better when considering a front rest. You should be able to touch the front stop of the rest without the rest moving. The original Farley rests came with a lighter base, which has since been replaced with one a bit thicker. The newer rests weigh about 22 pounds.

Cam Operation & Rest Rotation

If you have a pedestal type rest like the Hart, Sinclair, Bald Eagle, Loh, Dodd, Wichita, Hayes, or any other, and use a cam or speed screw for moving between the sighter and record target, you have one other issue to consider. You must rotate your front rest during the initial setup so when operating your cam, the crosshairs move straight up and down on the target when going between the sighter and the record. On my personal pedestal rest, as shown in figure 11, I went the extra mile to make sure the rest rotation was correct. I adjusted the rotation of the top so the crosshair movement went straight up and down between the record and sighter target, when the rear leg was directly under the stock of the rifle. I should note here that no amount of rest rotation will fix a bent rifle stock. If your stock forend and butt are not parallel you have other problems which cannot be corrected by turning the front rest.

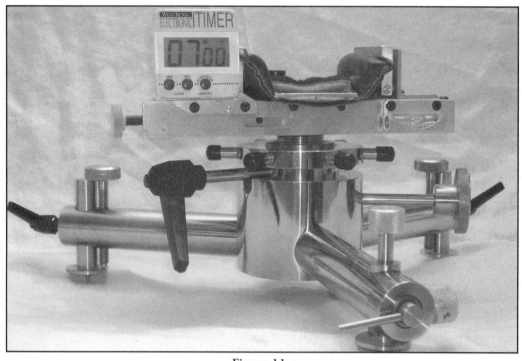

Figure 11.
Ratigan pedestal rest, with cam in rear leg, custom front feet, preloaded rest top, with bearing slide. Labor of love, about 80 hours for top and about 240 for the pedestal.

Figure 12.
Cam in rear leg of my rest.

Figure 12A.
Mr D's Cam.

The all Important Rear Bag

Arguably the rear bag is one of the most important pieces on the bench. Its function is to hold up the rear of the gun without moving on its own. Properties your bag should have are: they should be as heavy as possible, must not move, should be inert, and not contain stored energy when holding the rifle.

Figure 13.
Rear bag with Otto Stabilizer.

To make the rear bag heavy, you can fill them with extra heavy sand from Sinclair International. There are other heavy sands such as Zircon: The sand itself has properties which should be considered. The Zircon is very fine, round in shape, and white in color. The sand from Sinclair International is black, is small broken pieces which fit together nicely and will not flow or run like a pile of ball bearings. Ever try to make a pile of ball bearings and put something on top? They aren't stable. The ultra fine white sand will leak from the stitching in many bags. If given a choice, pick the black sand which is broken shards in a larger size. You might be thinking about using lead shot, this is specifically forbidden in the rules. Even if lead was legal, it's unstable because of the round shape.

Bag Stabilizer

The rear bag MUST NOT ROCK, either front to back or sideways.

Figure 13A.
Prototype Edgewood rear bag.

Figure 14.
Skip Otto bag stabilizer i.e. "Prairie Dog Life Raft."

To stop your rear bag from rocking USE AN OTTO BAG STABILIZER, referred to as a "Prairie Dog Life Raft." The Otto bag stabilizer is a raft shaped bag that holds sand and conforms to the bench, no matter what the contour. The hard bottom bags do not conform. Each bench has its own shape, and although your bag might fit your shootin' bench at home, you will still need the bag stabilizer come match time, especially when rotating benches at the majors. This is a good time to rehash "Democracy is NOT used in Benchrest." If your bag jiggles like a belly dancer on a shaker table, the stabilizer will help remove that feeling. Otherwise it's like shooting off of a waterbed.

Breakaway Friction

The rifle should not stick when it first starts to move to the rear when recoiling. Super slippery is also not wanted because of the higher recoil. Test by grabbing the rifle and pull it to the rear. If it sticks at first you will need to treat the stock and bags. I like to use a liquid wax (Liquid Glass) on the stock, any liquid wax will do, and a powdered carnauba wax on the bags. The age old trick of using baby powder will get sticky on the average afternoon. Wax stays more consistent from group to group. Wax does not absorb water from the air as does the baby powder. Wax simply makes the breakaway friction more consistent from shot to shot, and group to group.

Slippery Bag on Bench?

Many shooters complain of the bag sliding on the bench, and then use a material which is used for shelves in kitchen cupboards, as shown in figure 15. This stuff will stop the bag from sliding on the bench, but causes a problem much worse than the original. Bag instability. When putting your bag on this material it compresses somewhat, which is just like setting your bag on a spring. Some benches become slippery from the presence of a very fine dust. Phoenix Arizona is one of these ranges. Just wipe the bench where the bag will sit with a wet towel. This will get rid of the dust add helps the rear bag stay put.

Figure 15.
White Easy Liner for cupboards and tool box's, not under rear bag.

Common Bag Problem

One of my first epiphany's as a Benchrest nut came about one month after shooting my new used bench gun. I had all the right stuff--so I thought. After gently tapping the rifle into the rear bag, I watched in awe as my crosshairs moved slowly down on the target. How could that be? I was not touching any part of my setup! After about 2 minutes I figured out what was causing the problem. The stiff sides of the bag were applying force up on the ears when the gun was pushing down. The energy stored in the stiff sides was enough to actually pick up on the rear of the rifle. Now for those reading this you should be wondering... how many shots fall out the bottom when shooting free recoil? There was a small space under the ears and between the top of the sand. You're probably thinking about adding sand, but this will just mask the original problem of the sides being too stiff. To fix this, get a bag which has flimsy sides and no kinetic or stored energy that could possibly cause this problem again.

Bag Ear Material

Another thing to consider about your bag is the material the ears are made of as well as their height. I have seen every ear height used with success, and have no opinion on better or worse concerning heights. I have used and had success with both. I now use tall ears, as seen in the photo figure 13. Although I have no opinion on height I do have an opinion about cordura material used in ears. I feel they are "alive," as previously mentioned. I have shot several bags with cordura ears, and for me, I had to re-aim the rifle more than I like. This never changed with continued use. I don't feel they negatively effect accuracy, other than being a nuisance, which can slow the shooting process. I just don't like them. I also feel with the demonstrated inability to hold any shape, they might add to the Jell-O gelatin syndrome, but this is just my opinion.

Ear Stability

With the gun on the front rest, and rear bag set properly, and bag set so the ears are in line with the sides of the butt stock, slide the gun back and forth while observing the ears of the rear bag. The ears of the rear bag must NOT move to the front and rear when moving the gun back and forth. If they do move slightly you will need to correct this. This is normally caused by not having enough sand in the body or ears of the bag. If the ears are full of sand you most likely have an air space under the ears of the bag. To test, remove the gun from the bags and gently grab the ears on the sides. Try to lift them or rock them back and forth. Many bags with stiff side panels exhibit this problem. The sides of the bag are able to hold the ears up off of the sand inside the bag causing an air space under the ears. Rear bags are the most common cause of the Jell-O gelatin syndrome by far.

Carpet and/or Elbow Pad

Most shooters use a carpet or towel on the bench. Whatever you decide, do not set your front rest or rear bag on the carpet or towel. Most cut out where the rear bag will go on their carpet, and cut holes for the rest feet. I have cut holes for the feet on my rest and made a cutout for the rear bag, as seen in figure 16.

Figure 16.
Carpet the author uses on the bench.

No matter the range, the relationship between the rest and bag stays about the same. My carpet, which has been cut for my benches at home, has worked fine everywhere I have ever shot. Carpet helps keep your loaded rounds and fired cases from rolling around in the wind and onto the ground. Your carpet should extend around your rear bag to help keep your elbow from rubbing the concrete bench during recoil and during your reloading motion. Those with sensitive skin should consider buying a mouse pad. Yep, that thing you use under a computer mouse to help the roller move. It is sure smooth under your elbow. Jack Snyder of Edgewood Bags makes a very nicely made elbow pad out of leather, which also does the trick.

Snake Bag

When using my left-port left-eject rifles, on the normal T shaped benches, there is not much bench for the cases to eject onto. I used a rolled up towel to catch my cases from the time I started using an ejector. I considered making a sand bag the diameter of a fifty cent piece and about two feet long to use as a dam to stop the cases from rolling off the bench. As if it weren't bad enough the towel would blow off, I would have to roll the darn thing up again. After rolling up my towel about 4500 times, I finally had had enough.

Jack Snyder to the rescue. I met Jack for the first time at Raton, NM, in 2000. He made leather products with his brother Don Freeman. Beautiful English riding leather for horses. I asked Jack about making the bag described above. He looked at me like I was crazy (trained observer), but made one anyway. A couple years later Jack admitted thinking he would never sell one. Today you find many of these long slender sandbags at registered tournaments--thanks Jack! Mine, made of Elk hide, is pictured on the left side of the rifle in figure 1 of this chapter.

Umbrella as a Sunshade

It can be hard to see with the sun shining on your face and scope objective lens. When the sun shines under the awning you can use an umbrella to provide shade for your head and scope. There are many contraptions to provide shade. Some are small rectangular pieces of plywood, with some elaborate clamping systems to help change the height and tilt of the board.

Figure 17.   Rex Reneau, trying to keep the sun out of his eyes at the
1995 NBRSA Nationals.

Umbrellas are used only as a last resort to shield from rain. When rain droplets accumulate on the umbrella you will get soaked when firing the rifle. The muzzle blast releases the rain drops from the surface of the umbrella. They come sliding down onto you and your equipment. While it's raining you just do the best job possible to keep the water out of the muzzle of your rifle. You are going to get wet. Don't worry, you ARE waterproof.

Location of Extras

Locate everything the same on the bench every time you set up. This will pay big dividends when you need something in the heat of competition. I like to keep my extra chamber and action cleaning tools at the bench when not cleaning at the bench, as you sometimes do at smaller matches. I don't like going back to my loading area after I forget to clean the solvent out of the chamber.

Mark Your Spot

When sharing a bench (or rotating) you'll need a magic marker to mark the position of your rest and rear bag. This saves time when you set your equipment up for subsequent groups. Wait until finishing your group to mark the rest and bag in case you make any minor adjustments. During tournaments where you rotate benches, such as at the Super Shoot or Nationals, you will repeat this process five times, once for each bench you will shoot on, and maybe another five times for the yardage change. At some ranges the targets are in a completely different line when changing yardages.

Bench Moving?

After all the troubles we go through to prep our cases and reload, it would be foolish to sit down and shoot over a rolled up sleeping bag across the hood or your car or truck. A stable bench is an important foundation on which to start, and is a must when trying to shoot accurate rifles of any type. Many benches move when leaning against them. Some have loose tops and yet others have inadequate pedestals that move. Even the guys who shoot off hand during competition evaluate equipment and components shooting off of a bench from time to time.

Test the bench for movement. Set up your equipment and get comfortable, set your chair to a comfortable height. Look through your rifle scope, then lean against the bench. Watch for any movement of the crosshairs. If you notice movement, you must exercise caution in how you touch the bench. Many shooters will lean against the bench when shooting. I would suggest you don't lean against the bench if doing so will change your point of impact.

Posture

Keep both feet on the ground. At Raton, NM, and the right side of Fairchance, PA, it can be difficult unless you are 6'8" tall. About everywhere else you should be able to keep your frame or body stable. Position yourself around the gun and get in a comfortable position. Practice your posture, keep both feet on the ground at all times. Do not rely on the bench for your stability.

Don't sit on a spring. If your stool has rubber feet, remove them and throw them away. Their purpose is to keep from damaging interior floors, if you shoot on interior floors, can I come over and shoot?.

Figure 18.
Both feet planted on ground helping keep mid section stable.

Bench Stuff

Keep in one container with the exception of the front rest.

Front rest	Rear bag
Prairie dog life raft (Otto donut)	
Towel or carpet	Timer
Snake bag	Plastic hammer
Bolt lug lube	Bolt body lube
Stool	Elbow pad (mouse pad)
Marker	Brick bag or equivalent
Wax for bags, or baby powder.	

Steve Brown and Phil Jones (Australian team members) Demonstrate working together. Phil holds the rest while Steve shoots a group.

So Many Choices...Which Rest?

I am frequently asked about which rest to buy. I have personal preferences, but about every rest you can conceive of has been used with success. The most important property needs to stability.

I would like to see more match directors include the rest and rear bags in the equipment lists from the tournaments that the top competitor's use during the matches, until then...

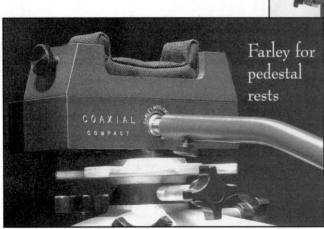

Butch Lambert's rest top

Farley for pedestal rests

Superman Bullets

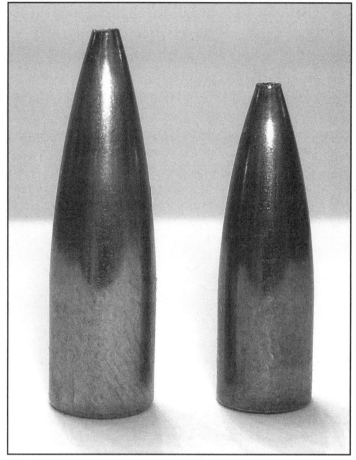

Figure 1. Ratigan custom made 6mm and 22 bullets.

Bullets! Bullets! Bullets! Bullets are everything to the competitive Benchrest shooter. If you shoot long enough, you will become very aware of the fact that once in awhile a lot of jackets are made that produce bullets that are head and shoulders above anything else. This phenomenon is very easy to see. Shooters who normally finish in the middle of the pack, finish in the top and win. When you inquire about the bullet used in the exemplary shooting performance, you will often find they are using some of the new found magic bullets.

These bullets are so good they <u>seem</u> as though they add nothing to the factors which cause dispersion. Superman bullets agg in the zeros--much better than the aggregate capability of a good Benchrest bullet. Bullets range in aggregate ability from the illusive Superman bullet, to good, poor and BAD. I would venture a guess that the aggregate capability of the average good Benchrest bullet to be just below about two tenths of an inch (say .160-.180). The Superman bullet seems to have aggregate capability much smaller, maybe .040 (forty thousandths) of an inch.

I've had bullets which fit nicely into the BAD category. This is not all bad, (pun intended). With BAD bullets it takes very little time and effort to figure out something is wrong. I tested bullets in nice conditions at Kansas City, which averaged 1.6 inches at 200 yards. That's an aggregate of .800, good enough for last place about anywhere. There was no doubt something was terribly wrong. I borrowed five bullets from a neighbor and shot one group at 200 yards which measured about .500, and that was just guessing on the seating depth. The problem was found with less than two hours invested.

Bullets between good and bad can be a challenge. These gems will tease you by putting some of the shots together, but never seeming to agg very well come the end of the day. If you live in a part of the world with nice weather, you won't have any problems discovering the quality of the bullet. You will have many shots out of the group for no reason. For the rest of us it takes a bit longer. Usually at a tournament, when everyone is spanking your behind, is when you first realize something might be wrong. The search is on; scopes, powder, primers, cases, barrel, or just maybe the BULLETS!

I've had three opportunities with bullets I would characterize as Superman bullets since I've been shooting accurate rifles. I had one box of jackets, when starting to make my own 6mm bullets, which were head and shoulders above average. I still have the first five targets shot with them. The aggregate was .1480, and life was good. I also had the chance to shoot one box of 500 from around 2002 from another maker, WOW, they were great. I have also had some 22 jackets which have shown excellent performance.

Finding such a bullet is the "holy grail" of Benchrest. When a shooter finally figures out what I am trying to describe is true, there will be endless hours spent trying to find more.

When a bullet maker who sells bullets happens onto jackets which make the ultimate in Benchrest bullets, that bullet maker will quickly dominate the match report equipment lists. Our most recent example of this phenomenon was in 2002, when Bart Sauter, of Bart's Custom Bullets, released upon us a batch of bullets which helped create a new bunch of Benchrest experts… at least until the bullets were gone. Soon after the discovery of such bullet quality, the bullet maker is overwhelmed by orders. And then about as quick as the Superman bullets had appeared, we are again relegated to our normal quality of bullets. Which, I must add, are pretty good.

Occasionally a shooter will obtain some Superman bullets and one of two things happens. They step to the podium and proclaim they are the new Tony Boyer, or they quickly tell stories of all their new barrels being the best they ever had. In a recent conversation where a shooter friend began to tell stories of super human barrels, and not just one but everything he had received lately were GREAT, he suggested the lot of barrel steel was good enough to warrant a second mortgage to buy all they had. After listening intently for a few minutes I could not help but ask "whose bullets are you using?" This question usually prompts the question "why do you ask." I continued by commenting about how odd it is that all of his equipment was performing better than it ever had, and the only new thing was a recent change in bullets, either lot or manufacturer.

The point of this whole chapter is to help you recognize when you have this illusive bullet before shooting them all during practice or in the smaller matches. After you discover you have had Superman bullets, <u>write down what the feeling is like when shooting them!</u> Record the feeling of knowing exactly where they will go every time you pull the trigger--how others talk about 2.5 inches of wind drift at 200 when you see much less, just to name a couple. Hopefully by doing this you might recognize them next time, before wasting them.

Analysis

Larry Engelbrecht and I have spent many hours talking about this phenomenon. Larry retired as a Troubleshooter for the CEO at Cessna Aircraft after more than fifty years. Larry was charged with solving any problems in materials and Engineering with any of the aircraft lines at Cessna. He also has been a past regional director of the NBRSA Mid-Continent region, past NBRSA President from 80-81, custom bullet maker for over 40 years, and my friend. Larry has been shooting Competitive Benchrest since 1956. Only Mike Walker, Walt Berger and George Kelbly Sr., have more experience.

Any shooter worth their weight in Benchrest will tell you gentle reader of the truth of this chapter, but as common as this knowledge is among the top guns in the sport, it's equally understood we don't know how to tell if a box of jackets will produce the uncommon performance, without shooting them.

Mike Walker, formerly of Remington, stated, "In his experience the quality of the gilding material determined the final accuracy performance of the bullet." Mike was not privy to what was regarded as acceptable. Remington had metallurgist's who took care of that quality control, and whether or not the material would be accepted or rejected. The bullet dies alone are not a factor in the accuracy potential of the final product, other than they need to be concentric and straight. Many things which are relatively simple go into the making of bullets--many of which can be varied--all of which can effect the bullet's accuracy potential, we are talking about making all of the bullets correctly, having one particular jacket being better accuracy wise.

We do know the die in which these gems are produced is not the determining factor when considering the uncommon accuracy. When the Superman jackets are used up, those same dies which produced the "holy grail" of Benchrest bullets, return to previous production quality. Likewise, the rifles and equipment used to shoot these bullets return to their previous performance level before the Superman bullet was introduced. These two facts also point to the jacket being the factor, but not to any specific property of the manufacture or gilding material.

To help explain why this observation is fact, we need to spend a moment and talk about bullet dispersion. Without rewriting the chapters in Harold Vaughn's book "Rifle Accuracy Facts," dealing with the effect of core stripping and bullet imbalance caused by the Center of Gravity (CG) offset caused by the core being off to one side due to the run out of the jacket or because of inconsistent core density.

Who knows what property of the jacket is responsible? One thing we do know is that whatever it is, it's not something that you can measure with simple inch measuring tools. Many shooters and bullet makers use a ball micrometer and claim they measure jacket concentricity. This property can be measured, but measuring the jacket at one point over its height does not tell the story of how uniform the jacket thickness is. It's just one sample, and it's not reasonable to assume the error at the point measured will be consistent throughout.

To get a representation of jacket concentricity or run out, you must look at the jacket over the majority of its height. To get a representation of the CG offset, you should measure the whole area of the jacket where the lead core will be, including the base thickness around the circumference. The CG offset is a measure of the mass being off center. Again this cannot be measured or represented in a measurement of jacket measurement at one point on the jacket.

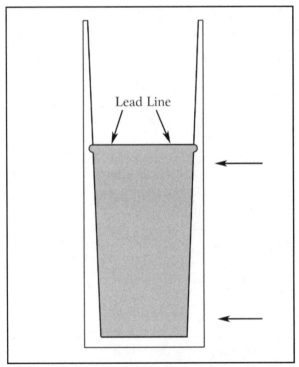

Figure 2. Representation of jacket with core seated.

My lot of 6mm jackets, when measured with the ball micrometer, showed run out at the measurement point of about .0004, which if measured alone, would cause many to turn up their nose and go on to the next bunch looking for something better. But let me tell you I would pay a small fortune for more of those jackets!

Mass spectrometry is used to analyze the quantity of different materials contained in a material sample. We can sample jacket material from Superman bullets, and samples of jacket material from other good quality Benchrest bullets. It's unlikely we would see any correlation in the graphs of the Superman samples. I'm not sure the graphs would tell us which property of the material was responsible for this uncommon performance. It's possible that differences in the mixing of the molten material are responsible for the magic, which would not show as anything unusual on the graphs. That's where an electron microscope might come in handly.

During a discussion with a long time bullet maker Don Gentner, at the 8th World Benchrest Championships at Kelbly's in 2005, this subject came up again. Don also surmised the chemical composition might be responsible for the occasional magic jacket lot, but he also did not have any idea what to look for, or if the difference in chemical composition would be different enough to tell by comparison to the average good jacket.

The chemical makeup of the gilding material can vary due to a number of reasons. The finished product, or copper sheet, used in the making of the jackets, can have grain structure differences, which can be caused by the mixing process at the foundry. The wire can have inconsistent hardness from the same, raw copper from the smelter and can vary in quality, purity, and hardness specification. The people in control of the alloying process might not care enough to correctly control the process (shovels and containers full of material). The annealing process can be inconsistent and out of spec. It's possible the sheet can vary in hardness even across the sheet producing jackets of different properties from the same sheet run. Hell, I could go on for another hour, but one thing should be clear--making the jacket material is more involved than first meets the eye. You don't just order the material and expect to get the exact same material every time.

To summarize this section, you **MUST** shoot the bullet, and let the performance provide you with the quality information. We may never know why they are, or what makes them the way they are, but this doesn't negate the fact that THEY ARE....MAGIC!

The net effect of the occasional Superman bullets is apparent. They have the ability to quickly transform a shooter with average flag reading skill into a superhero. Above average shooting ability is not going to overcome a bullet's accuracy potential, which is sometimes less than perfect. I wasted two years trying to make a lot of jackets shoot that would not. I thought by messing with the dies, I would make things better, but to no avail. They were no good. Different methods are now used to evaluate my bullets. Finishing place isn't one of them.

If we have two shooters with different flag reading skills, and one with the lesser skill is given the Superman bullet's and the shooter with the greater skill level given the normal bullets, we observe something interesting. In the following example, a novice shooter has the flag reading skill of about .200 and the pro is twice as good in reading the flags with a normal resolution of about .100 at 100 yards.

When both shooters have the same bullets, the pro in my example will often shoot aggs about .100 smaller than the novice. But give Superman bullets, capable of shooting aggs in the .050 range, to the novice shooter, and good bullets which are capable of shooting just about the .200 level to the pro, the outcome will be much different. The novice shooter with the same ability now can agg about .250 with the same shooting skill, but the best you could expect from the pro would be about .300. This helps show what an advantage the shooter has with the better bullet. The only way the pro could expect to compete with the novice would be to better his average performance by a factor of two. Now, that is hard to do.

You can imagine how difficult it would be when you come to the firing line and a couple of the top guns of benchrest appear with the illusive Superman bullet. You are shooting for second or third, at best.

Don Powell came to my loading area at the 2002 Super Shoot to tell stories of a new bullet that seemed to possess the powers of the illusive Superman bullet we all look for. Don was instructed to go and buy all he wanted, and then let me know. I would buy what was left. Don did just that. He let me have one box of 500 which absolutely fit the description. They were used at Raton in a sporter match, a run away finish. Life is great when armed with this type of bullet.

There are many custom bullet makers who spend hours making these things we shoot for very little profit. Thanks to everyone for your dedication to our sport. Many top shooters make their own bullets. The thought is to have control over the whole process and to know what you have for sure. But, I would buy bullets from any bullet maker demonstrating the aggregate capability of a Superman bullet. No one knows what causes the phenomenon, referred to as the Superman bullet, but it is a FACT of Benchrest, just as the earth turns from west to east.

$1.00 US reward for each jacket which produces the illusive Superman bullet, but until then the search continues.

Happy hunting!

Loading Box Contents

Figure 1. Authors loading tools, setup at the range.

Anyone, from the hunter to target shooter, can benefit from reloading at the range. It's a MUST for any Benchrest shooter. The process of rifle tuning is made faster and easier by reducing trips to the range trying different bullets, powders, and seating depths--not to mention the time saved to set up and tear down all of your bench stuff and flags. Once you embrace loading at the range you will wonder how you went without for so long.

Everyone who reloads can load at the range with minimum effort. Presses and powder measures can be clamped to a board or bench at the range with a couple of C-clamps. Varmint shooters and hunters can resize and re-prime the empty cases at home, then simply travel to the range with a press, bullet seater, bullets, caliper, powder measure, powder and scale, bullet puller, and loading data.

Having loading tools at the range makes changing powder charges, seating depths, primers, neck diameters, bullets fast and easy. Mobile loading tools also allow the use of a minimum number of cases for each barrel. Most Benchrest shooters use 15 to 20 pieces of brass for Varmint and Sporter class rifle barrels, which are used to shoot 5 shot groups. About 20-30 cases are needed for unlimited barrels when shooting 10 shot groups.

Preparing brass to Benchrest specifications is time consuming and they're expensive to purchase. If you shoot Benchrest for any amount of time you will have multiple barrels for each action. Making brass in large quantities for every barrel is uneconomical. Most shooters will shoot between 9-16 shots per 5 shot group. You will shoot a couple shots to foul the barrel, some sighter shots, and five shots on the record target. A grand aggregate is 10 groups. A two gun aggregate is made up of 20 groups, a three gun aggregate is 30. To preload for a weekend two gun match you will need between 180-400 pieces of brass. If you purchase ready to fireform brass from one of the Benchrest suppliers you will spend about $1.50 each. This is about $270.00–600.00 for each barrel, just for the brass. Starting to get the idea? The brass will cost more than the barrel. Not all Benchrest barrels will be good enough to shoot in competition. You will spend a fortune on brass for barrels which are not good enough to shoot in a tournament.

Benchrest shooters have many tools or "do-dads". Some things are required and others are just nice to have. The equipment you need will fit into a small tool box making transport easy.

Figure 2. Scharny's loading Box

Must Have Tools

If you full length resize your brass, you will need a press for full length sizing, full length die, neck bushings, "Otto" die shims, and sizing die wax. If you are neck sizing, you will need a neck die, neck bushings, and die base for your neck die.

Regardless of neck or full length sizing, you will need a loading block, arbor press, (could use your full length press) priming tool, primer pocket uniformer to clean pockets, nylon brush for cleaning inside necks, chamfering tool, bullet seater, small screwdriver, inexpensive calipers, bullet comparator, shoulder measuring gauge, powder measure and bracket, bullet puller, small assortment of Allen wrenches, rule book, record book for barrels, and pens or pencils.

Nice to have

There are a few tools many shooters acquire which will fit in the category of things which are nice to have. They are tools like a case trimmer, flash hole deburring tool, cleaning swabs, small piece of emery cloth, small file, spare decapping pin, ear plugs, band aids, Never Dull for cleaning necks, spare trigger, neck turner, and neck sizing mandrels with sizing body (these are for home use, unless you are Jack Neary, Jack uses about 500 pieces of brass at each match, I will explain further in the match report for the World Benchrest Championships later).

The photo in figure 3 shows about everything needed to shoot. The case is small enough to carry and will meet the weight requirements for air travel. All that will be needed are the flammables like powder, primers and solvent. They also travel with a front rest which has a hollow pedestal which is filled with lead or something heavy upon arrival, very clever indeed.

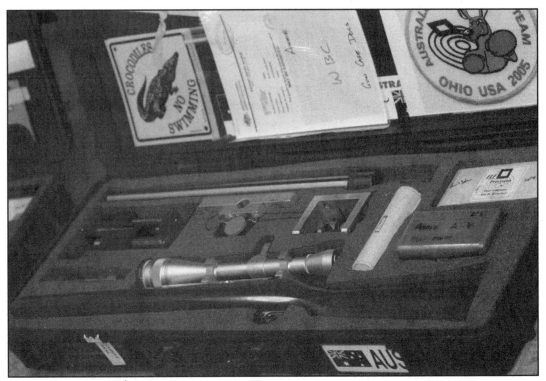

Figure 3.
Stuart and Annie Elliott's gun case, prepared to travel to the USA to shoot.

Other Loading Box Stuff

It's very easy to fill a tool box to the point of being too heavy to lift. With a little experience, you'll remove the tools from your loading box which aren't used at the range. When packing to travel to a tournament, as long as you bring your full length die you will be able to borrow about anything else you might need, from bullet pullers to case trimmers.

I carry a few other things such as brass, extra scope rings, assortment of small parts, springs and pins, extra action parts and springs, small calculator, powder scale, and extra timer (for bench).

Having a scale in your loading box can be an asset. Digital scales are nice in one respect--they eliminate errors reading the scale. It's a common misconception that because a digital scale has a digital readout it must be correct. In the price range of scales used at the range, we get what we pay for. Many of these scales are not able to measure to the resolution of the numbers displayed on the display. Measurement of many scales in this price range is not much better than 1%. Just because the readout reads two or three digits right of the decimal does not mean it can measure that amount accurately.

Sebastian Lambang from Indonesia, maker of the Seb front rest.
Photo taken while he shoots from one of his rests during a trip to Australia.

6PPC & 22-100

Figure 1. 6PPC left, 22-100 middle.

The Palmisano Pindell Cartridge (PPC) simply is the most inherently accurate cartridge ever developed. It's been the undisputed heavy weight champion in rifle accuracy for over a quarter century.

It's hard to imagine a cartridge could have such a profound effect on the accuracy world as has the PPC. The success of the PPC has even astounded Dr. Lou Palmisano and Ferris Pindell, the creators of the cartridge. Almost 100% of the shooters on the firing line at any tournament are using a PPC in 6mm or a cartridge based on the PPC, such as the 22-100. The reason is quite simple. The availability of good brass, it's user friendly, and it's easy to tune. Everything about this cartridge seems to work well together. Many powders, primers, bullet shapes, and weights perform well in the PPC. When using good components, even an out of tune rifle can perform remarkably well.

It's hard to imagine that any future cartridge could have such a profound affect on the Benchrest community as has the PPC, given the current accuracy levels.

History

Rifles used in early organized Benchrest matches, prior to the introduction of the Sporter rifle class were predominantly 22 caliber. Life was good for the accuracy nut and varmint hunters alike after the introduction of the 222 Remington in 1950. A high percentage of shooters used the 222 Remington in the Light and Heavy Varmint matches, or a wildcat based on the 222 (.222 magnum, .222½) until the late '70s and early '80s.

In 1958 the NBRSA established a new rifle class called the "Sporter." Sporter class rules were similar to the Light Varmint class with two distinct exceptions. First, it must be 6mm or larger. Second, scope magnification was limited to 6 power.

Before the removal of the scope power limitation from the Sporter class, many shooters used different rifles for each of the NBRSA Varmint classes. After the scope magnification restriction was changed, many shooters were compelled to find a way to shoot one rifle in both the Light Varmint and Sporter classes. This would help reduce the workload trying to keep two and sometimes three rifles up and running.

In the days before the PPC there was no one dominant cartridge. Shooters experimented with many different cartridges for the Sporter such as the 6x47, 6mm International, 308 Winchester, 6mm Remington, 6mm x 225, 6mm x 224, 6 x 43, and many others. The most popular Sporter class cartridge of the day was the 6 x 47, and most shooters found this cartridge to be finicky at its best.

Testing by Dr. Lou Palmisano showed consistent powder ignition with a small rifle primer that had a slightly smaller flash hole diameter, and a shorter powder column, about 1.5 inches long.

With this test data the search was on for a short case with a small flash hole. The 220 Russian, a machine gun cartridge, was used as the parent case for the PPC. The 220 had several of the properties which made it attractive. It had a small rifle primer, smaller flash hole (.066), and it was short. The body was severely tapered to aid in the automatic feeding of the cartridge. This was easily fixed with a reamer which had most of the body taper removed and the shoulder angle changed. The neck diameter of the chamber was reduced so you could neck turn the cases to correct any concentricity or wall thickness problems. All the shooter need do is neck turn the cases and then fire form them in the new chamber. Easy.

The 22PPC showed excellent accuracy potential from the very beginning. Ferris Pindell had success with the new 22PPC at the 1975 Super Shoot. It didn't take long before the 22PPC was sized up to the 6PPC, which we are so familiar with today. This was done to meet the requirements of the NBRSA Sporter class.

Dr. Lou Palmisano   Figure2.   Ferris Pindell

After the Sako 220 Russian brass became available in the Untied States, almost all of the other cartridges vanished from the Benchrest scene. Today it's rare to find anything else being campaigned at Benchrest tournaments. The reason is very simple--the PPC is the best all around cartridge available.

Manufacturers of the larger hunting calibers are finally getting the idea of short and fat. Today you find many short and super short magnums in factory chamberings. These shorter hunting cartridges exhibit some properties of the PPC--easier to tune with lighter recoil. Who would have guessed it? Only took more than 20 years for the manufacturers to pick up on that. Even though the short magnums shoot very well they're bound to have feeding problems to some degree because of their size.

The accuracy capability of the 6PPC allows the shooter with one 10.5 pound rifle to participate and be competitive in all of the bag gun classes.

Larry Engelbrecht asked Ferris Pindell about the amazing similarities between the PPC and the Donaldson Wasp. Ferris replied he had used the tried and true method of taking the best properties of each cartridge of the day, and designed the new cartridge out of them. Compare the 219 Donaldson Wasp to the PPC. You will notice they are similar in many ways. It is amazing how long the basic case body design has been around the Benchrest shooting scene.

22 Waldog (.125 short 22PPC)

The 22 Waldog, an idea of Dan Dowling, first used at Phoenix in 1980.

Until the introduction of the PPC the 222 was king. After the original 22PPC was made into the 6PPC and replaced all of the sporter cartridges being used there was another problem. The 222 and the PPC were different bolt faces. By this time the Sporter class had evolved into a 6mm Light Varmint rifle. Using one rifle in 222 and the 6x47 was common by changing barrels. Now with the two different bolt faces it wouldn't be practical. Dan Dowling to the rescue.

To Dan, the 22PPC seemed just a bit too large for the powders of the day. Dan shortened the case, reducing the capacity to better fit the powder. Several world records have been broken by the short versions of the 22 caliber, including Rex Reneau's .1399 100 yard aggregate in Heavy Varmint from 1982--the smallest yardage aggregate by a bag gun to date.

Figure 3. Logo from Dan Dowling's business card.

As with many ideas, the name for this new cartridge had humble beginnings. Dan used to chew a bit of tobacco. A friend, Jack Shipiro, who worked in an add agency made several drawings for Dan, one of which you see above.

Fred Sinclair helped Dan with the forming of the first shortened cases. A 22PPC die was used but would swell the front of the case. Eventually Bill Pond came up with the idea of shortening a 22-250 die. The front of the 22-250 die is about the same taper as the original 220 russian taper. More about this later.

I first met Dan in 1997 at the Cactus Classic in Phoenix. Dan was shooting a rifle with a very unique rifle barrel. The outside of the barrel had a hex machined onto the outside. The hex was twisted to one turn in 14 inches. I inquired about the machining time to make that twisted hex. Dan confirmed it took many hours in the CNC mill with an automatic indexing head. He said the barrel was "rifled on the outside." With his sense of humor I could tell we would get along just fine.

Figure 4. Dan Dowling

My first opportunity to shoot next to Dan at a tournament was at the 2006 Cactus. We had a wonderful time trading stories. I inquired about the "Waldog" name. Dan told me the story of how he came up with the name. Just as with many ideas, it started in a joking manner while at home and visiting about a local friend. Dan named his new design after a friend, Waldo G. Woodside, thus the Waldo-G or Waldog.

22 Performance

While any velocity can be used indoors or in a tunnel, you should use the highest velocity that produces usable results without being too sensitive and which doesn't cause too many problems with the cases and action operation. 22-100 muzzle velocities over 3500 fps are typical. This powder charge will not fit into the shorter .125 or 1/8 inch short case (Waldog) with the N133 of today.

In order to get enough powder in the case to get up to the next higher tuning node (higher than the .125 short PPC), Rex Reneau started making the case longer. My first 22 short was -.100 and shot very well. I was reluctant to call this cartridge a Waldog and it certainly wasn't a 22PPC. Being of a lazy nature, I did not want to write some long description of the cartridge on the equipment list for the match reports, thus, the 22 short and subsequently the 22-100. Short and sweet.

Using a ballistic program you can see the relative similarities of the wind sensitivity between the 6PPC and the short 22's. When changing between the 6PPC and 22-100, I do nothing different when holding at 200 yards with similar flag readings. In fact, I often find that I will over hold when shooting the 22-100. Over holding is a very nice problem to have and is very easy to correct.

Early on at the start of my competition shooting, I watched Rex shoot his 22 short PPC. Rex never seemed to have any problem shooting it. I felt he would never go to a large tournament with a self imposed handicap. Many believe that the 22 is more wind sensitive, which is absolutely false. The velocity of the 22 short is well above 3500pfs and has the same wind sensitivity as the 6PPC at 200 yards. I do not change the amount I hold when alternating between the 6 and 22. This is one more variable which would just complicate matters.

Legalized Cheating

In my opinion the short 22 caliber is so good, it is akin to cheating, but is entirely legal. Thus the term "legalized cheating."

Many shooters have inquired about the short cartridge. I convey my love for this cartridge for several reasons. First, the reduction in recoil is significant. This helps in the gun handling department. The first one tenth of an inch of recoil must be the same every time. Secondly, I feel the tune-up is less sensitive. In my experience shooting the cartridge, I've had less trouble chasing the tune than with any of my 6PPCs, ever. Third, I find the wind drift to actually be comparable and sometimes even less at 200 yards than the 6PPC. Fourth, good bullets are easier to make. When you have the same error in the jacket, the 22 will be better, you'll have less mass off center or less CG offset. The 6 bullet must be better in jacket concentricity to be of equal quality.

Two drawbacks to shooting the 22-100 are making the cases and the inability to shoot the 22-100 in the Sporter class.

Is the 6PPC better?

Why not let me shoot the 22 in the Sporter class?
What's everyone afraid of?
Think about it!

Powder is as important in the 22-100 as the 6PPC. Rex has been shooting BLC-1 in his for many years before I started shooting. This powder was unobtainable (unobtainium) and is unrealistic for many to obtain. I was advised to try N130. For 6 months I tried to shoot the 22 with this powder. I was able to shoot some small groups, but never a competitive aggregate. I tested several different powder lots. Although I shot some good groups with the N130, the aggregates were less than impressive. At the end of my rope, I was ready to abandon all my 22 stuff, bullet dies and all. In desperation I loaded some N133 powder for my 6PPC into the 22 case, WOW, did things change. I shot 56 groups over four days on two weekends. All groups were shot at 200 yards in our normal Oklahoma weather, which is usually WINDY and not too great. The aggregate of all of the groups, (not leaving any out), was .2204

You must understand, cheating when evaluating equipment or components only benefits the competition. Again, the agg of all of the 56 groups at 200 yards was .2204. Yep, that's a 5.5 gun agg of .2204, all at 200. WOW, THAT WILL WORK! The N133 produced only a couple of groups in the twos, but NO big groups. I shot one group about .900, one .800, one .700, some six's, some five's, lots of threes and four's and a couple two's. I've used this cartridge ever since with several different lots of N133 with great success.

It didn't take long to realize I was leaving my best stuff at home by not bringing my 22 to the line during the major tournaments. I began shooting my 22 at the Super Shoot in 1998 and don't see this changing any time soon.

My only regret shooting my 22 was in Sweden at the World Benchrest Championships. My rifle was shooting very well--one of the best at the range. My 200 yard practice groups were small, very small, in tricky conditions. I was victimized by the cleaning solvent. The more I shot the rifle, the larger the groups became. I was unable to clean the rifle. The solvent we were provided was so old it had crystallized in the bottles. We might as well have been using water. We finally received some good solvent but it was too late. I continued in the Championship sharing Gene Bukys' rifle in 6PPC which shot pretty darn good.

"With so few 22's being brought to the firing line, why do they seem
to be at, or very near the top so often?"

George Kelbly, Sr.

Figure 5. George Kelbly Sr. and your author.
George, one of the true ambassadors of the sport, with more than 50 years experience.

If the 6mm restriction of the Sporter class were removed, I would bet in a few short years we would see the death of the 6PPC, at least at the matches or tournaments.

Case Forming for the 22-100

When considering a short 22PPC you will need to purchase or make some cases. If you decide to make the cases yourself, you will need a couple extra tools to facilitate the manufacturing of your new cases. Starting with 220 Russian cases, you need some way to shorten the case or push the shoulder back. The easiest way I have found to shorten a 22-250 full length die. This will be used to push the shoulder back about .105 for a .100 short 22PPC. Then trim the neck length back to about .100. At this point your standard neck turning tools will be used to turn the necks to the thickness needed for your chamber.

Two passes with the neck turner at different depths of cut will ease the turning process and give greater control over the final wall thickness. I use two different turners--one set to about .011 thickness and then my finisher set to about .0087. After the turning process, continue with the standard case prep, chamfering the neck, primer pocket uniforming, then flash hole deburring. My chamber neck diameter is .243. The necks are turned to a uniform thickness of about .0085-.0090. The final outside diameter of the loaded round with a bullet installed is between .241 and .242, which will give between one and two thousandths clearance. When using these chamber dimensions and neck thickness, your range of neck bushing diameters needed will be from about .239, .2395, .2400, .2405, and .2410. This range will give you neck tension from light to heavy.

Measure the outside diameter of every loaded round where the pressure ring of the bullet sets in the case. Oil the case with light weight oil on a patch and fire. Fire form just like any cartridge. Then trim to final length and you're ready to shoot.

Why didn't you hit the middle?

Extremely rare,
Back to Back sub .100 groups during a registered tournament.

Why didn't you hit the middle? Something every competitive group shooter hears when practicing. Hunters and varmint shooters alike often wonder why the groups aren't in the middle. Well first I don't want any chance of shooting out my aiming point. Second, I want the bullets downwind of my crosshair.

Precision does not equal Accuracy

Precision = Five bullets in the same hole.
Accuracy = Putting a single bullet where you want it.

You cannot have accuracy without precision.

With a rifle that shoots every shot into the same hole, don't ya think I could hold over and hit the middle? Don't judge a group by where it forms.

Shooting Techniques

With the small aggregates being shot today, you need every advantage possible. For the new shooter, I recommend you learn to use different shooting techniques, each has advantages and disadvantages. It's important to use the proper technique at the correct time, which is dependent on the range conditions at the moment. Be flexible when refining your strategy in regards to your shooting techniques. At certain times you'll need to be very careful with your gun handling or "table manners," and at other times you'll need to shoot at the correct time. How carefully you handle your rifle won't be as big of an issue. There are 2 different basic shooting techniques--free recoil and holding/pinning. I will attempt to give you a comprehensive explanation of each technique.

Figure 1. On the firing line at the 2005 Nationals St. Louis.
Photo by Todd Tyler

Posture

First things first. Get comfortable while seated at the bench. Adjust your chair height where you feel natural and not bent out of shape. Keep your head down when shooting, as though you are looking through scope all of the time, even when the rifle is recoiling and during reloading. Keep both feet on the ground unless it's not possible, as seen in figure 2, to help stabilize your body.

Figure 2. Both feet on ground.

Watch Your Flags!

Be consistent on where you keep you loaded rounds. You should be able to reload without looking down. Keep your eyes focused on the flags during the reloading process. You should have your loaded rounds situated on the bench so you don't have to look down to pick up a loaded case. I use a block mounted in front of my loading port, as seen is figure 5 of this chapter.

If you look away from the flags it can be difficult to tell if the flags have changed slightly. You will be required to remember exactly what they looked like. It's difficult to identify small changes after looking away. This applies to any of the shooting techniques you might use.

Free Recoil

Free recoil is the most common shooting style and is used by approximately 70-80% of Benchrest shooters. Free recoil is when your trigger finger is the only part or your body that touches the gun. When shooting free recoil you keep your shoulder about ½ inch away from the stock. Don't touch or hold the pistol grip. Your cheek should not touch the rifle.

This style of shooting can yield some incredibly small groups. Your table manners or gun handling technique must be very precise when shooting free recoil. Any gun handling mistakes when shooting free recoil can really make your groups big.

Common Mistakes When Shooting Free Recoil:
> Shouldering the rifle as you pull the trigger.
> Shoulder too close.
> Hand or thumb hitting the bolt handle.
> Heavy coat touching rifle without knowing.
> Slapping the trigger instead of nice even pull rearward.
> Pushing on the side of the trigger shoe instead of the front.
> Deliberately pressing down with your cheek to aim the rifle and get the last little bit movement in the crosshair.

Figure 3. Mike Kavanaugh shooting free recoil at Raton, NM.

You must have a stable rest setup when attempting to shoot free recoil. The rifle will recoil about one tenth of an inch before the bullet is set free from the bore. The rifle must go through this part of its recoil movement the same every time, without touching your shoulder or cheek, or without the bolt handle hitting your trigger hand when the gun starts to move.

Shooting Fast When Using Free Recoil Technique

Keep your body still when shooting and hopefully you won't flinch. When you have the condition you wish to start in, aim at the correct spot on the target. With trigger finger on the front of the trigger, gently pull the trigger to the rear. Hold your ground. Do not move until after the rifle hits your shoulder, or until the sight picture through your scope goes black. If you blink, or are unable to see the scope picture black out, just wait until the rifle hits your shoulder before starting to reload.

Move the rifle forward with your shoulder while keeping your head still until you contact the front stop. Hold the rifle up against the stop. At the same time you are moving the rifle forward, use both hands to reload if you can. The configuration of your action will determine whether or not you'll be able to use both hands when reloading. If you have the loading port opposite the bolt handle, you'll be able to use both hands. With the loading port and bolt handle on the same side, you will use one hand to operate the bolt and reload.

Figure 4. The author showing where to place your thumb when reloading.

On a right-bolt, left-port gun, open the bolt with your right hand, and reach for a loaded round with the left while holding the rifle against the rest keeping your head still while watching flags. When opening the bolt, regardless of your action configuration, place your thumb behind the bolt shroud or "tang." Don't use the scope or scope ring as a lever. This is unnecessary movement which will slow the process. Proper placement of your thumb is shown in figure 4.

Continue to hold the rifle against the front stop with your shoulder, remove the fired case (mine ejects), install the loaded round into the loading port, and close the bolt. While closing the bolt, return your left hand to the joystick on the Farley rest (or rear bag if you squeeze the bag).

After closing the bolt, return to the trigger while moving your shoulder back away from the stock. While moving away from the rifle, you will make decisions on whether the conditions are the same or not, and where to hold for the next shot.

If the flags are okay, re-aim the rifle with the joystick or by squeezing the rear bag. Then look at the last shot on the target. (this should be the first time you have looked to see where the previous shot hit). About the time you're ready to shoot you should have moved your shoulder back to the starting position. Your trigger finger is now on the front of the trigger and you're ready to shoot again. With practice, about 3-5 seconds is all that is required to reload, re-aim, and shoot again.

During nice weather, which would be considered a trigger pulling contest, I will shoot free recoil, being very careful and deliberate. I slow down the process of reloading and focus on not making any errors in my table manners. By slowing down and being more deliberate, you will not disturb the gun in the bags quite as much as when being rushed.

Pining the Rifle

This shooting technique uses your shoulder to hold the rifle against the front stop without holding the pistol grip or touching the stock with your cheek. Don't relax your pin against the rest when shooting. Hold your ground.

It's difficult with a lighter front rest to use this technique. The lighter rest will scoot forward when shooting. I like to pin my rifle against the stop with so much pressure it will lift the rear leg of the lighter rests. Often times more than 20 pounds of force is applied to the front stop on the rest to hold the rifle.

There's no faster shooting technique than a firm forward pressure to get you back on target for the next shot. Just like any shooting technique which involves touching the rifle, you must practice and become proficient so it becomes second nature. Changes in pressure, or forgetting to apply the forward pressure, will not yield acceptable results. If you're able to hold the same pressure against the front stop, you can actually drive your aiming point slightly with your shoulder without effecting your group size. I cannot emphasize how important it is that you hold your ground. The most common mistake when using this style, is the shooter relaxing the hold against the rest about the time he fires the rifle, anticipating the shot. Be honest about your ability when shooting this or any type of holding. If you're not able to learn to be consistent, free recoil might be your best choice.

When shooting uphill, consider holding your rifle up against the rest stop with your shoulder. When shooting free recoil uphill, it's possible for the rifle to move from pulling the trigger. A definite accuracy problem.

My Preference

After more than 10 years of Benchrest competition, my preference is to pin the rifle against the stop while shooting. During a trigger pulling contest, I will shoot free recoil and be very careful, deliberate, and not rush. Any other time I prefer to pin my rifle to the rest stop. I will and do shoot whatever style is needed when it is appropriate. I've been shooting more free recoil as of late, because I've been making too many mistakes pinning my rifle, such as relaxing the pressure against the rest or pushing forward when pulling the trigger. These mistakes are a direct reflection of my reduced practice time. My practice time is less frequent because of family demands. When I am able to practice more, I'll be back to pinning my rifle more often, especially in normal to bad weather.

Shooting Fast, My Technique

Before I start explaining the process some perquisites are in order. Everything about my rifle and bench setup is geared toward the ability to shoot fast--my action design, front rest, rear bag, where I put my cases, flag setting, everything. Having full length resizing die allows reloading without disturbing the rifle in the bags, or rocking the rifle back and forth. The full length die makes opening and closing the bolt easier, as will shooting lighter loads.

Let's shoot a group one step at a time. When I see a favorable condition coming, I fire a shot on the lower right corner sighter, or lower right bull, to see what the shot placement looks like relative to my hold. If everything looks as expected I go to the record, try to stabilize the rifle by moving it back and forth in the rest, and push forward to the stop. I aim at the appropriate place, hold onto the handle (using a Farley rest, you must not apply any force while holding the handle either up, down, or sideways, just hold it still), and pull the trigger to the rear. The rifle fires, hopefully without flinching or blinking. When the sight picture through the scope starts to black out as the rifle moves to the rear, I start the reloading process. If everything goes as expected, I will know exactly where the crosshairs were pointed when the rifle was fired.

While keeping my head down, body relaxed, still in the shooting position, I simultaneously reach for the bolt handle with my right hand, and reach for another loaded round with the left. During the reloading process, I watch the flags while keeping my body still. I have no reason to look down. My loaded rounds are right in front of my face in a loading block next to my loading port, as seen in figure 5.

Figure 5. The author using both hands while reloading.

To open the bolt I put my right thumb, as seen is figure 4, on the rear of the action and rotate the bolt counterclockwise. I rotate the end of the bolt handle in an arc. I see many shooters who try to lift up on the handle. You don't lift anything. Rotate the handle around the center of the bolt.

When the bolt opens, I have another loaded round from the loading block just in front of the loading port. I move the loaded round over to the loading port while sliding the bolt to the rear. When the empty round ejects out of my left port I stop pulling the bolt to the rear. I do not pull the bolt all the way back to the bolt stop.

I'm not testing to see if the bolt stop works. I'm just trying to get the fired case OUT. My stroke of the bolt to the rear is as short as possible, which saves time. After the empty comes out I put the loaded round into the action. The empty case often hits my left hand on the way out, and sometimes hits the ground. I focus on reloading and don't worry about the empty case. I will pick up the cases after finishing my group.

After putting the loaded round into the action, I carefully push the bolt forward and rotate the bolt closed. While closing the bolt I move my left hand back to the joystick of my Farley. After the bolt is closed, I move my right hand back to the trigger.

When the rifle is ready to shoot, I look to see where the previous shot impacted. If the height and windage are as expected, I am ready to shoot. I evaluate where to hold. If I am satisfied I know where to hold, I hold for the new condition and start the trigger pull again… bang… repeat.

If everything works according to plan, less than 10 seconds will have elapsed from the first shot to the last. Yep, that's 5 shots and 4 reloads in less than 10 seconds. This type of speed is unrealistic for most shooters. Most shooters will be able to shoot five aimed shots in about 20-25 seconds.

Practice

In order to practice your technique, it's best to actually fire the rifle. You can practice loading at home if you have somewhere you can setup your rifle and rests. Load up some dummy rounds with no powder or primers and with heavy neck tension. These dummy rounds will feed easier than empty cases. The difference will be ejecting a bullet in the case. I know of many shooters who have set at the kitchen table practicing their loading technique.

Keep Your Body Still

In this next series of pictures, figure 6-11, you'll see proper bench technique. The first photo shows me using both hands at the same time, right to operate bolt, and left to insert the loaded round, head down, smooth.

I would like to emphasize again how important it is to keep your head and body still. These photos weren't staged. They were taken of me by Todd Tyler at the 2005 NBRSA Nationals. I didn't know I was being photographed.

I believe that it's VERY important to stay still when shooting. These photos show exactly that. My body and head were not moving, only my hands were moving in these photos. Practice keeping still. It is the foundation of very good table manners and will help you remain focused on the flags, which are usually moving.

Figure 6

Figure 7

Figure 8

Figure 9

Figure 10

Figure 11

I must relay a story about Tony Boyer and Wayne Campbell here. Tony is very critical about you not moving your head when he is trying to coach you. Tony has been overheard saying, "Move your head one more time and I'll hit you with a stick." Imagine Tony standing behind Wayne holding a stick over his head saying, "Alright Wayne, move your head one more time, just one more time!"

The reason Tony is so critical is simple. Staying still is the building block on which many more good habits are formed.

Hold

Holding the rifle can take on many different forms. Some shooters only hold onto the pistol grip and keep the shoulder in the free recoil position. Others hold the pistol grip and hold their shoulder against the rifle stock to varying degrees. Even others will hold the pistol grip, shoulder the rifle, and lay their head down on the stock. Holding the rifle will usually result in a bit larger groups and aggregates, caused by the inherent problems of trying to hold the rifle consistently from shot to shot. However, major mistakes common when shooting free recoil are often eliminated. This style of shooting also enables your group to be fired quicker.

Figure 12.   Larry Lesser at Raton, NM., photo by Todd Tyler.

When holding, you must be conscious of holding the rifle consistently from shot to shot. Changing down force or forward force will introduce vertical into your group. The amount of vertical can be severe. Also, it's common that your impact point will be lower on the target when holding or pining the rifle. Another definite accuracy destroyer if you change while shooting a group.

US Benchrest Hall of Fame member Ron Hoehn from St. Louis, said this best while we were visiting one evening in the stat house at Mill Creek Rifle Club at Kansas City. Ron said, and I quote, "I shoot smaller groups shooting free recoil, but shoot smaller aggregates while holding on to my rifle. Now you (Ratigan) must decide, if you want to win the small group trophy or the grand agg trophy."

This style of shooting requires practice to perfect the ability to hold. If you have little time to practice, consider free recoil. You might be surprised to learn that many very successful shooters do not shoot free recoil. Some pull the rifle to their shoulder, some pin to the rest, some hold pistol grip, and yet others use every way you could touch a rifle. The idea behind pinning or holding the rifle is to attempt to eliminate handling mistakes common when shooting free recoil.

Notable Shooters Who Shoot Free Recoil
Lee Euber, Jef Fowler, Tony Boyer, Pat Byrne, Dwight Scott, Smiley Hensley, John Brown Jr., Wayne Campbell, Glenn Newick, Ed Adams, Russ Boop, Skip Otto, Bart Sauter, Billy Stevens (98%), Clay Spencer, Bob White (90%), Mark Buettgen, Lou Murdica.

Notable Shooters Who also Shoot by Holding or Pining
Lowell Frei, Speedy Gonzales (variable), Allie Euber (variable), Charles Huckeba, Dennis Wagner, Rex Reneau, Allen Arnette, Don Creach, Larry Engelbrecht, Dennis Thornbury (variable), Ron Hoehn (variable), Jim Borden (variable), Walt Berger, Mike Bryant, Clarence Hammonds (firm), Lester Bruno, Gary Ocock, Dale Boop, Larry Scharnhorst, Don Powell, Red Cornelison, Gene Bukys, Don Gentner, George Kelbly, Cecil Tucker, Tom & Carolyn Libby.

Extra Steps When Shooting Fast

When shooting free recoil you will add another step to think about. You will need to get your shoulder away from the butt of the rifle.

I would like to add just a note about shooting fast with free recoil or any kind of intermediate hold. It will slow the shooting process slightly.

The intermediate hold adds steps to the shooting process, such as having to grip the stock the same way <u>every time.</u> This will require specific focus on that one thing which must be done properly and the same from shot to shot.

Pinning and holding the rifle will require more practice in order to build your muscle memory. When shooting by pinning or holding, you are required to apply the same amount of force the same way each time in order to have shot to shot consistency.

Scope Is Not Used As a Lever!

Do not use the scope eyepiece or scope ring for leverage when opening bolt. Place your thumb behind the bolt shroud and firing pin (or tang) to hold the gun down while turning the bolt to open it (as in figure 4). This is a good time to mention the bolt handle is not "lifted," which is mentioned in many writings and articles. The bolt handle is rotated around its center. This is why you place your thumb on the back of the action. Besides a firm anchor point, you will not have to lift your arm. Keeping your arm down will help speed up the loading process, eliminating unnecessary motion. Downward pressure on the action will help stabilize the rifle in the bags, a definite accuracy enhancer.

Figure 13.   Wayne Blackketter, shows how not to open your bolt.
Wayne's first Nationals was in the early '60s at Knoxville. He's shot several NBRSA records, most recently, the smallest group ever fired at 200 yards in Heavy Varmint, a .102.

Flinching and Follow Through

When practicing any of the shooting techniques, you need to be aware of flinching while you fire the shot, and whether or not you follow through. Flinching will adversely effect your group size. Many shooters must make a conscious effort to keep from flinching.

Common flinches are, moving away from the rifle anticipating the shot when pulling the trigger, becoming tense. Second, pushing the rifle forward with your shoulder when anticipating the rifle firing. Third, slapping the trigger, etc.

Flinching can be easy to identify by video taping. Annie and Stuart Elliott, from Australia, have many shooters on video from their many teaching sessions, many of whom move back when pulling the trigger. Many shooters become tense and move when pulling the trigger. In most cases, the shooter's face will clearly indicate this. Many shooters close their eyes in anticipation of the shot. It can be hard to identify when you develop a flinch. Flinching can be reduced with a conscious effort, but not by dry firing the rifle. When dry firing the rifle you know the rifle will not fire. Have a friend help you load the rifle. Once in awhile place a empty case into the rifle. You'll pay more attention, but might learn to hold your ground.

Eye Dominance

Eye dominance is your brain's propensity to use one eye more than the other and is mostly involuntary. Approximately 70-80% of the population is right eye dominant. About 20% are left eye dominant and a small percentage have no dominance (like me). Dominance can be from almost insignificant to extremely profound.

Your ability or lack of ability to use both eyes will determine your ability to keep your head down behind the rifle scope while in the shooting position. I'll discuss shooting right handed (the issues will be reversed when shooting left handed). There are three different eye dominance possibilities which everyone will fall into. You are either right eye dominant, left eye dominant, or have no dominance, with the ability to use either eye at will (ambidextrous). For a right handed shooter, no dominance, or being left eye dominant, is a great advantage. Many times throughout this book you will be reminded of the importance of watching your wind flags.

If you're left eye dominant and shoot right handed, your brain will favor the information from your left eye, and unless you force yourself to look through your scope or right eye, which usually takes a conscious effort, your brain will favor the flag information. Being left eye dominant and right handed, you will have a hard time looking through your scope for extended periods of time, which I believe is a good thing. While you stare at your crosshairs the flags are changing. Many shooters who are profoundly right eye dominant have problems using their left eye to look at the flags. These shooters will often raise their head to look over the scope at the flags. This is referred to as the "Turkey Neck Syndrome," because of the up and down motion of the shooter's head. When helping new shooters, I recommend closing their right eye lid instead of lifting their head. This will keep you in the shooting position and enable you to shoot faster, but it will require practice.

Easy Test for Eye Dominance
Make a circle with your thumb and index finger and focus on a distant object centering it in the circle. Close your right eye. If the object appears to move, congratulations, you are right eye dominant.

My non-dominance has caused problems shooting a shotgun. I must cover one eye (left), or I get confusing data that will often cause me to miss. I spent hours at a friend's house during my youth trying to play pool. I made thousands of wrong decisions on which line was correct because of the constant misleading information from both eyes. To play pool, I must cover my left eye. If not, I have trouble trying to decide which line is correct. However, my lack of eye dominance is an advantage in Benchrest.

For profoundly right eye dominant shooters, there is hope. With practice you can train yourself to use your left eye. If you are unwilling, you will need to adopt another style of shooting, maybe lifting your head to look over your scope. Ignoring the flags and not looking will not work, long term.

Improve Your Techniques by Watching Others
Just as I have mentioned many times is this book, improvement in your ability will come by observing and closely studying the consistently good performers or "Top Guns" in Benchrest. It's a good idea to watch someone who has good technique or table manners. Physical techniques can be video taped and/or photographed. You can learn many things by watching: Bench setup, posture, shooting techniques, proper gun handling, etc.

Prepare for Bad Weather
Just when you thought you had it made by shooting free recoil with no influence from you to the gun, you have a very high humidity or rainy day come match day. No matter how much powder or wax you use, your rest and bags are just too sticky. You will start to get vertical shots. Many shooters think this is caused by an out of tune rifle, when it is actually caused by sticky bags. When you notice bag trouble, try pinning the rifle up against the front stop. This will stop the wild vertical shots. You might introduce some minor gun handling errors, but they will be less than the wild shots caused by the sticky bags.

I remember a fun match at home in 2005. I was running the match, scoring, changing targets, etc. One shooter was having some vertical from the high humidity of the day. After hearing him describing his follies for the second time, I offered some advice. I recommended pinning the rifle to the rest, and that it might reduce the vertical from the sticky bags. He was uncomfortable pinning the rifle to the rest. I understood he was uncomfortable with changing his shooting style. Several targets later he was still struggling with the unexplained vertical. During another quiet moment, I reiterated my advice. He was still apprehensive about changing his shooting style. I asked him to give it a try. It couldn't be much worse and might actually help.

Keep an open mind when encountering situations where you find yourself out of your element. If your shooting is suffering don't be afraid to try something different. I was genuinely interested in helping the shooter in my above example, but to no avail. He was inflexible and unable to adapt as needed. This situation goes right to the heart of being comfortable with different shooting techniques.

Look Last

When conditions change faster than you can look through your scope to check your aiming point and fire, consider shooting without looking through your scope when the time is right. I call this technique "look last." Ed Adams uses this style regularly. He looks over the scope making the flags easier to see. Looking last can be used with any of the shooting techniques mentioned earlier, but you MUST have a stable rest and bag setup. Your rest and bags must hold your rifle still without moving, even when your neighbors are shooting.

Figure 14. photo by Todd Tyler
Ed Adams using the "Look Last" shooting technique at Raton, NM.
Ed is a good friend and one of the best shooters you will find anywhere.

When using the look last style of shooting, aim your rifle about where you intend to aim. When your condition returns, pull the trigger without delay. When the conditions are bad enough, gun and trigger handling problems will not hurt in the aggregates as much as shooting at the wrong time.

It's impossible for an observer to tell if I am using this shooting technique because I stay in my normal shooting position. I remain down behind my rifle, use my left eye to look at the flags, shoot when the time is right. I often employ the look last technique at Luther, OK.. At Luther the conditions change so often and so fast, shooting at the wrong time hurts much worse than aiming in the wrong place.

Examples of When To Use What Technique

Use free recoil when conditions are mild and stable, and when the sight picture through your scope is good, as is common when shooting in overcast conditions.

Benchrest heaven is defined as a five mile per hour crosswind from either direction with heavy overcast skies. This is also known as a "trigger pulling contest." In these conditions you must be very careful with your gun handling. Your aim needs to be very fine and repeated from shot to shot. Records are often broken during trigger pulling contests. When you have these conditions at major tournaments, many shooters will have the equipment necessary to shoot at world record levels, provided they don't introduce any handling mistakes. When shooting free recoil during trigger pulling contests, slow down, be careful and deliberate.

Pinning the rifle to the front rest has all of the advantages of holding, and in my opinion, is the fastest way to shoot a group. Heavy pin of your rifle can also reduce the shock loading to your scope. I don't recommend pining your rifle in a trigger pulling contest. I pin my rifle when I need to shoot fast. This technique has made the difference between getting all five shots off when other shooters might only get one or two. I am talking about 5 shots in about 10 seconds.

At ranges where you will be shooting uphill, this technique will help reduce mistakes by the rifle moving while you pull back on the trigger.

Figure 15. Bob Brackney's shooting technique. Notice coat removed to stop interference with sleeve. Bob is a great gunsmith and friend from Arizona.

Figure 16.   Dave Turnbridge showing his shooting technique. Notice Dave's thumb is a bit close to the bolt handle. It will not effect the bullet flight but might disturb the rifle in the bags on recoil.   Photo by Todd Tyler.

Figure 17.   photo by Todd Tyler
Aaron Segura, Ed Adam's step son, showing his technique at Raton, NM, in a crosswind.

Proper Brass Resizing

Proper full length resizing is the single hardest mechanical thing we do. To properly size our brass we must determine what needs to be done. Once the brass fits the chamber properly we will benefit from proper body sizing of the case. The main benefit of sizing is to make the rifle easier to operate. After the brass is up to full size, reducing the length and body diameter by about .0005 is all that is required. Again, all that is required is to *push the shoulder back AND reduce the diameter of the shoulder and base of the case about ½ of one thousandths.* Wow, that was easy to say, but hard to do. This is represented in the figure 1.

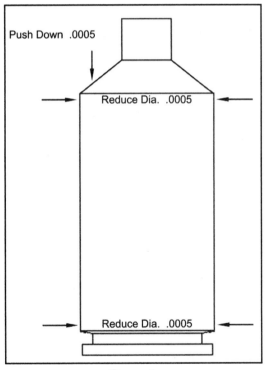

Figure 1.

Why They Tighten Up

Cases get tight for several reasons: Brass too soft, load hot enough to exceed the specified minimum yield strength(SMYS) of the brass, various powder burning characteristics, action lugs or bolt lugs out of square, or simply the stretch of the action front and barrel when firing, just to name a few.

Every so often a lot of powder is produced, which just doesn't seem to effect the cases no matter how high the velocity. Darrel Loker, from Tulsa, OK, said it best. Darrel calls this type of powder "Soft Start." Conversely you'll find powders when shooting at normal velocities cause the cases to get tight after only one or two firings. I have had both types of powder--the Soft Start and Hard Start. This falls into the category of things we don't completely understand. However, incomplete understanding doesn't mean the effect is not real. It just means we don't understand why. Time concentrating on why or why not would better be spent at the range.

Setting the Die

To facilitate the setting process you'll need a shoulder gauge. This is used to measure the shoulder to base dimension on the case. The primer will protrude below the base of the case after firing and must be removed before attempting any measurement. Remove the primer with a neck die, hand depriming tool, or by running the case far enough in the full length die to just remove the primer. Place the shoulder gauge on the brass and measure the length from the base to the end of the gauge.

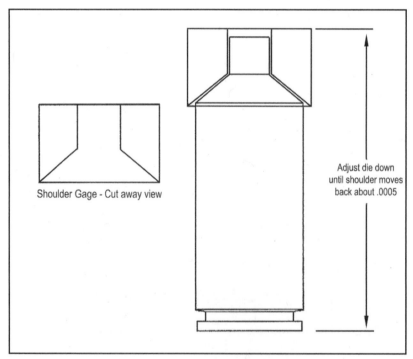

Shoulder Gage - Cut away view

Adjust die down
until shoulder moves
back about .0005

Figure 2. Drawing of shoulder gauge.

Figure 2 shows the gauge in place over the case. It should be noted that the gauge should not start down the body. A chamber reamer can be used to make the gauge with two exceptions. First, don't run the reamer in far enough to make the shoulder body junction, and second, the fired case should not touch the end of the neck cut. Bore out the neck diameter a bit and make it deeper.

Just as with any full length sizing operation, you must properly lube the case body. Most Benchrest shooters use Imperial sizing die wax applied with their finger. This wax comes in a small tin container, and easily fits in a loading box. A small container lasts for years of normal use. For the hunter it would last a lifetime.

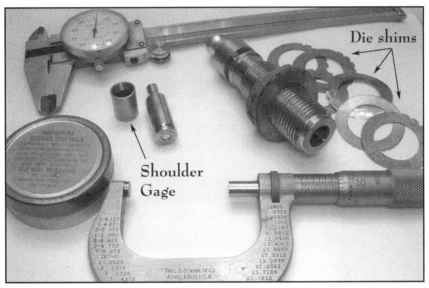

Figure 3.
Shoulder gauge, tools, wax, die and die shims for full length sizing.

Die Shims

Die shims manufactured by Skip Otto, as seen in figure 3, help in setting the full length die after the initial setup. Install about .020 - .030 of shims under the die, before setting up for the first time. After the die is adjusted using the adjusting nut around the die you can add or remove shims to obtain the exact amount of change in height you desire. These die shims are great when changing from barrel to barrel with slightly different head spaces. You will not have to loosen the locking ring on the die, and you'll just add or remove shims. What a time saver, thanks to Skip Otto. Turn down the full length resizing die until you push the shoulder back about .0005, which is just about where you see it move with a calipers. Then lock the collar around the die. Record the shim and die used in your record keeping for each barrel. After resizing the case in your new die setup it should now fit into the chamber, correcting any bolt lift problems you were having.

Proper full length sizing won't correct something which is moving or out of square, action out of square, lug contact problems, bolt face out of square, or a moving thread joint.

Do Not Adjust by Feel

Don't adjust the die by how the bolt feels. This will almost certainly lead to excessive headspace. After you determine the shoulder set back of between .0005 and .001, you can lower the resizing die another .0005 to .001, which may or may not change how the bolt closure feels.

Again, NEVER use the feel method without measuring to see what is actually happening. After determining you've pushed the shoulder back about .0005, the case should now fit into the chamber with a marked reduction in the force necessary to operate the bolt.

To test whether you have changed your bolt operation you must remove the firing pin assembly. By removing the firing pin assembly, the only thing you feel as resistance to closing the bolt will be the case itself. Again, after setting the die for the proper shoulder reduction, you can test for a change in feel. You should test feel before and after using the same case. First remove the primer as discussed earlier and try it in the chamber with the firing pin assembly removed. Then lube and resize with the full length die. Remove the wax and try the case again in the chamber. This should have reduced the force needed to operate the bolt if you have sized properly.

If the case still doesn't fit at this point, this die will NEVER work!

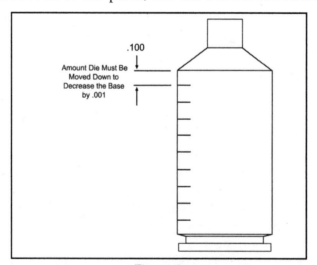

Figure 4.
Visual of the amount the die must be moved up or down to change diameter .001.

Adjusting the die farther down will not change the body, it will just make the case shorter. There is only about .010 taper per inch in the bodies of the PPC and 22-100 cases. This means in order to get a body reduction of .001 by moving the die farther down, you must move it down by .100 or ONE HUNDRED THOUSANDTHS! Now that's a headspace problem, don't you think? This is represented this in figure 4.

Again, if you move the shoulder about .0005 to .001, AND you don't get the desired results, this die will NEVER work with your chamber. You must change the size of die or chamber. Dies are cheaper and faster to obtain. As you can see, getting the die to work with your chamber can be quite an exercise. This discussion emphasizes the need to have your own chambering reamer in order to keep your chamber size similar from gunsmith to gunsmith. Changing gunsmiths will often start your search for a die all over again. Preplanning will save lots of time, money, and frustration.

After finding a full length die of the correct size, use it from the start when making new brass for a barrel. You should not wait until the cases get tight before getting out the full length die. If the cases are allowed to work harden at the larger size they (the cases) will not want to go back to the smaller size and will need to be replaced. In order to get the most life out of your brass you need to be proactive about the full length sizing process.

Shoulder Bump

Shoulder bump dies do not work. You cannot push the shoulder back on the case without supporting the shoulder diameter. If you push the shoulder back without supporting the diameter, the case will get bigger in the front. When you push back the shoulder the brass gets thicker just at and below the shoulder body junction. If you push back and do not support the outside diameter, the diameter will increase, which then causes problems with interference, which is what you were trying to correct. You must hold the diameter, which isn't possible when pushing the shoulder back without supporting the outside diameter.

Frequently, shooters ask about having a die made using the chamber reamer without thinking the matter through. If that is all that is required, just put the case back into the gun, then neck size. Even if the die made with your chamber reamer was shorter, it will not hold the diameter at the shoulder and would act as a shoulder bump die.

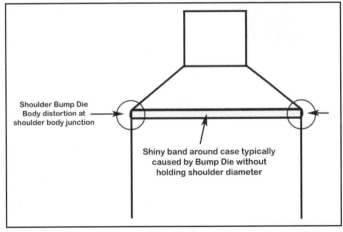

Figure 5.
Effects of using a shoulder bump die.

Resize Reamers

When considering the making of a resize reamer you need one that is undersized. This is complicated by the elastic properties of the brass. It will spring back after being reduced in size. Just how much resizing is dependent on the chemical composition of the brass, the thickness, how old it is and how many times it has been fired. There is no easy answer for what size to make the resize reamer. The ammunition manufacturers and die manufacturers make the new cases and resizing dies small enough that the cases would fit into any chamber of the same caliber. As you have discovered, this is not an accuracy enhancer, and is something to avoid with any accurate rifle.

With no intention of complicating the matter further, the elastic properties of the case change from the top to the bottom. The top portion of the case, which is thinner, will not spring back as much as the bottom of the case. This means when ordering a new reamer to make a full length resize die, you also need to change the taper of the reamer to obtain the perfect resizing of .0005, at the top and bottom when just pushing the shoulder back. Case width and length will determine the final dimensions of the resize reamer, but in the end the finished product will determine success or failure of the resize reamer. For a PPC case with a body length of about one inch and a taper of .010 over that length, you can get usable results by opening up the taper by .001 at the top of the die at the shoulder body junction. Sorry for getting carried away on such a seemingly simple subject.

Loading Tech Tips

Extreme rifle accuracy requires carefully assembled ammunition with attention to EVERY detail. I don't want to rewrite things which have been covered in great detail about reloading for accuracy. I recommend Sinclair International's "Precision Reloading & Shooting Handbook" and the "Precision Shooting Reloading Guide" available from Sinclair International. The "Benchrest Shooting Primer" published by Precision Shooting has many good articles covering many aspects of precision reloading from case prep to neck turning. This chapter will cover some subjects not previously covered in any significant detail.

Figure 1. Shooter seating some bullets, getting ready for the next relay.

The properly assembled cartridge starts the bullet on its way to the target the same way every time, at the same speed. Cases are made as identical to each other as is practical: Neck concentricity, neck tension or grip on the bullet, neck length to let go of every bullet at the same time, powder charge, primer pocket depth, flash hole size and length, and chamfer on the inside, etc.

Bullet Alignment

It's of the utmost importance when loading for an accurate rifle to have the bullet properly aligned with the bore centerline. This allow's the bullet to start down the barrel perfectly centered. A bullet won't self align with the bore when fired. If the bullet is misaligned, it will enter the barrel off center. This will cause the center of gravity (CG) to be eccentric and the bullet will leave the muzzle out of balance. Not the best accuracy enhancer.

The case must properly fit the chamber without being too loose. While using the full length sizing die, you want to reduce the dimensions of the case a minimum amount so the brass is stay in contact with the chamber. This help's properly align the bullet, assuming the neck is the same thickness around the circumference.

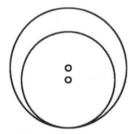

Figure 2. Error from off center alignment, bullet to bore.

Proper alignment is critical. The bullet will not align itself when entering the barrel. As was covered in the chapter on proper resizing, we learned it's common when using a full length sizing die that the front is sized a bit more than the back. This changes the taper of the case. If you've oversized the body, the case will lay down on the bottom of the chamber. This will cause a misalignment between the bore centerline and bullet centerline as shown in figure 2.

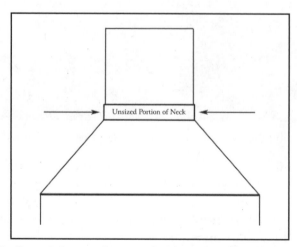

Figure 3. Incomplete neck sizing helps maintain bullet alignment.

One easy way to help align the bullet to the bore with a concentric neck thickness is to leave a small portion of the bottom of the neck unsized. As seen in figure 3, the unsized portion will closely fit the neck of the chamber and help hold the front of the case in proper alignment, and help get the bullet started straight down the barrel.

Seating Depth

Bullet seating depth is adjusted for best accuracy. Every different style and manufacturer of bullet barrel combo can have a different optimum seating depth. To measure seating depth you'll need a bullet comparator. Sinclair International Inc., makes a popular bullet comparator which accommodates different calibers.

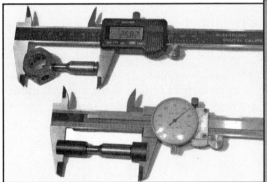

Sinclair and Davidson comparators in use

Figure 4.
Bullet comparator from Sinclair.

To Start

Without a primer or powder, seat a bullet into a resized case so the bullet just starts into the neck of the case, say about .050. Measure the overall length from the bottom of the case to bullet nose. This is the only time you can measure to the bullet nose. Also you must continue to use the <u>exact</u> same bullet when measuring to the bullet nose.

Chamber the empty case with bullet seated and close the bolt. The bullet will be pushed back into the case by the rifling. Remove from chamber. Re-measure the overall length. It should be shorter than before you chambered it. Pull the bullet back out slightly with a bullet puller. Repeat the process until obtaining three similar readings. This measurement is referred to as the push back distance or the "jam" length.

Zero

I like to find where the bullet is just touching the lands, or about where the rifling marks just disappear on the seated bullet. The neck tension, or grip on the bullet, does not effect where the bullet first touches the lands. This point (zero) is just a point where the bullet starts to touch the lands. This can be hard to see without the use of a loupe or magnifying glass. Doesn't really matter anyway, it's just a place to start.

I set my seater die to push the bullet down into the case about another 10 thousandths or .010 of an inch farther than the measured push back distance or jam length. I clean the bullet with "Never Dull," 0000 steel wool, or something similar, and then chamber it again in the rifle. If there are still rifling marks on the bullet, push the bullet into the case another couple of thousandths and repeat. I repeat this process until the rifling marks just disappear. I record this bullet seating depth in my records as my zero point, for that one bullet type and manufacturer.

When tuning the rifle, the bullet can be moved out from this point without being pushed back into the case. The total amount the bullet can be advanced without being pushed back is determined by the amount of grip on the bullet. The tighter the neck bushing the more neck tension, at least to a point.

With my normal amount of grip, or neck tension, I can usually advance the bullet out about .010-.015, without the bullet being pushed back into the case.

Jam Length
Many shooters record what is called the jam length. This measurement is dependent on the neck tension. The more grip, or neck tension, the farther out the bullet will stay, or the farther into the lands it will go. Whichever method you use to find your starting point, the end result will be the same. The seating depth will be set where the rifle shoots its best.

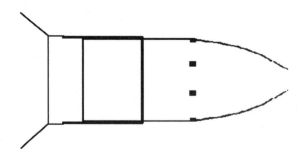

Figure 5.   Rifling marks on bullet (6 grove barrel).

Overall Length (OAL)
Measuring the overall length of a loaded round is of no value in Benchrest. Overall length is only needed when the loaded rounds must fit into a magazine. Single shot rifles make this measurement unimportant. Furthermore, the length of the finished bullet (distance from the base to nose) is the only dimension not controlled in the bullet making process. Bullets can vary in length more than .005 from the base to the point.

Seating Depth Tools
Use of an external tool with a case attached will not give accurate readings, at least for the purposes of shooting Benchrest. The reason is simple. The case is not fired in your current barrel, and will have a different head space, (the distance between the shoulder and base).

If the case used on the measuring tool is larger than your chamber, you'll not be able to get it completely into the chamber, causing errors in the measurement. Use a fire formed and resized case and the rifle to determine your seating depth.

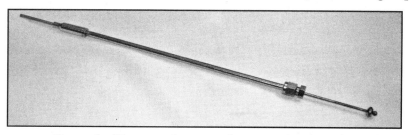

Figure 6. Home made external seating depth tool.

Occasionally you'll see a barrel stub which has been chambered with the same reamer as the barrel. The idea is to use the barrel stub in determining your seating depth, like the external tools. This will not provide good enough depth measurements. Use the barrel for which you would like to find the seating depth. To obtain accurate starting data, you must use the barrel and the bolt in the rifle you are wanting the data for.

Variable Seating Depth?

Now and then, 2-3 thousandths change in seating depth can make the difference between average and peak accuracy. Careful observation of the seating process will assure the exact same seating depth of every loaded round. There are several reasons why you might be a victim of variable seating depth. The most common are; the primer protruding beyond the bottom of the case, case which is bigger than the bullet seater, and having something lodged between the shoulder and the die.

Primer Not Seated Properly.
Most bullet seaters are chambered a little deeper than normal headspace. This allows for minor changes in chamber lengths. The bullet seaters job is to seat the bullet the same distance ahead of the bolt face. If your seater touches the shoulder of the case (case sticking out of the bottom of the die) you will have different seating depths depending upon how much you push the shoulder back when sizing.

A protruding primer can push the case into the die causing the seating depth to be shorter. The use of the die base will eliminate this problem, until you chamber the round. If the primer protrudes it will be seated when it's loaded into the rifle. A protruding primer usually makes closing the bolt more difficult.

Cases too Tight.
The seater must fit completely over the case when seating a bullet. If not, the seating depth will be longer. It will be easier to determine if you don't use the small die base. The seater will wobble on the arbor press when seating a bullet, and the case will be stuck in the seater after seating. If you use a small screwdriver to remove the loaded round from your seater, you might need a larger diameter seater.

Something Between Shoulder and Die?

Wilson bullet seaters come with a piece called a die base. The idea's to keep from the primer from igniting when seating a bullet and blowing up the die and case in your face. This is a great idea if you use a hammer to seat your bullet into the case. However if you use normal neck tension and arbor press, you'll not be able to press hard enough or fast enough to ignite the primer.

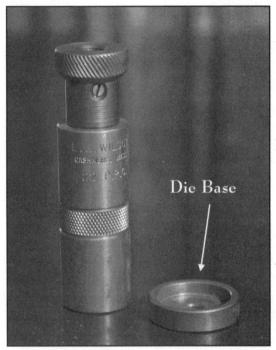

Figure 7. Wilson seater and die base.

The die base can be a potential source of seating depth problems. Every so often you will have a kernel of powder lodge between the neck of the case and the bullet seater. A single kernel of powder can increase your seating depth by 10-15 thousandths or more.

I've found it much easier to tell if I have a kernel of powder between the shoulder and the die when I don't use the die base. Figure 8 shows my bullet seater with a single kernel of powder preventing the case from fully entering the die. You can see the die is being held up off of the arbor press. When the die fails to go all of the way down onto the case I instantly know there's something between the shoulder and the die. I start the bullet into the case, then remove it from the seater and remove the kernel of powder then finish seating the bullet.

Figure 8.
Shows kernel of powder preventing proper seating.

Bullet Will <u>Not</u> Self Align

Again, this is important. The bullet won't straighten itself in the barrel when fired. The tooling should be straight and not cause the bullet to be pointed in any direction other than straight down the middle of the barrel. Once you have determined the tooling is good, this section will be forgotten about until the next time you drop the bullet seater, purchase other sizing dies, or the newest high dollar bullet seater. Remember to retest.

Tool Problems

Just as with bullets, barrels, powder, primers, scopes, and about everything in Benchrest, our tools can be a potential source of accuracy problems by introducing misalignment. Evaluation of the loaded rounds can indicate problems with the tooling. Run-out measurements taken throughout the loading process are used to indicate mechanical problems with the loading tools.

After the brass is fired, it will be reasonably centered. Deprime the case without sizing the neck or the body. Measure the unsized neck for run-out with a concentricity checker. If the fired case is not concentric after being fired, you have problems which are beyond the scope of this chapter. Call your gunsmith. It is assumed the necks are concentric, most all modern bench guns use brass which is neck turned to the proper uniform thickness. Either neck size with your neck die or size only the neck with your full length resizing die. Recheck the run-out of the neck. The sizing die should not bend the neck. I don't like to see run-out in my cases of more than .0015. If the die is causing excessive run-out it can be repaired.

Figure 9. Sinclair concentricity checker.

Water Test

Throw the die into the bottom of the deepest lake you can find and be patient. It takes awhile. After about 17.324 years, retrieve the die and retest. If it still causes a problem, repeat the process. These tools are inexpensive. Don't waste time trying to fix them.

After you determine the sizing dies are okay, seat a bullet with your bullet seater and then recheck for any new problems.

Test the run-out at the neck, then check run-out up on the bullet, up on the curve behind where the folds are in the bullet jacket. Both measurements should be okay if your neck wall thickness is concentric. The higher up you measure on the bullet the more exaggerated any errors will be, making them easier to see. I don't have a particular number which is a "line in the sand" so to speak, but my good shooting 22 will show run-out at the bullet ogive of about .001 to .0015. I would not let the run-out get much more than this, just a feeling. Seater die trouble can be repaired, see water test above. If it floats it's good.

Figure 10.   Neck bushings, carbide, coated, mild steel.

Neck bushings are not immune to improper manufacturing and can be the source of tool problems. They can also be off center and have the hole non-perpendicular to the end of the bushing, causing neck to be tipped after sizing. The bushing should float from side to side when installed in the die. Floating will not help if the hole is not perpendicular to the end of the bushing. Steel and coated bushings have a higher frequency of problems. Carbide sizing bushings are more difficult to manufacturer. They must be finished by grinding. This gives a better chance that the hole in the bushing is perpendicular and round. The nature of the grinding process produces better end products.

Note: Carbide bushings can vary in overall height. This may cause problems in some dies. Shake the die, you should hear the neck bushing rattling.

Case Head Squaring

Case head squaring is a WASTE of time. After firing a couple of times it will be square if the action is. You'd better find out what is out of square if your case heads are out, maybe a shell holder, or bolt face.

Neck Sizing with Wilson Neck Die

Wilson neck sizing dies only size one half the neck as delivered. The bad news about this is that the bullet pressure ring (largest part of the bullet at the bottom), will often be sitting below the sized portion of the neck as expressed in figure 11.

In my opinion, this isn't how to properly resize the neck. Enough of the neck should be sized to hold the entire bullet inside the neck. Neck dies can be reworked to size more of the neck. You can size all of the neck when using just the neck die, but you do not want to size the entire length of the neck when using the full length die. Leave a small unsized portion to hold proper bullet alignment, as seen in figure 3. When neck sizing, the body of the case will aid in bullet to bore alignment.

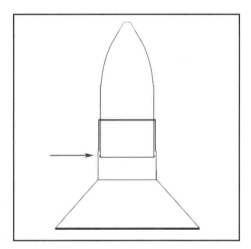

Figure 11. Bullet shown below sized portion of the neck. A No-No.

Powder Measures

Let's dispel one myth about powder measures right away, There is no significant difference in the ability of any one measure to drop charges of the same weight. There's no method you can use to make the powder measures throw charges with zero weight deviation every time. The reloading process depends on the weight of powder. Powder measures dispense by volume. The weight of the charge will vary depending on the temperature and how the powder kernels fall into the adjustable hole of the measure. Again, there's no powder measure or powder measure barrel which will give the desired end result of the same exact weight in every case. The measures commonly used in Benchrest will drop charges varying about +/- .2 grains, having extreme spread typically 3-4 tenths of a grain.

A powder which is sensitive to minor changes in weight will force you to use a scale. At the very least, this is a significant challenge when reloading outside. Often the very table you are loading on is not stable enough, not to mention you're sharing a table or picnic table with shooters who are constantly bumping, getting up and down from, and using their presses with full length dies to resize cases.

Digital Scales

Digital scales are often not as good as the readout would suggest. For example, if your scale will read to .01 grain, you might find by reading the specs, they often have accuracy no better than .1% of full scale, which means that if the scale can read to 750grains there can be an error of +/- .75 grains. .01% of the same full scale is still +/- .075 grains (close to one tenth of a grain). Confusing eh? The cheaper the scale, the worse the measurement, sorry.

Most accurate scales are of a balance type, and when used in a controlled environment can be amazingly accurate. Some balances are so sensitive they can measure what a "." weighs. You weigh the paper without the period, add the dot of ink, then weigh paper again. The difference is what the ink weighs. Scales costing a mere 100-200 dollars are much less capable, plus we use them in about every different environment on earth. The cheaper scales are also not very repeatable. This means that when weighing the exact same charge, they will often indicate a different measurement. All of that said, a scale can improve the accuracy of the loading process. Just be aware that test equipment is merely equipment, it can be good, bad, drift, have power problems, thermal drift and many other things, just be smarter than the test equipment.

Fire Forming Secrets

Done properly, cases will get shorter after being fired, and will measure about the same length, assuming they were the same length to start with.

This is an easy process which starts by sizing down the neck using a neck bushing smaller than you normally use. Prime and put some powder in the case. To fire form a PPC or a 22-100 from a 220 Russian case, use the powder you normally shoot in the full size case. No funny business here, no shotgun powder or extra stuff lying around the loading bench, just use the N133, T322, N201, or H322, or whatever you would normally use. Seat the bullet very long so it will be jammed into the rifling. This will help hold the back of the case up against the bolt face. This helps facilitate hitting the primer hard enough to start the ignition process.

Before getting anywhere near the rifle, measure the diameter of every loaded round where the pressure ring of the bullet is setting in the case neck. Check to make sure every round is smaller than chamber neck diameter. You should have .001 to .0015 clearance between the outside of the loaded round and the chamber. Any less clearance than .0015, and you have a fitted neck, or worse, interference.

Fitted necks were popular 20 years ago. They have good accuracy potential. They typically have a total clearance of about .0005. After being fired, the case neck springs back to the same size it was before it was fired. With the fitted neck, you remove the fired primer, re-prime, add powder, seat a bullet, and shoot again. The undesirable attribute of a fitted neck is the requirement of a specific size bullet. Small increases in the size of a bullet can cause interference problems. If you change bullets when using a fitted neck, you can cause a dangerously high overpressure or worse.

Figure 12. Cutaway showing typical location of case separation.

Put a few drops of light weight oil on a cleaning patch or a small towel. I use 3-in-1 oil. Wipe the outside of each loaded round with the light weight oil. It's okay to get oil on the bullet. Oiling the case allows the case to slip in the chamber. When the firing pin hits the primer, it will drive the case forward. When the case starts to pressure up, it won't grip the sides of the chamber because of the oil. This will allow the case to be forced back up against the bolt face, and it will stay there without stretching in the web area, as shown in figure 12. The neck of the case will be pulled back to fill out the shoulder area, which will reduce the effect of the dreaded donut, as seen in figure 13. I don't think this bulge inside the neck hurts your accuracy but it's a nuisance if it grabs hold of your decapping pin on your 22 caliber.

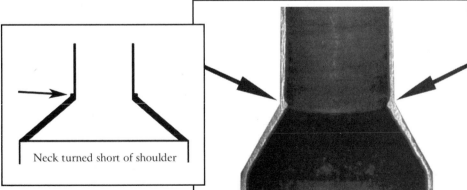

Neck turned short of shoulder

Figure 13 Material pushed inside of neck after fire forming.

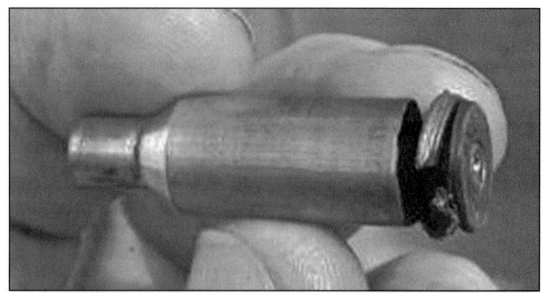

Figure 14. After effect of excessive headspace, after multiple firings.

Without the oil, the case will pressure up and grip the chamber around its circumference, causing it to stretch somewhere. The case grips the chamber with more force than the web area of the case can tolerate, which causes the case to stretch in the web area just above the base. This can lead to case head separation, a spectacular event that should be avoided. Figure 14 shows the effect of excessive headspace, which will lead to stretching the case above the web.

After fire forming, the finished product (fire formed cases) will be very close in overall length, assuming again they were similar before fire forming. Finish with your normal case prep procedure from here. Trim to length, primer pocket uniforming, flash hole deburring, etc...

Common problem...

Returning to the firing line without sizing or repriming.

It's easy to eliminate the problem of going to the firing line without new primers in your cases. Never turn the cases neck up, until after you've install a live primer. This is Benchrest 101. After shooting your group, put the cases back into the block neck down, and leave them that way until they have a live primer installed.

I overheard a friend returning to the loading area at the Super Shoot. She was talking to her husband about not being able to finish her group because she had cases which were not primed. Go figure. They were talking about this when walking by my loading area. I approached and asked if they would care to know how to eliminate that problem in the future. Both were all ears, and agreed that would be nice. You guessed what was said, I turned her cases neck down and instructed her not to turn them up until a live primer was installed.

Figure 15. Cases neck up contain live primer, others have no live primer.

Reload first, it just takes a few minutes.

It's easy to be distracted during the reloading process. Shooters visit between relays when they should be reloading. Start the rifle cleaning process, then reload. Most everyone loves to visit. It's very easy to become immersed in conversation with any number of friends. By reloading first, you won't get caught by the command "shooters to the line" without reloading. Sure is a feeling of anxiety.

Jack Sutton (Hart Rifle Barrels)
ready to test more reloads during the IBS Nationals 2006.

Skip Otto, Arnold Jewell (Jewell triggers), BR Hall of Famer, Dwight Scott.

Chuck Miller, from Phoenix, AZ.

Tuning

Summary

Seat your bullets so you have about a square mark from the rifling. Load several different powder charges. Start with the lightest load (powder charge) and work your way up. Aim at the same place every time, the bullets should go with the changes in flag readings or conditions. You should see a load which shoots better than the others. Shoot groups with that load and try to learn to use your flags. After you find a load which shoots well, shoot through a chronograph. Record your findings for future reference. When changing powders you can return to the chronograph to see if the velocity has changed. If so, change the powder charge to get back to your original speed.

Topics in this chapter.

Predictability
Tuning Is Not Practice
Change One Thing at a Time
Getting Started
One Group Evaluation?
Broad Tune Window
Balancing Razor Blades
Multiple Sources of Inaccuracy
Remove Variables
Proven Components
Proven Equipment
Example of a Mechanical Problem
Barrel Vibration

Miscellaneous
Effect of Seating Depth on Pressure and Velocity
Effect of Rifle Weight
Humidity?
Preloading
Chronographs
Clicks?
Tunnel Range

Handloading is potentially dangerous. With the many idiosyncrasies possible between each rifle, treat each rifle as an individual and proceed with caution. Data from one rifle will often not apply to another. The purpose of tuning the rifle is to get the best accuracy performance with the combination of components. Most serious competitors use proven components when trying to tune a new rifle barrel. After the barrel's performance has been established, the proven barrel can be used to test new bullets, powder, and primers.

Rifle tuning involves adjusting component variables for optimal performance. How to tune a rifle is the subject of much controversy. There's many different approaches to rifle tuning. No matter what method you choose, the goal is the same. Each shot should hit at about the same spot at 100 or 200 yards (200 yards is preferred).

This chapter contains information about several controversial subjects. I believe this information to be as accurate as possible. Much of the controversial stuff is supported by data collected by Harold Vaughn and Dr. Jack Jackson for Harold's book "Rifle Accuracy Facts."

Predictability...

Predictability is the one word which best describes a perfect tune up. Once you have the rifle tuned, it should be predictable every time it's fired. A properly tuned rifle will go with the flags. When wind going to the right gets stronger the bullet will go to the right and down a bit. When the wind from right to left gets stronger the bullet will go left and up (as shown in figure 1, commonly expressed as 10 o'clock to 4 o'clock). This information is only valid for the a right hand twist barrel. A left hand twist barrel has the opposite tilt. This effect is referred to in some writings as the vertical component of wind drift.

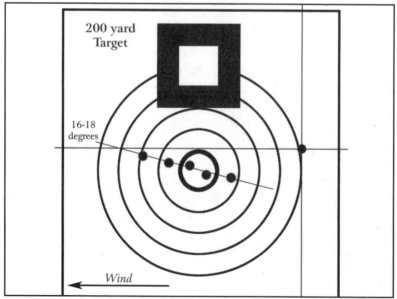

Figure 1. Mock up target of good tune shooting in a cross wind.
Bullet slope while holding in same place with different wind intensity.

Tuning is Not Practice!

One thing you must realize, tuning is NOT practice. When tuning, you're not shooting groups to be measured. You will need wind flags in order to make informed decisions about whether or not every shot goes in the correct spot on the target. Tuning your rifle by trying to shoot little tiny groups can take forever. Which is why I recommend to simplifying things by tuning at 200 yards in a cross wind, no angling stuff. Shooting the 45 degree stuff can drive you crazy. There's an almost endless list of things to account for; angle changes, intensity changes, and if the gun is shooting. Take the cross wind. If you have no flag reading skills, ask someone to help you who does. They'll watch while you shoot. It's much easier if the shooter holds in the same place for every shot for the observer to be able to tell if the shots are going where they should. Just learn to do it; the Top Guns of Benchrest understand this very well.

Rare calm overcast days can be nice, sometimes. Many days which look inviting often times cause problems (aiming errors). Calm days at my home often produce less than acceptable groups. I've learned to avoid days with no wind and reserve such days for a picnic. You'll find yourself tuning your rifle, or at least trying to tell if it's shooting in normal weather conditions. Get started right and you will soon become used to tuning in normal weather. After awhile should become proficient tuning in a nice cross wind. Shooting and tuning in a crosswind drives many shooters crazy. Remember, predictability is the name of the game. If you see a condition change, the bullet should go with it.

Change One Thing At a Time

When progressing through the tuning procedure it's very important that you change only ONE THING AT A TIME. It's common to select a starting bullet seating depth, and then vary powder charges.

Getting Started

Without primer and powder, seat a bullet into a resized case so the bullet just starts into the neck of the case. Measure the overall length from the bottom of the case to bullet nose. This is the only time you can measure to the bullet nose. Also you must continue to use the exact same bullet when measuring to the bullet nose.

Chamber the empty case with bullet seated and close the bolt. The bullet should be pushed back into the case by the rifling. Remove from chamber. Re-measure the overall length. It should be shorter than before you chambered it. Repeat until you obtain several similar readings. Adjust the seater to push the bullet back a couple thousandths farther than the measured push back distance. After setting the bullet seater use a new bullet and seat into another unprimed case, measure the length and chamber to make sure the bullet is not being pushed back into the case. If the bullet doesn't move back inspect the rifling marks on the bullet. Adjust the bullet seater to obtain a square mark. This is usually about .010 into the lands. A magnifying glass or loupe is commonly used to see the rifling marks. I clean my bullet with "Never Dull" before chambering which makes the rifling marks easier to see. If you change bullet makers or bullet styles you must start this procedure over again. Before long you'll be a pro at quickly finding a starting place. It's taken longer for me to write this than it actually takes to find a starting point.

With my 6mm bullets, I start 'em just touching the rifling. I've shot many bullets that liked about a square mark. With mine, I start with them just touching the rifling. Where-ever you decide to start with the seating depth, you will then try a starting powder charge. Start low for each new barrel, then work your way up.

There's an overwhelming majority of rifles that when tuned to there best, the bullet will be in contact with the rifling.

Ok, now your rifle seems to be shooting pretty good and going with the changes in the flag readings, shoot some three shot groups. If the rifle won't shoot three shots in a small group, it will not shoot five. If the bolt opens okay, and there's no pressure signs, shoot a group with the next higher powder charger. If this group is better, shoot the next higher load. If the group is bigger, shoot a group with a lighter powder charge. After your gun looks predictable and the groups start to naturally look better, it's time to start learning to read your flags. While this might not be the absolute best the rifle will perform, now it's time to shoot some groups. After you get comfortable with your rifles performance, you might try to make further improvements to its grouping ability.

Once you have found a powder charge that looks good, use that powder charge and load up the next series of test loads with different seating depths. Try to lower the bullet in the case (down) 3 thousandths (.003) from the square mark setting. If the rifle shoots better, go down farther. If the groups get bigger, shoot the bullet seated farther out a three thousandths (.003).

After arriving at the optimum seating depth, run the powder charges up and down again, to see if you can make any improvements. When you think you have found the load for that bullet in that barrel, its time to shoot five shot groups. The rifle should now be predictable. There should be an explanation for every bullet that doesn't go into the group.

One Group Evaluation?

It's impossible to evaluate your rifle's performance with one three shot or five shot group. You'll also need some shooting skills or table manners along with good flag reading skills to properly evaluate the performance of your equipment during normal conditions. Without some skills you will wonder why the bullets were not in the group. Possible causes for wondering bullets could be conditions, gun handling, component and/or mechanical problems.

Many times during a tournament you will overhear shooters telling stories of changing some small thing (seating depth .001, or 1/4 click on the measure) and the source of all of their troubles vanish. Usually it's after shooting just one group. Shooting one group doesn't mean you have accomplished anything. You must shoot enough to properly evaluate the tune and setup. For me this takes a couple of aggregates (20 groups), slow learner I'm told.

When I change powder charges, I use whole number changes on my Jones powder measure for the initial testing, which is about .5 - .7 grains when hunting for the load on my 6PPC which changes the velocity about 50-70fps. I make changes of 3/4 clicks for the .100 short 22 PPC. I look for a bullet and barrel which will shoot well over a broad range of powder charges or velocity's.

I'm very critical of a bullet and barrel combination which is finicky. If the load window is narrow or very narrow, I will not shoot this combination in a tournament. It's very difficult to stay on top of such a set up to keep the tune-up competitive. Record your findings as you go.

Seating Depth (#'s using my comparator)	Powder Charge (clicks, or numbers on scale)				
2.753	51	(52)	(53)	54	55
2.750 (square mark)	51	(52)	(53)	(54)	55
2.747	51	52	(53)	54	55

Above is an example of how I keep track of what I'm doing as I test. Note the three shot groups which were predictable and went with the flags by circling them. Start with the square mark seating depth. Find the best powder charge. Use that charge then change seating depths. Load the seating depth which shows the best overall performance. I'll then shoot between the whole numbers at 52.5, 53.5 and 54.5 and again try to sort out whether anything stands out in predictability. Let's say that the 52.5 had shown the best performance on the second try. Load up groups of 5 at that seating depth and 52, 52.5 and 53, shoot them at 200 and again evaluate the groups for predictability.

Often one charge will perform just a bit better. When everything is working properly with good bullets, you'll see the changes you are making on the targets in the form of vertical (not condition induced) in your groups. Make sure you record the tuning information on your data sheet for that barrel. After the tuning process is complete you're ready to practice testing the different conditions.

You can drive yourself crazy trying to tune in conditions. I am able to evaluate my tune in bad weather. I realize many shooters have difficulty doing so. My ability is partly because of where I practice and shoot groups. Most shooters would pack up and go home and try and wait for the perfect day, which in my case might take a year. Then I might miss the chance because of other obligations, such as work.

I can't tell you how many times I have been visiting in the loading area during a match and comment on needing to change my load in conditions where it's hard to get two bullets to touch at 100 yards. I also have errant shots because of the conditions, but I can't tolerate a rifle tune that doesn't go with the flag readings.

Broad Tune Up

If you find a combination which shoots well over a broad range of powder charges and seating depths, consider yourself lucky. This type of combination is rare but does exist. Bullets are probably responsible for the uncommon performance, but who cares, just shoot. I've been blessed with this very problem. It's rather embarrassing. The best way to describe this very unique problem (luxury) is, it's hard to find a tune-up. I've had combination's that were so good I could not find a tune up. It would shoot at about any powder charge, 51, 52, 53, 54 and at any seating depth. Many shooters will have this unique phenomenon once or twice over their shooting career. This type of tune up is well understood by most of the successful benchrest competitors, if this paragraph has been confusing, you might want to reread the chapter on Superman Bullets.

Balancing Razor Blades

Every so often you'll encounter a combination which shoots very well but is very sensitive to small changes in powder charge, seating depth, temperature, etc. I call this type of tune-up "balancing razor blades." Just as the name implies, try balancing one razor blade atop another, it's very difficult at best. I would never bring this combination to a match. It's hard to survive a single day with a sensitive tune let alone a multi day tournament, no matter how good it is.

If your powder and/or measure is the cause of the temperamental tune you can reduce the frustration caused by your powder measure by using a scale and weighing every charge. There's been a couple lots of powder that Benchrest shooters use, which have been sensitive to minor changes in weight. Find another powder lot. If this is not an option, weigh every charge. A scale will not fix a combination sensitive to seating depth changes or a bullet seaters performance.

Test the powder measure to make sure it's not causing problems by dropping wildly different charges. There are several problems common to measures. Something might be causing powder kernels to stick in the measuring barrel. You also might have a problem with kernels sticking to the top of the drop tube. Simply drop a charge by raising the handle up and down without tapping on the measure. Then hold your hand over the bottom of the drop tube and tap the handle at the bottom of the stroke. If any kernels fall out you've got more investigative work to do. Powder in the burning rate used in the 6PPC effects the speed about 100 fps per grain or

Powder for the 6PPC   1gr = approximately 100-110 fps velocity

Multiple Sources of Inaccuracy

It will be impossible to tune a rifle that has mechanical problems or when using substandard components. To put the statistical problems in layman's terms, if you have a rifle which has multiple problems causing inaccuracy and one item is corrected, it can be very hard (if not impossible) to tell you've made an improvement. The rifle will only start to show its true accuracy potential after all the sources of inaccuracy have been removed. For example, the finest bench gun in the world will perform badly when topped with a scope which moves every time the rifle is fired.

The rifle will only perform to its potential after you have markedly reduced or eliminated all of the problems whether mechanical or component related. The math is quite simple. The sum of inaccuracy is equal to the square root of the sum of the squares of the individual inaccuracies or

$$X = \sqrt{(A^2 + B^2 + C^2 + D^2 + E^2 + F^2 \ldots \ldots \ldots)}$$

.....this assumes that the sources of inaccuracy are unrelated to each other and do not add to, or subtract from one another. A full analysis is beyond the scope of this work. You can read a bit more about the relation of the inaccuracies in chapter 4 on barrel vibration in "Rifle Accuracy Facts" by Harold Vaughn.

It's common for shooters having equipment or component problems to change things. For example, let's imagine having a moving scope which moves about .100 every time the rifle is fired and bad bullets which will shoot about .280-.300 at their best. If the scope is changed, the rifle's performance will not improve much because of the bullets. Many shooters will change the scope, fire a few groups with little improvement, and then change back to the bad scope. Until the last source of inaccuracy is eliminated the rifle will not perform to Benchrest standards. This is why competitive Benchrest accuracy can be difficult to achieve, even with Benchrest equipment. This is why Benchrest accuracy is almost impossible to achieve with factory equipment, given the added mechanical problems common with high quantity production rifles.

> *Quality*
>
> *≠*
>
> *Quantity*
>
> **"The only thing Quality and Quantity have in common is the letter Q,"**

Remove Variables

It can be difficult to understand how tough it can be to work through all of the possible problems with equipment and components. Let's consider just a few of the things which can contribute to inaccuracy; flag reading skills, barrel, action, bolt, firing pin, firing pin spring weight, trigger, scope, scope mounts, scope lens movement, bullets, powder, primers, dies, front rest, rear bag, shooting techniques, flinching, and target movement. These are a few of the literally dozens of things which must work together in order to shoot well.

It's difficult to keep track of one powder and bullet combination, let alone many different bullets, powders, barrels, rifles, rear bags, etc. I received good advice when starting my adventure into benchrest that I feel the need to pass on again. KISS, or "Keep It Simple Stupid" and make it easy on yourself. Buy one powder, a couple bullets, and primers in enough quantity to learn how to shoot them. Use advice from other good shooters about what current powder lots to use, and which bullets to buy, then wear out two or three barrels learning to read your flags.

Proven Components

I recommend you remove as many of the variables as possible. When starting with a new rifle barrel or rifle, use known good bullets, scope, powder and primers. You will spend less time troubleshooting. You might ask a fellow shooter with known good components to sell you a few.

Proven Equipment

The following approach to testing new equipment would not be possible for a beginner. New shooters would not have proven good barrels bullets and scopes laying around just to name a few. If your new and need help to evaluate your equipment don't be afraid to ask any experienced shooter to help. Have them shoot a couple groups with your rifle and components.

This is my approach in evaluating new equipment. For example when I purchase a new stock, I will install a proven action, barrel, scope and use proven components. Then I can evaluate just the stock. If I am unable to make the rifle perform to my standards I will be pretty sure the new stock or the bedding is the cause. This can be a slow process when building a new rifle. For me, I feel it's faster and cheaper than starting with a complete new rifle than spending days, or weeks troubleshooting. I must admit, I am on the extreme conservative end of the scale when it comes to changing equipment. After you have proven your equipment (rifle, barrel, scope, loading tools, etc.) to be good, test away with new bullets and powder.

Example of a Mechanical Problem

I went to Luther, OK in April of 2006 to test a new scope mount prototype from Gene Bukys. I had tune data for my barrel, and I'm comfortable with how to shoot this range. I shot only two groups prior to match start time. The rifle tune looked good. However, when the time arrived to shoot the first record target, something was terribly wrong. When fouling my barrel and shooting a couple sighter shots, my rifle was changing impact points, more than the conditions were responsible for, about 3 times more. I knew I was in trouble. If this were a major tournament, I would have borrowed a rifle. This was just a weekend match for fun. I shot my group, as seen in figure 2, the biggest group I have ever shot in a registered tournament. Something was terribly wrong.

I emptied enough cases on the sighter target so as to have enough empty cases to change bullets. What I was shooting was NOT working. After changing bullets, seating them way out so they will be pushed back when closing the bolt, I returned to the rifle. I haven't felt so bad about my rifle in a long time. Was something loose? I just added the new scope and mount. Could something be wrong with the new mount? I reached up and touched the side of the bell of my scope while looking through it at the target—WOW did the crosshair move a long way with very little pressure. The crosshair moved three inches to the side and only came back about 1/2 inch. I touched the other side of the scope bell and the crosshair moved about 5 inches to the left, then came back about a half inch. The front scope ring was loose on the bending beam. Even experienced shooter's make mistakes in judgement under the pressure of the clock during match time. I sure made the wrong first choice in this example, I was there to test the scope mount. Had I not shot a couple good groups before match time my choice might have been different.

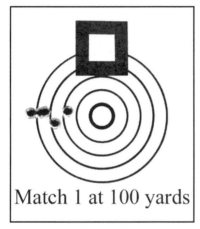

Figure 2.
Target shot with loose scope ring.

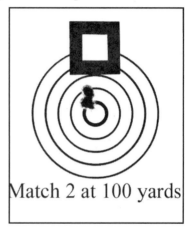

Figure 3.
Target shot with rifle out of tune.

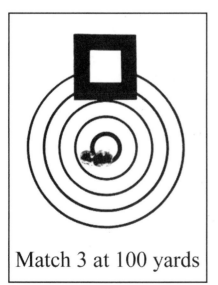

Figure 4.
Tunes ok. Just shot at wrong time.

I only had time to change the scope, so I did. I stayed with the other bullet seated long. You can see from the next target (figure 3) that the rifle is now just out of tune with vertical in the group. This was to be expected because of the bullet change and seating depth change. I tightened the loose scope ring and changed back to the load which I knew would work and shot target number three (figure 4). Everything was back to normal. You can see there is now very little vertical, just what is caused by the difficult wind velocity changes.

I finished in the top 30% at 100 yards, won the 200 by a good margin and was third in the grand. The top three in the grand aggregate were very close. This real life example is a good reminder to not give up and have fun.

Barrel Vibration

When the trigger breaks, the process of firing the rifle starts and the barrel begins to vibrate. Ultimately, as the barrel vibrates, it's desirable for the bullet to exit the barrel when it has reached the top of its stroke or just past the positive peak. The barrel vibration can be expressed as a sine wave (figure 5). By changing the powder charge you can change where in the cycle the bullet exits the muzzle. When the barrel reaches the end of its stroke it's velocity decreases and changes direction. Small differences in velocity won't have much effect when the bullet exits at the end of it's stroke, when the barrel velocity is at its minimum (or stopped).

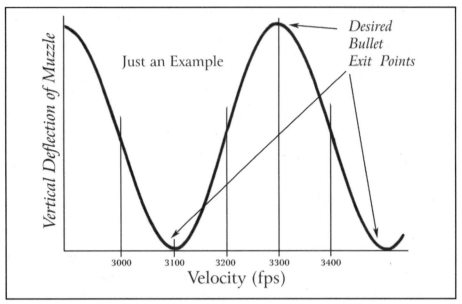

Figure 5. Sine wave drawing, illustrating barrel vibration.
Refer to "Rifle Accuracy Facts" by Harold Vaughn for an in depth explanation of vibration.

You want to tune your rifle so the average bullet exits the muzzle just after the positive peak, when the barrel just starts to go back down. Minor changes in velocity will be compensated for. Higher velocity, lower release from muzzle, lower velocity mean higher release from muzzle.

Miscellaneous Considerations

Effect of Seating Depth on Pressure and Velocity

Tuning involves changing powder charge weights, bullet seating depths, powder types or lots, and primers etc.. One common misconception is that changing seating depths will change the pressure and velocity. The data collected by Harold Vaughn and Dr. Jack Jackson while working on Harold's book, "Rifle Accuracy Facts," found conclusively that changes in bullet seating depth had no significant effect on pressure or velocity. Their testing was using an instrumented 6PPC and involved small changes of +/- .010 into the lands and off of the lands with light neck tension, typical of benchrest loads.

Effects of Rifle Weights, Rifle with Weight Systems

As rifle weight increases the amplitude of the vibration increases but the frequency does not change (this is expressed in figure 6, the difference in the amplitude is exaggerated for the purposes of explanation). This means a couple things. The tune up for the rifle with a weight system, and the weight installed, has a sharper peak, making the tune point narrower or more critical. Secondly, this means when tuning a rifle with a weight system, tune the rifle with the weight installed. Then remove the weight for LV or Sporter. The rifle will be on the same tune point, it will just be a bit more forgiving because of the lower amplitude of the vibration.

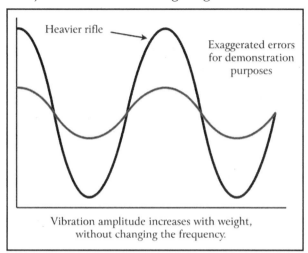

Figure 6.

Conversely, if you tune a rifle as a light and then install the weight system, you can be in real trouble if your tune point is on the side of the slope of the curve (as shown in figure 7 & 8). This is why I tune my rifles as a heavy (13.5lb), then pull the 3 pound weight and I have no problems with tune.

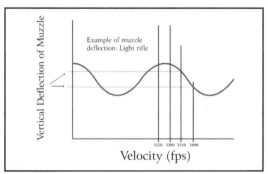

Figure 7.

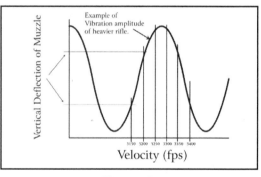

Figure 8.

Figure 9 shows demonstrates a tune point at the peak and with a muzzle velocity that varies 50 feet per second. This clearly shows my point. If you tune the rifle correctly as a heavy configuration then remove weight your tune will be ok. This assumes the rifle will ride the bags as well in the lighter configuration. Heavy rifles are typically easier to shoot because of the extra weight.

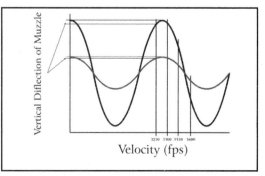

Figure 9.

Humidity?

Powder is not hygroscopic. This means the powder neither absorbs moisture nor gives off moisture. However, it does adsorb (accumulates on the surface) moisture which is a consideration in the loading density. Rifle powder is basically a flammable plastic. As you know, plastic does not readily absorb water or give off water, it is non-hygroscopic.

That being said, I think relative humidity, or the amount of water vapor in air, can be a factor when tuning a rifle. Just visit a tournament and you'll find many shooters with temperature and humidity measuring do-dads. These devices attempt to measure the relative humidity, though it's a bad attempt, often with errors approaching 20%. I have many years experience measuring the amount of water vapor in air, a multipurpose tool costing a mere 19.95 will not do the job. Many try to correlate the relative humidity to needed changes in powder weights. I have not been able to make any correlation, but if it makes you feel good, what the hell. I prefer to spend my time trying to read flags.

I only mention this to tease your brain. Dr. Jack Jackson, while attempting to test temperature velocity effects, discovered another abnormality. Powder charges were carefully measured to .01 grain. Jack was to test half of the loads in about 45 degrees and the other half in 95 or better. The expected result was to be 1 feet per second (fps) per degree F. The test results were much different however. The powder charges were all measured at one time, and stored in vials toward the end of the summer in Albuquerque, NM.

The day arrived to start the testing in the ZIA tunnel range in NM. Jack set up the chronograph with the artificial light sources and started the testing one hot 95 degree afternoon. Jack collected the temperature and velocity information, then waited about four weeks for the outside temperature to drop. About four weeks later Jack returned to the tunnel range to test the powder charges at the lower temperature. With temperatures about 45-50 degrees F the expected results would be about 45-50 fps slower than previously measured.

When the pre-weighed powder charges were fired, the measured velocities were about 50 fps higher than the data from the 95 degree afternoon. These velocities were almost 100 fps faster than were expected. Dr. Jackson was surprised by the data, which began the search for the cause. Back at home, Jack reweighed the remaining dropped charges from about one month earlier. These carefully measured charges were .02-.03 grains lighter than previously measured. Jack surmised the difference in measured weight might be the loss of surface moisture. Dr Jackson did not know for sure that the difference in weight was due to a loss in moisture, this was assumed. The powder was about 3 years old and opened for months before the test, making it difficult to assume that it was solvent that was lost.

Jack repeated the temperature velocity test and shot the test over one day. This yielded the expected results of 1 fps per degree Fahrenheit. Jack started the test at 4am when the temperature was about 45-50. Later that same afternoon when the temperature reached about 95, the second half of the testing was conducted. The higher temperature showed an increase in measured velocity of 45-50 fps. Not enough data has been collected to reach any conclusions about this experiment, with one exception. The results of this bothers Jack to this day.

Preloading

Dr. Jack Jackson shoots benchrest and although loves the competition, it's supposed to be fun. Jack removed the one thing he liked least about the tournaments--loading between each target. He'd rather use the time for visiting and relaxation. Jack deduced that by decreasing the weight variations in powder charges and ultimately reducing velocity variations that this would make your tune point less critical. The down side is, if you show up at the range with the wrong load, nothing can be done to change it. For Jack, preloading makes the matches more enjoyable.

One disadvantage of preloading is the large number of cases you must have for each barrel. I've already covered the economics of having several hundred cases for each barrel, but preloading can be done successfully.

When preloading, you should accurately weigh every powder charge, to less deviation than .05 grain. This type of resolution can only be accomplished by a very good scale in controlled conditions. Jack, a MD and PhD chemist, has had years of experience using micro, analytical and top loading balances for making standards. Jack's high quality balance has accuracy and precision of +/- to .01 grains.

Chronographs

A velocity measuring tool, or chronograph, can be a valuable asset, as long as the user understands the shortcomings of the test equipment. Just having an expensive piece of equipment does not mean it will perform under all conditions. Chronographs are no exception.

Chronographs require light to operate properly and if you vary the intensity and direction of the light, the measurement results will vary slightly. When attempting to conduct controlled experiments, those shooters with access to a tunnel range have quite an advantage. To use the chronographs indoors, they need an external light source which is much more controlled than using ambient light.

When testing Benchrest equipment and shooting over a chronograph outdoors, many times the rifle will be more stable than the speed measurement from the chronograph. I did not say that you could not get good measurement, just be aware that test equipment is not perfect. When shooting outside, it is hard to measure the powder accurately and hard to get good measurement from the tools. It's amazing that these rifles shoot as well as they do, given all of the things that can go wrong.

Clicks?

Many of the powder measures used by benchresters have adjustable cylinders and have what is referred to as "click" adjustments. The powder measure click adjustments, even from the same manufacturer, can be the source of disaster. Shooters trade powder charge information using the click value. Don't listen to anyone telling you how many clicks to use on your measure. Different measures meter dif-

ferently. There's a couple well known shooters from the northeast who are famous for using powder charges no other modern man can get close to. They regularly talk of shooting 56 and 57 clicks. This number on my measure would destroy my rifle. If you weigh a powder charge from them, you would be surprised to find they weigh about the same you've been shooting all along.

Figure 10.
Sinclair powder measure barrel, set at 50 1/2 clicks.

Tunnel Range

In order to remove conditions as a variable you can try and shoot on calm overcast days. These can be rare at the very least. Another option is to shoot indoors or at a tunnel range. No matter how nice shooting indoors may sound, indoor ranges have their own unique challenges to overcome. At the very least, you will need to learn to deal with mirage, which can be severe. Unless there is good ventilation, differing air densities and exhaust problems will present special problems. That being said, a tunnel can help in component and equipment evaluation. You will also learn how important "table manners" are. Having good table manners or shot to shot consistency handling the rifle, trigger, rest, and bags can be learned in a tunnel or shooting indoors.

Shooting in a tunnel or indoors will not teach you to read flags or make you a better shooter, but will help with your table manners as previously mentioned. Tunnels and indoor ranges help speed the equipment and component evaluation process. If the tunnel itself could improve your shooting ability there would be many more of them scattered around the world.

Most of the best shooters in the game are so accomplished with flag reading skills, there's almost no need to travel to shoot indoors to test equipment or components. I recommend, for those unable to evaluate your components or test indoors or in a tunnel, that you tune your rifle in a 5 mph crosswind on a heavy overcast day if possible. Of course, I recommend shooting at 200 yards when tuning, the errors are magnified and easier to see.

Record Keeping

Records of loading data and ranges are essential in your pursuit of extreme rifle accuracy. They allow you to return to previous performance levels, saving valuable time. After tuning your rifle to peak performance, record your tuning data.

Even though recording information about your rifle, components, tool settings, and conditions can be tedious, the information will be needed when returning to the range with your rifle. If you elect to skip the record keeping, you are required to have a better memory than most, or at least better than mine, and guess or start from the beginning. Which is far worse than keeping records in the first place.

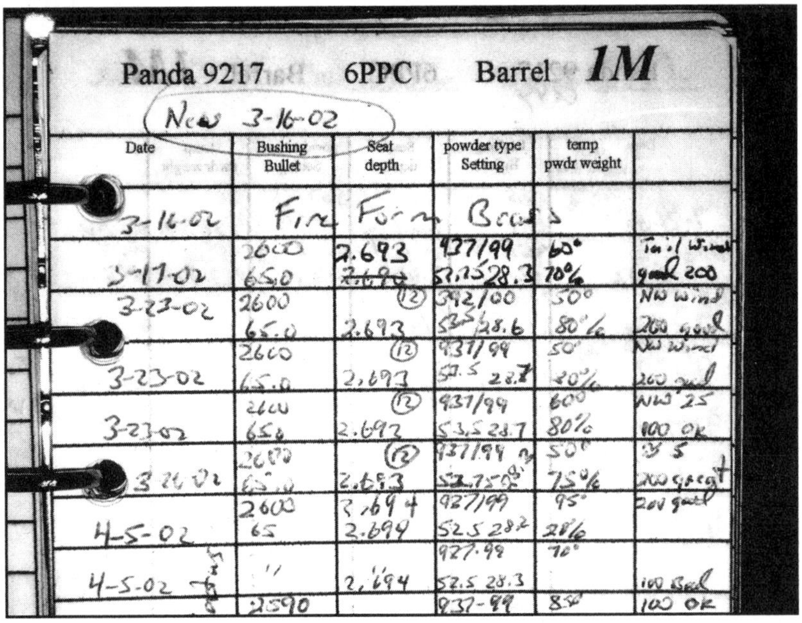
Panda 9217 6PPC Barrel 1M

New 3-16-02

Date	Bushing Bullet	Seat depth	powder type Setting	temp pwdr weight	
3-16-02	Fire Form Brass				
3-17-02	2600 65.0	2.693	937/99 53.75 28.3	60° 70%	Tail Wind good 200
3-23-02	2600 65.0	(12) 2.693	392/100 53.5 28.6	50° 80%	NW wind 200 good
3-23-02	2600 65.0	(12) 2.693	937/99 53.5 28.7	50° 80%	NW wind 200 good
3-23-02	2600 65.0	(12) 2.692	937/99 53.5 28.7	60° 80%	NW 25 100 OK
3-26-02	2600 65.0	(12) 2.693	937/99 52.75 28.3	50° 75%	35 200 great
4-5-02	2600 65	2.694 2.694	937/99 52.5 28.2	95° 28%	200 good
4-5-02	"	2.694	937-99 52.5 28.3	70°	100 good
	2590		937-99	85°	100 OK

Figure 1. Copy of my record book.

If you buy a used rifle or barrel that was a good performer, you'll benefit from information about how to load for the barrel or rifle.

When you gain some experience with different barrels, powders, and bullets you will notice the barrels will have many things in common, such as similar powder charges, and bullet seating depths, at least when using the same chamber reamer.

Keeping records about barrel performance makes discovering the illusive Superman bullet easier to recognize. Great bullets stand out when looking through your record keeping of different rifles and barrels. When I have good bullets, I have many entries of good or great performance, even when shooting in rough conditions.

Barrel Records

Start by keeping your records indexed by barrels. Serial number and keep data on every barrel in your inventory. When moving a barrel from one rifle to another, the tuning data will follow the barrel, not the action or rifle. The varmint hunter who has only complete rifles will do just fine to have rifle-specific records. Whatever method you decide, keep all your records together, and filed in numerical order. By keeping your records together, you will have your loading data when needed at the range.

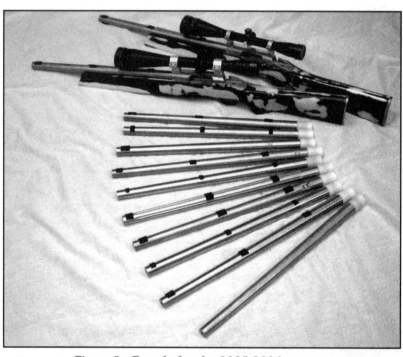

Figure 2. Barrels for the 2005-2006 season.

My rifle actions are close enough to move barrels from one action to another. This requires tracking the barrel rather than the action. My records are numbered to match the barrel, and filed in numerical order. This makes finding the records easy. I don't have to remember which action the barrel was originally fitted to.

Some shooters keep entire record books for each barrel. This works fine until you bring the wrong book to the range. I recommend you keep ONE book and have all of your records in it. You'll have your information when it's needed.

The information you keep will fall into two categories, fixed or variable.

Fixed Data

Some of the data about your barrel won't change. I record this data and use it in my index starting with the barrel number. When adding a new barrel, I number it with the next available number in the sequence with no regard of the caliber. Many shooters use only one caliber. I use two. Included in the fixed data is the action the barrel was originally fitted to, caliber, manufacturer of the barrel, weight, and twist if you have different twist barrels (I only use 14 so this is assumed). You might also record things such as the inside dimensions of the barrel, for example the button size might be .236 or .237 for a Krieger barrel. If you know the major inside diameter (groove) you might want to record that as well. You might record the reamer info, gunsmith, and date the barrel was chambered, etc.

Barrel #	2C
Action #	Panda 9217
Caliber	6PPC .262 neck, 22-100 .243 neck
Barrel	Hart 14
Weight/Length	4lb 14oz/ 20.5in
I.D.	.2580
Reamer	JGS 1042
Gunsmith	Ratigan
Chamber Date	4-15-08

Variable data

The record book will be primarily used to record the data which is dependent on the powder, bullets, dies, neck bushings, etc. This would be the tuning information for each barrel and will vary, often during the day, depending on temperature, humidity, altitude etc. Record the data as you make the changes or immediately afterward. Be vigilant about recording the data, only takes a minute to do. I personally hate the paperwork and must make a conscious effort to do it.

Just as in goal setting, evaluate the rifle barrel in terms of performance, not finishing place. In bad weather it's possible to finish first with a barrel which is not properly tuned. I call every shot when shooting. Any shots that give me the thought "why did that go there" cause concern. In this situation, I would be cautious of my evaluation and never record "great 200 yards" in my records, even if I finished first. If EVERY shot goes exactly where it should, my record keeping entry will warrant a "great" comment. If I make strategy mistakes and finish fifth, that's not the barrel's fault, or any fault of the tune up or equipment, be honest.

I record the following data in my record book while at the range: I only shoot a couple of powders, which allows me to become familiar with its specific performance characteristics. When I start to compile data for a barrel, its performance will usually become more predictable. My entries get smaller with fewer variables. When I have been using the same seating depth, I will leave following rows blank, same for bullets. Eventually I get down to changing dates, recording die shims, powder charges, and how it shoots at the yardages.

Date
Place
Match or tuning? (practice uses previous tune data)
Full length die #
Die shim for above
Neck bushing
Bullet (manufacturer, style & lot)
Seating depth
Powder type and lot
Measure setting
Powder weight
Weather conditions, temperature, humidity, rain, etc.
Wind conditions
How did the rifle perform? Great, good, so-so, bad
Chronograph speed when available
Aggregate
Finishing place (not so important).

Leaving your records at home can really increase your level of anxiety. By keeping all your data within one small book, you'll always have it. My data has a home in the top of my loading box. I keep my data in a form of shorthand. I've considered making a bigger log book, but I'm afraid of forgetting it at home. My method has worked. I've never arrived at the range to discover a missing book. Guess I'll keep the status quo.

Range Information

It's a good idea to keep records on the different ranges you shoot. When making observations on conditions which were not good to shoot in, note any mirage conditions which moved too slowly to see without studying through your scope. At home (Mooreland Public Range), we do not know how to shoot the calm. Be afraid, very afraid. Some ranges have benches with good prevailing conditions (honey hole) and some have benches where no shooter has ever survived an aggregate without a bad group or two. Some ranges have conditions to avoid. Ask the locals what to look for. Many will offer advice. By keeping data on the ranges and observations, you will find it easier to remember.

Consider recording the conditions you've shot. Like what the predominant condition was, how the bullets reacted, whether or not you outsmarted yourself by going up on load. Memory fades, which is the reason you record the data at the time. Records of range information are important to affirm your observations during your next visit. You won't have to relearn certain peculiar range conditions if you record your observations the first time. Mark Buettgen says he uses this information about ranges, and I quote, "So I don't outthink myself."

Many shooters change their rifle tune, powder charges, or seating depths when the range is responsible for spitting shots on the target.

Make or purchase a small record book, you will not regret it.

Action # _____ Cali _____ Barrel _____
Barrel Manu. _____ Barrel Wieght _____ Date New _____

Date	Where	Die & shim	bullet/ bushing	seat depth	pwdr lot# setting	pwdr weight	temp humid.	Speed fps	Performance & Conditions

Morning dew and calm weather at Canastota NY.

Nelson, New Zealand, sight of the World Benchrest Championships 2001.

Practice to Learn

What's practice? Practice is when you take all your best gear to the range and set up as you would to shoot a match. Shoot some groups on record targets under the normal time pressure of your clock to develop your flag reading skill. You must learn to shoot in the wind, control your rifle with proper table manners, and follow through.

Many shooters call tuning their rifle "practice." Tuning a rifle involves testing of components to make the rifle shoot to the best of its ability by changing powder, powder charges, bullet seating depth, barrels, scopes and trigger, trigger hangers, etc... Early morning hours and overcast calm conditions with a nice 90 degree crosswind should be used for tuning, testing bullets, powder, primers and barrels.

Practice and tuning are two completely different things and should never meet. During practice, take the rifle to the line and shoot it to learn what the rifle, loads, and shooter can do in the conditions at the time. The tougher the conditions the better. Practicing in tough conditions helps build your confidence in your equipment and shooting ability.

Figure 1. Lacey, ready to practice at home.

What will the Equipment Do?

With all your flags in place, it's time to test your equipment, learn what it is capable of shooting through, and what will cause trouble. Practice is the time to learn from mistakes, either your mistakes or the mistakes of others. Practice should be a learning experience.

Prerequisites

I recommend you do not dial windage into the scope. This means when the wind is from the right the bullets will go left, etc. By using this approach, you will learn, by watching your flags, how much flag deflection is how much drift on the target. You must learn during practice what the conditions are worth, and which changes won't have much effect on the target. Practice is not the time to shoot zeros (small groups). Make mistakes in judgment reading flags during practice, and apply this experience during match time.

Use match targets when practicing. You'll gain valuable experience when firing the first shot on the record target, when the shot doesn't hit where it should. This is covered in detail in the strategy chapter. You won't see this when just moving around on the multiple bull targets, yep they save money but limit your experience.

Set Goals for Practice

One important goal for the newer shooter is to become familiar with tournament procedures. Depending on conditions, set specific goals for group sizes and aggregates during practice. I go so far as to guess what a winning aggregate of the day would be and try to shoot smaller than my estimate. You will need to apply proper strategy and shooting techniques in this pursuit.

Practice Together

Having a practice partner helps gauge the quality of your practice, and adds a bit of competitiveness in a normally non-competitive environment. Sit side by side. During practice you can talk about when to start shooting, the range conditions, missed shots, etc. Both shooters shooting poorly can be an indicator of conditions which are unpredictable. If one shooter is shooting bad, and the other good, the conditions might not be the problem. Shoot different conditions during practice which you would normally avoid during match time. Shoot and test your ability in conditions you're not comfortable with will give you an advantage come match time, if and when you're forced to shoot a non favorite condition.

Get Uncomfortable

To practice being uncomfortable, you can play a game when practicing. Fire a shot on your practice partner's target away from any normal impact area. Then have the other shooter fire the four other shots. This will help you familiarize yourself with that feeling of "OH NO!" When your first shot hits someplace unusual, you'll have practice trying to make the most of the situation. Often you might be surprised how good it will turn out.

Yardage

The majority of your practice time should be spent shooting at 200 yards. Why? The farther distances are the most important. You can lose a match at 100 yards but it's won at 200, 300 etc. Strategy at 100 and 200 yards is different. You must adapt accordingly. One Hundred yards requires more finesse, while aggressive usually describes the 200 yard stage. The beginner usually thinks the value of the wind at 200 yards is only double that of 100, but in fact it is more like 2.5 to 3.5 times, which makes the 200 yard performance more important to your grand aggregate.

The recipe for success, as it's been for many years, is to stay in the hunt at 100 yards and shoot good at 200. It would be nice to lay down the smallest group on the first relay and never look back, but this rarely happens.

Flag & Equipment Setup

Set up your flags, rest and bags, loading gear, and everything that you'll use match day. During a match is the wrong time to learn how your equipment is to be set up and used. Again, when match time arrives, the only thing that should be different will be more shooters to visit with while waiting for your relay to begin.

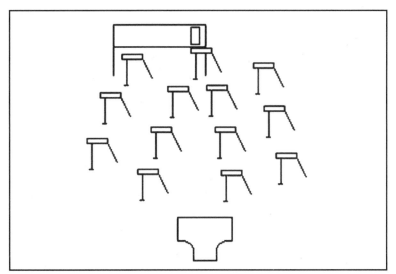

Figure 2. Proper Flag Setup for practice. Note flags to right of frame.

Target Selection

Use match targets and shoot them as you would in a match, barrel fouling shots, sighters on bottom, and group for record on the top. You will obtain valuable practice holding up after the first shot on the record target, and you will be more confident when required to repeat this during a tournament. The goal of this is to be familiar with your setup when match time arrives.

Scope Setup

In my opinion, one important aspect to learn is how far bullets are being blown around in the wind when conditions are bad. Practice is time to learn what your rifle is and is not capable of. In my opinion you should not dial in windage on your scope. Let the bullets fly, or Kentucky windage. At those ranges where wind can come from every conceivable direction at one time, you will not get caught having no idea where to hold when your condition fails to return. With your scope set at zero windage, when wind dies, you hold over to the bullet holes and allow a bit for the vertical from the loss of wind and shoot.

Kentucky windage is the best way to learn what your flags are <u>trying</u> to tell you. This is easier to keep track of than trying to dial. When using the Kentucky windage, bullets will always be down wind of your cross hair, unless you are shooting in a calm condition. Many shooters will dial in windage to hold at the middle or 12:00 and hit around the mothball. The only problem with this is that in a letup you need to hold down wind, which can be confusing. In the heat of the moment, when forced to hold, many shooters hold the wrong way. If you only shoot when the flags are the same, hold at the same place for every shot. It doesn't matter what method you choose. Good luck!

Spotting Scope Use

Watch others through a spotting scope or a rifle scope during practice. You will learn things about your rifle's relative performance. Watch from directly behind the shooter while using a spotting scope. You can "go to school" and learn from others, what conditions they preferred to shoot in, and if they were able to make it work.

Don't stare through the spotting scope, Watch the conditions and the shooter. Look at the target through the scope after a shot is fired. Ask the shooter about the groups and where they were holding. When I watch someone shoot in changing conditions, I will guess on where I thought they were holding before asking.

Different Shooting Styles

Practice using the different shooting styles: Free recoil, hold, pin, look last, etc., during practice. Let the conditions determine which type of shooting style to use. Don't be afraid to shoot a different style from group to group. You must learn to shoot fast. Make sure your operation of the rifle includes everything you will need to shoot fast. This includes any special loading blocks, case placement, etc...

Calling the Shots

When shooting, call every one of your shots. You should know where the crosshairs were pointed when you fired the shot. Be honest about your follow through and about any bad table manners you might have had. If you have done your part, be honest about it. If not, you might have influenced the rifle with a flinch. If you have done everything right, watched your crosshair until after the rifle is fired, and the rifle still shoots stupid (not with the flags), you'll need to re-evaluate your tune up, rifle, scope, and maybe your components.

You should have an answer for why any shot was out! Having one bullet out the side, when it should have gone in the group (no problem on bench, flags okay), could mean your tune is going away. Check the target for a bullet which is unstable. This hole will not be round and will give you some indication of what is happening. Others having similar problems, tells of the range causing trouble.

Figure 3. Tony Boyer.
It would be a safe bet that he's practiced more than any shooter in history.

Match Simulation

After you've reloaded and are ready to shoot, find your way to the bench, and set your gun up and prepare to shoot. When ready, start your timer before placing your bolt in the rifle, foul the barrel, and shoot as many sighters as you want, then shoot one group just as if it were a match. Practice should simulate match conditions as close as practical. Remember this is not time to be tuning your rifle. Its practice with rifle and equipment, i.e. practice.

Flinching

When practicing any of the shooting styles, you need to be aware of flinching and conscious of your follow through. Flinching can adversely effect your group size. Just as with an addiction, the first step to correcting a flinch is to be honest. Dry firing the rifle will not eliminate flinching. You know the rifle will not fire. It's not the same as practicing when shooting.

Many of my shooter friends must make a conscious effort to keep from flinching. Follow through will help with your flinching. Focus on the crosshair. By knowing where the crosshair was pointed when the gun goes off will delay any flinch or movement. Any movement after the scope blacks out is too late to effect the bullet impact by flinching. I <u>try</u> to hold my ground, and do "Nothing" behind the rifle until after the sight picture goes black, then I start the reloading process.

Focus on the Bad

Improvement cannot and will not come if you only shoot in nice calm overcast conditions. After you are happy with your equipment and with how your rifle shoots, practice in whatever conditions you have at the time, just like shooting at a match. Don't be afraid to shoot in almost any condition including rain, and the subsequent nice weather. You'll be required to shoot in almost any type of weather during match time. You might be surprised how good you can shoot with the proper frame of mind when conditions are bad, and other competitors are complaining. Learn from the mistakes of others, by talking with and watching them.

Figure 4. George Kelbly Sr. has time for a little practice for the 2006 Eastern Regionals.

Range & Bench Etiquette

How we conduct ourselves at the range is important. Our rifles and components are dangerous. Practice safety at all times when at the range. Don't be afraid to ask questions of anyone you find at the range. Keep bolts out of rifles unless the firing line is open, AND you're ready to shoot, or until instructed by the range officer during match time. Never leave a rifle unattended without removing the bolt. Bolt action rifles are easy to disassemble. Just do it.

Figure 1. Author helping Lowell Hottenstein set up in Sweden.

Loading Area

The first item on the agenda when arriving at the range is to find somewhere to set up your reloading gear. Many ranges have a loading area with tables or benches. It's rare to have more loading area than is needed, especially at the major tournaments. It's common for local shooters to reserve loading areas for themselves and for shooters who call in reservations. Problems arise when shooters arrive late and find all of the loading space has been used by shooters who have taken more space than is really needed.

Proper etiquette requires us to share loading tables. A 6 foot long table has enough room to accommodate two shooters, loading and cleaning. If you see someone searching for a spot to load, offer to share a table or bench with them. I often travel with Butch Fjoser, we share a 6 foot table for loading and cleaning. By doing so we are comfortable all the time. Shooters who feel they need two tables feel crowded and uncomfortable when they're required to share.

Practice Time

When practicing, be aware and alert when coming back to the line to shoot. Several times at tournaments shooters have been so involved in what they were doing they didn't notice a cease fire had been called to change targets. They sat down, and shot before they discovered people were down range. If nobody is shooting, and it's quiet on the range, assume a cease fire has been called. Please, just be aware.

When practicing at major tournaments like the Super Shoot, you will share a bench. Find some friends and use the same bench to practice. When you are finished shooting, remove your equipment from the bench before heading back to the loading area so others will have a chance to shoot. During small matches, set up on your assigned bench and share with your bench mates.

Match Day - Flag Etiquette

Many flags will be found on the range come tournament time. Where you put your flags is not specifically spelled out in the rule book. The rules describe how high you may have your flags. They must be lower than a line that extends from the bench top to the bottom of the target card.

Where you put your flags, or in what line, is a matter of manners. As a general rule, where you can put your flags, is half way between your bench and your neighbors on both sides. Any flags that are set farther away from your bench are encroaching on your neighbor. This is clearly defined in the World Benchrest Championship rule book, but not by the IBS or NBRSA rule books of the United States. Cooperate and work together. It's bad manners to wait until another shooter on your bench rotation has finished setting flags, then set your flags directly in front of theirs, covering them up. It's not the best way to make new friends.

Compromise and cooperate with the others on your relay. While I was preparing to host a National championships, a friend put it best. He said "There's nothing in the rule book to keep me from setting up my flags." I could not help but respond, "Yep, there's also nothing in the book preventing the others on your rotation from planting you 6 feet under behind the firing line."

Distractions

One new rule addresses cell phones and pagers. If you have a cell phone or pager on the firing line and it rings or alarms, you'll be disqualified. Leave'm in the loading area.

Firing Line

After the first shot is fired on match day, no competitor is allowed in front of the firing line until the end of that yardage aggregate is complete. The firing line is generally considered to be the front edge of the bench. You will be disqualified for violating this or any other safety rule come match time. At some tournaments the front edge of the roof is designated as the firing line. This allows competitors to move equipment in front of the benches, which helps ease the congestion so common at the Super Shoot and Nationals. You should know where the firing line is.

Relays

It's common at tournaments to have relays. Relays are required when you have more shooters than benches, or when shooters are sharing equipment like rests and rifles. At the end of your relay, after the "cease-fire" command, quickly remove your equipment from the bench. The person following you on the bench needs to get their equipment set up. It's bad manners to visit with your neighbor about your groups after your relay is over while the shooter who follows you waits for you to remove your gear. When you come up to the bench after the previous relay, be courteous and give the shooter ahead of you a moment to remove their stuff.

Figure 2.   Ron Breedlove waiting to approach the firing line for his relay.

As you can see in figure 2 at the Super Shoot, with seven relays there's a lot of gear behind the firing line. At the Super Shoot there are six sets of gear behind every bench. It's necessary to leave walkways through the gear behind so shooters don't have to crawl over all the shootin' gear.

Disabled Shooters

It's common at about every large tournament to have one or two shooters in a wheel chair. It's absolutely necessary to leave the concrete walkway or runway behind the benches free of gear and carts, as seen in figure 3.

Figure 3.   Runway behind benches at the Super Shoot.

Coaching

Coaching of any kind is prohibited while you are shooting during the tournament. This includes from behind the firing line or from your neighbor. You can help a fellow shooter find his/her target or with a rifle or components, you're not allowed to give advice on when to shoot or where to aim.

Firing Line Etiquette

At certain matches you will be required to remain seated at the bench until the end of your relay. Respect the people around you while they are shooting. Keep visiting to a minimum. If you were shooting while your neighbors were carrying on, you would be upset. Be proactive and show the respect you would demand. There's no rule in the book requiring to throw down a few choice words everyone on the firing line can hear if you shoot a bad group. If you happen to shoot a bad group, it's not the end of the world. Throwing your loading block or headphones is also not necessary. Many onlookers have commented to me after some of my bad groups saying "how can you sit there with no reaction after shooting a group that bad?" I just tell um "practice, plenty of practice."

Sighter Target Manners

If you'd like to test conditions or different loads after you finish your group, give your neighbors a chance to finish their record group. Doubling (shooting at the same time) with your neighbor can cause a major change of impact. Who cares if it's on the sighter, but if you give your neighbor a nice .350 on his record target at 100 yards for no other reason than you wanted to test conditions, it's just bad manners. If you are hurt by your neighbor messing around on the sighter after the fact, you might be a bit upset too. Be courteous. It doesn't take long to get a reputation for being someone you don't want as your neighbor.

No shooter is allowed to occupy any bench on any relay when not shooting. Everyone is required to stay behind the firing line while not shooting. Generally, this is considered to be the concrete pad. During the World Benchrest Championships there is line or fence which is designated as the point that shooters are not allowed to cross during any relay. Figure 4 shows the fence which was used as the demarcation point behind the firing line in Umea Sweden.

I've seen spectators walk right up to a bench and stand opposite a shooter who is trying to shoot a group in a tournament. I've asked several spectators to step back behind the firing line until after the cease fire.

Figure 4. World Benchrest Championships 2003 in Umea Sweden, scopes and barrier.

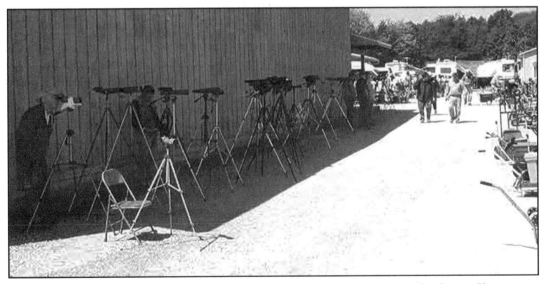

Figure 5. Some of the spotting scopes behind the firing line at the Super Shoot.

Spotting Scopes and Watching

When watching through a spotting scope, keep your comments soft spoken and to a minimum. Very few shooters like to hear you screaming and hollering while they are trying to put that last shot into the group.

At the 2005 NBRSA Nationals, several shooters were watching Lester Bruno finish his last group in the unlimited 200. Lester's aggregate was well under the current world record. We were quiet until after the time had elapsed so as to not disturb any other shooters on the firing line. After the cease-fire, about ten shooters who had been watching gave Lester a standing ovation.

Psychological Warfare

Now and then shooters will seek you out and let you know how you have been shooting. They realize many shooters are vulnerable to psychological warfare and will fold under the pressure. I don't agree with this type of psychological warfare. Don't trash talk to those shooters you know are susceptible to it. Most of those who are vulnerable don't win on a regular basis. You'll hear comments like "if you shoot another good group, you might just win this thing." These folks need our silent support. Wait till the match is over to visit with them.

At the Super Shoot 2003, while shooting very well on the last day, I was visited by several shooters who would have liked to see me fold and give them a chance. One Hall of Fame member came out of his way to visit and give me a little trash talk. I invited him to stay, as he knows I am not bothered by knowing how I am shooting. I told him, "Pull up a chair and stay awhile, we can talk trash all you want." Oh, by the way, I won the yardage by a good margin.

At the 2004 Super Shoot, Dick Wright happened by the Wailing Wall where the targets and stat sheets are displayed. Ken Hottenstein and I were looking at the stat sheets. Dick did not know he was leading the 100 yard aggregate after four targets. Dick, rifle over his shoulder on his way to the firing line, asked Kenny and I how he was doing. We told him to go shoot his group and don't worry about it. Dick insisted we tell him and that he wouldn't be bothered by knowing, I would not tell and replied "how can you say that!" Kenny finally broke down and said "you're winning this thing." Dick insisted it didn't bother him and went to shoot his last group. I watched Dick shoot his two previous groups, his gun was really shooting. Dick's first two shots on his last record target did not touch. He shot about .250 and finished third. I scolded Dick about his insistence the following year.

Lend a Helping Hand

If you see a fellow competitor in trouble during a relay with time left, loan your rifle to them so they can finish their group, or at the very least, help find someone with enough ammo left in order to finish their group. Don't be afraid to ask someone if you can borrow a rifle if you have gun trouble.

While reloading after my third shot on the record target during the 2002 Nationals at Midland, TX, I felt a tap on the shoulder. I turned around to find Dennis Wagner standing over me. He asked to borrow my rifle. I agreed he could use my rifle, but asked "could I finish my group first?" The look on Dennis' face was priceless. He finally realized I was in the middle of my group and thought it would be okay to finish. I finished with a .469, a reasonable group at 200 yards. Dennis bettered my group with about a .425. I told Dennis what Rex Reneau told me after I shot a nice .124 with his rifle at Luther after my gun trouble, "That will be enough of that. Next time you can borrow a rifle that doesn't shoot!" I was kidding, of course, and would have loaned my rifle to Dennis the next relay.

If you have knowledge of someone struggling, offer to help. If you're running a match and notice someone struggling, ask a fellow shooter to help. Many shooters are too timid to ask. Lifelong friendships are made with a simple action of offering to help. We certainly don't shoot Benchrest for a living. You might as well have fun and make some friends.

At the smaller local matches, help with the little things at the range. The local match hosts desperately need your help, but many are afraid to ask. Benchrest at a local level is a break even affair at best. Shooters hosting local tournaments are do so for the love of the sport.

Figure 6.   Wayne Campbell, just before receiving the citation for driving in the lobby.

Time to Visit

Take time to get to know your fellow shooters. The other shooters at the range are your friends who share a common passion. At our local matches we gather at my home after the match on Saturday for food and fellowship. This is a great time to get to know some of the folks away from the pressures of the range. The only downside is we tend to stay up way too late visiting.

Figure 7. Larry Kuse, is one of the nice guys, about 50 years experience.

Integrity

I was scoring a tournament at Raton when a competitor dropped of a sheet of paper with a simple request. I asked the shooter what he had observed. I was pleasantly surprised (again) to find out that the shooter who handed me the paper was shooter "52". After a short conversation, I insisted the target detail was inspecting the backers, and the backers for match two have already been inspected and that no problems or questionable backers were reported.

The competitor was Gene Beggs, and if you haven't gathered by now, he was wanting to make sure that he had fired the correct number of shots on his target. Yep he was telling on himself, and was a bit worried because he did not know for sure. This type of thing is common amongst the competitors in this game.

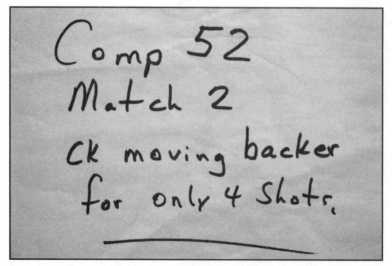

Figure 8. Request from Gene Beggs to make sure he had fired the correct number of shots.

NBRSA Nationals
Doing the Right Thing

During the unlimited stage at a National Championship, my neighbor waited until very late in the relay to fire his last shot. The range officer immediately asked who had fired late on our side of the firing line. Wayne Campbell <u>immediately</u> raised his arm and was ultimately disqualified.

I was looking right at Wayne and was pretty sure he did not fire late, but Wayne's actions were one of the ultimate in integrity and honesty. Many would have not been so quick to admit they were the one who fired. Wayne did visit with the Range officer but to no avail he was disqualified from the yardage. I agreed with Wayne, I didn't think he was late. Remember, I was looking right at him, but we both realized the call is up to the range officer. Wayne did not dwell on what had transpired, and I don't remember hearing anything about this since.

Could've been Handled Differently

I just happened to have a front row seat at these Nationals to witness about every rules infraction of the week. This comes from watching whenever possible. While approaching the firing line during a relay, I normally look to see who still has their bolt in their rifle. This often leads to some drama with the clock running down while waiting to get the last shot off. I noticed a competitor who was not finished after the 30 second warning, and of course I would be watching. The competitor was just to the right of the range officer's stand. I never dreamed of having the best seat in the house for the drama which was about to unfold, I watched intently while the time ran down and the range officer said "cease-fire," Cease. Bang. Fire. The range officer immediately indicated the shot was late and the competitor would be disqualified and wanted to know his competitor number and name.

The shooter was insistent from the outset he had not fired late. The competitor threw a fit, cursing and swearing. An hour later he could be heard a half a block away. This was one situation which I believe a competitor should have been ejected from the event for unsportsmanship like conduct which is addressed in the rule book. This was not a life changing event. No one was hurt. No money was lost. No careers were damaged. If you wait and get caught, just take your medicine.

Summary

Have fun,
Share the loading area,
Share benches for practice,
Work together setting flags,
Cell phones and pagers off or set to vibrate,
Be aware of the location of the firing line,
Leave runway behind benches clear of obstructions,
No coaching during any relay,
After finishing your group, go easy on the sighter,
Stay behind the firing line when not shooting,
Remain soft spoken when watching through spotting scopes,
Those who are shooting well don't need you to remind them,
Lend a helping hand where you can,
Keep your cool when a referee's decision goes against you,
Have fun; ask Wayne Campbell, "It's just a game"!

Tom Libby, proving you can have fun about any time.
Tom has provided many memorable moments during
opening ceremonies come Super Shoot time.

What's a Tournament?

Many shooters experience anxiety to some extent when match day nears. This simply means you're alive. The newer you are, the higher your anxiety level will be. These feelings are normal and rightly so. You are preparing to participate in arguably the most difficult shooting sport on the planet.

Match schedules for NBRSA Group, Hunter, 600 yard, 1000 yard, and Rimfire classes are found in the NBRSA News for registered tournaments which are contested in the continental United States and in Europe. The IBS schedules can be found in the March issue of Precision Shooting Magazine and online at the IBS web site at http://www.international-benchrest.com.

Both schedules are divided by region and listed by range at which they will be contested. Along with the dates and type of matches are the people to contact for each range. In most cases the match directors are shooters. They can help with directions to the range and recommend accommodations. If you're new to the sport, the match directors can usually help you contact shooters in your area who regularly attend. Don't pass up an opportunity to travel with a shooter from your area. It's a great time to learn about the coming event and everything Benchrest.

MID-CONTINENT REGION
Butch Fjoser, Director

MOORELAND PUBLIC RANGE – Mike Ratigan, 1116
Bel-Mar, Woodward, OK 73801 580-123-45673:
Email: 9823749123984.com   ***Bring Shooting Chair!***

Nov 24	SP State	100/200	1:00pm
Nov 25	HV	200/100	9:00am
Dec 5	LV/HV	100yds	1:00pm
Dec 6	HV/LV	200yds	9:00am
Jan 8	LV Rgnl	100/200	9:00am
Jan 9	HV or Unl 5	100/200	9:00am

MILLCREEK RIFLE CLUB, DeSoto, Kansas – Contact
Larry Kuse, 8112 W. 89th St.

Figure 1. Fictitious match schedule.

Reading the Schedule

Above is a sample of a schedule as would appear in the NBRSA news. This sample schedule is fictitious, but a good representation of what you'll find. As you can see from the November dates in the schedule, Nov 24 is the Sporter State. This tournament is being held in OK, so yep, it's the Oklahoma State Sporter. The tournament will be shot in the order listed, 100 yards first, then 200 yards, with a start time of 1:00 pm. Some ranges will leave the targets set up at the last yardage contested on the first day, then start with that yardage on the second day. In the example above, Nov 25 will be a Heavy Varmint starting at 200 yards at 9:00 am.

Saturday, Dec 5, shows both 100 yard stages for the weekend. First is the Light, then the Heavy Varmint; also, you should note the start time of the first match of the day is another afternoon start time of 1:00 pm. Typically the range would be open for practice before the matches with afternoon start times on Saturday. On Sunday the start time is moved up to 9:00 am. This helps the traveling competitors arrive home a bit earlier. Note the guns are reversed, a very common practice. You start Sunday with the rifle you finished with on Saturday.

In the third example for January, you can see that on Saturday there will be the Light Varmint Regional. The region is the Mid-continent, thus it will be the Mid-Continent Light Varmint Regional. The start time is 9:00 am at 100 yards. This match finishes the same day with 200 yards in the afternoon. On Sunday you have a choice of shooting Heavy Varmint, or if you prefer, you can shoot a 5 group 5 shot Unlimited. Notice the Sunday start time is 9:00 am and starts at 100 yards.

Preparations

It's common to double check equipment a couple days preceding travel to any tournament. Most writings on the subject cover only the shooting equipment, but lets consider personal needs first.

Whether traveling to a weekend match or a major tournament, consider your needs for food, clothing, shelter, and travel arrangements. I love to travel to the shoots with other shooters. Car pooling gives many hours to trade stories about all things Benchrest, strategy, and hunting stories, etc.

Many range facilities are in remote locations. Let's face reality for a moment. The middle of town isn't the most popular location for a rifle range, except in Buenos Aries, Argentina. The range is in the town center in Argentina's capital city, this is a rare exception.

Most ranges have no kitchen. Many are without drinking water. Plan on bringing food and drink with you. Even at the NRA Whittington Center at Raton, NM, we make plans for lunch. There's not enough time, when shooting 10 groups a day, to travel to town for lunch, even to retrieve something to go.

Plan to bring appropriate clothing. Bring rain gear, no matter where you plan on attending a tournament. I've been rained on at the Cactus in Phoenix (dry? desert? ya right!) about as many times as the Super Shoot. When traveling to different elevations you also should consider clothing for the different climactic conditions. Bring cold weather clothing when traveling to the mountains, even in the middle of summer. Mornings at Raton can be brisk even in July. You must admit, its not natural to grab a coat during summer weather when it's 80-105 degrees outside.

My normal plan includes rain coat and umbrella, medium sized coat and warm shirts, pants, short sleeve shirts, and shorts regardless of where we're going.

Inventory Your Shootin' Gear

Nothing will raise your level of anxiety more than forgetting something you need when competing, like your gun, bolt, flags, bullets, rest, bags, or loading box. I have made a list called my "Do Not Forget List."

Go over your list while assembling your shooting gear before leaving, half way to the range might be a bit late.

Do Not Forget List

Gun	Bolt	Extra barrel
Scope	Mirage shield	Empty cases (non primed)
Bore guide	Bullets	Bolt lube (synthetic)
Priming tool	Powder measure	Full length die
Neck bushings	Bullet seater	Primer pocket uniformer
Full length press	Arbor press	Otto die Shims
small screwdriver	scope	9/64 allen wrench
nylon neck brush	Never Dull	sizing die wax
Rest	Rear bag	Snake bag (empty)
Stop watch	Plastic hammer	Towels
wax -liquid	wax carnauba - dry	
Hearing protection	Ear plugs	Sun glasses
Solvent bottle	Cleaning rods	Patches
Brushes	JB bore paste	Action cleaning tools
Umbrella	Rain suit	Tape for gun case
Calculator	Note pad and pen	

Figure 2. Do Not Forget List!

Some tournaments require you to travel to the range the day before. Tournaments with afternoon start times allow the shooters who live within 2-4 hours travel time, to travel the day of the match. Tournament directors will be around before the tournament to attend to the many details that go with hosting the event. It's common to be able to draw for a bench if the tournament director is handy. Most of the folks hosting these shoots are in it for the fun and want you to be as comfortable as possible.

Experienced competitors like to know what bench they'll be shooting from. This helps in the decision of where to set up the loading stuff, where to unload the bench stuff and flags. Many participants want to practice and verify the rifle and tune up prior to match time. Being able to set up on the bench they will be shooting from means they won't have to move later on.

Unload your bench stuff and flags at your assigned bench, or pick a bench to practice on if benches haven't been assigned. Find somewhere to reload. If you have a choice, pick a spot where you can watch your flags while reloading.

At smaller matches with no relays you can clean your rifle on your bench, a very popular choice. Set up your cleaning gear and get your rifle out and clean it. While your gun is soaking, set up your loading tools and get organized to load your ammunition.

Before getting too involved in visiting, testing, tuning, and practicing, find the scale at the range and weigh your rifle, no matter how many times it has been weighed before. Things get changed like scopes and barrels. After the match starts you'll be disqualified if your rifle is over weight. Some ranges will weigh every rifle before the tournament starts, some spot check and some do both.

Figure 3. Rifle weigh in at the IBS Nationals

St. Louis

I remember attending a US World Team Qualifying Match at St. Louis in 2002. I wasn't feeling well. I had such a sore throat I couldn't talk. I did not shoot and volunteered to oversee the weighing of rifles. This saved the refs many trips into the stat house after every group. During the course of the random checking of rifles two competitors came to weigh their rifles that were not called for inspection. I asked if they were sure they wanted to weigh since they were not called to do so. Both shooters indicated they wanted to weigh, both were disqualified. One of the shooters was shooting a Heavy Varmint rifle in the Light Varmint class, the other was well over the 10 pound 8 1/2 ounce limit, weighing in over 11 pounds. This example should reinforce your desire to know before the start time. The only course of action is disqualification. After the fact, it's too late to lighten the rifle.

Practice

Set your flags. If the range is not open for practice, your first order of business, if you have been able to draw a bench is to set your flags. If the range is open for practice, attend to cleaning and loading. Remember, shooting without flags is a waste of time. If there are flags close by which you might use to practice, use them until the next cease fire.

When practicing at matches with relays, or more shooters than there are benches, you will be required to share a bench, even during practice. Don't be bashful, introduce yourself to the person you'll be sharing with.

Don't forget to bring your hearing protection when approaching the firing line.

Test your rifle tune. If your rifle appears to shoot okay then it's time to practice in the conditions of the day. I like to shoot in every condition I can find. If one or two conditions seem to yield smaller groups during testing, I would prefer to shoot those conditions during tournament time.

Matches with morning start times don't allow practice before the match, or any shooting prior to the match start time. Tournaments with afternoon start times will close the range before the scheduled start time to prepare the frame and range.

While the range crew is finishing up the target preparations, make any last minute flag adjustments. Check for the legal height, line up, and visibility. After the first shot is fired in the first match no competitors are allowed downrange. The tournament officials will be required downrange from time to time, but no adjustments to any flags are allowed. If a competitor's flags are higher than allowed they will be laid on the ground. It's the owner's responsibility to make sure they are set per the rule book before the start time.

Eventually you'll hear the call everyone has been waiting for "shooters to the line." The range master will welcome everyone to the range for the Mid-Continent Sporter Regional or whatever the match happens to be. The range officer will read the standard safety commands or play them from a tape recording or CD. Be sure to ask any questions you might have. Introduce yourself to your neighbors. If this is your first match let your neighbors know, they'll keep a watchful eye on you.

The range will either shoot a warm-up match or add three minutes to the first match of each yardage, it's up to the tournament director. Where you live will determine if you shoot a warm-up or not. In the part of the country where I live, most tournaments add three minutes to the first match of each yardage. After all of the safety commands are announced, the range master will say, "This is relay 1, Match #1 at 100 yards, it will be a 5 (or 10) shot match and you will be allowed 10 (7, 10, 12 or 15) minutes to complete your firing." Then you hear the commands, "Ready on the right?" (The range officer will look and pause) "Ready on the left," (Look and pause.) Then while looking onto the range to make sure there are no safety problems and no one is down range, the range master will then announce "Ready on the firing line?" (Pause) "Place bolts in rifles." (pause) "Commence firing." The official time starts after the command "commence firing." If you shoot during the commence fire command, you'll be disqualified.

Never put a loaded round into the action or onto the loading ramp until after the commence fire command. I hold my bolt up in the air so the range officer can see it until after the commence fire is given. This way, if someone shoots early I won't move a muscle and will still have my bolt out and holding it up so everyone can see it wasn't me (as seen in figure 4).

Sorry for the repeat, this is important!
Don't place any ammunition in the action or breach of your rifle until after the commence fire command is given. This again means that if you insert your bolt on the "place bolts in rifles" command your rifle shouldn't be loaded. You can be disqualified for having your rifle ready to shoot before the "commence fire" command. Wait until after the commence fire command to install your bolt and load your rifle. The only prize for shooting early is disqualification for a safety violation.

Figure 4.
How to hold your bolt until after the "commence fire command is given."

After the relay is started foul your barrel and shoot your group. You must shoot your group within the time limits, there's no provision for anyone to shoot after the time has expired. At the major tournaments leave your rifle setting in the rest and rear bag until the time runs down. Look at your target just as the time expires, make sure nobody has cross-fired on your target before getting up. If you're cross-fired upon, you must report it immediately to the range officer. After the targets are scored, it's too late to complain about a cross-fire.

Clean your rifle and immediately go and reload regardless of the size of tournament. After you're ready to shoot again, go and visit the other shooters, look at the targets, etc. Congratulations, you have made it through the first target of a registered tournament.

Target Crew

After it's been determined to be safe for the target crew, targets and backers will be changed. The targets are then handed off to the scorer. The moving backers are inspected to insure the required number of shots have been fired. If there are any questions with the backers, they are shown to the scorer. If the scorer can not determine whether it contains the required number of shots, the target is inspected. If the required number of shots can be seen on the target, no further action is required. If the target doesn't clearly show the required number of shots, the referees will be called for a ruling. It's rare to get this far into the process. Most of the time you will see five shots in the backer or target.

The rule is clear. If you can't see the required number of shots, a penalty will be assessed. In an NBRSA tournament the penalty is 1 inch for every 100 yards per missing shot. Or 1 inch at 100 yards, 2 inches at 200 yards, and 3 inches at 300 yards for every missing shot (NBRSA rules). In the IBS the penalty is different.

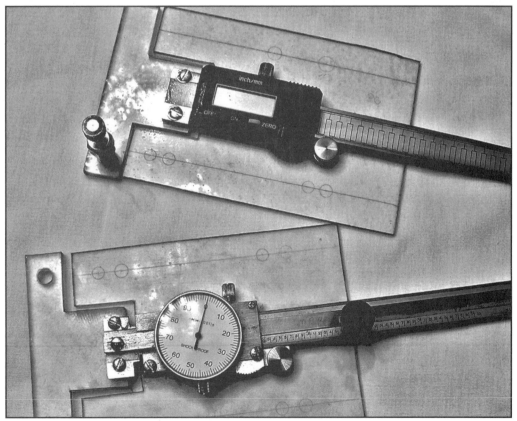

Figure 5. measuring tools.
Sorry for the doctored photo, but this made the scribe lines on the bottom visible.

Official Scoring (group targets)

The targets are brought to the Official scorer to be measured by a tool specifically designed to measure groups. Group targets are measured center to center of the two widest shots. Sounds easy. With the correct tools, it is. Many shooters believe you can measure how far apart two bullet holes are by measuring outside to outside with calipers then subtract the bullet diameter. This might sound like a good idea, but you will not get accurate measurements. You can get relatively close, say about +/- .040 or forty thousandths. There's so many variables which can't be accounted for with a pair of calipers.

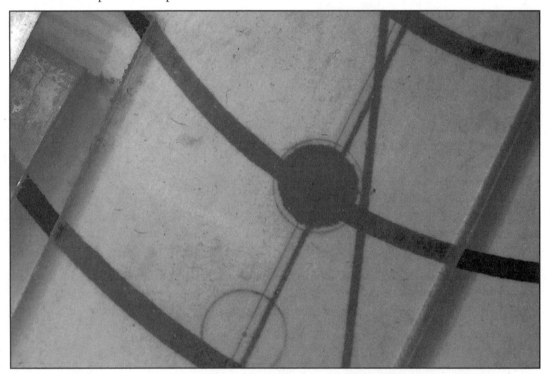

Figure 6. Measuring reticle over black dot.

My personal home-made measuring tools are shown in figure 5. You can see the scribe line on the bottom of the lexan plastic. There are two different sized circles, one for a 6mm, the other is for .22 caliber. You might be asking how can a home made tool accurately measure groups. Well, in 2005, I measured two yardage aggregate records. I measured one at .1845, the second measured .2354. After going through the measuring committee, the two records were Official. The first record returned as .1844, the second .2354. Record measurement is made by a three person measuring committee of experienced scorers around the country.

Figure 6 shows the reticle over a black dot. Bullet holes often do not exactly fill the reticle. What's important is to know how to compensate for the difference in size. In figure 6 it's straight forward how to obtain the center to center measurement. Just center the reticle over the holes as shown in figure 6

Small Groups with Overlapping Bullet Holes

When you have a small group, this simple idea becomes more complicated. In order to accurately measure a small group, examine a single bullet hole on the sighter. This reference will tell the scorer what the bullet should look like in reference to the reticle. Apply what was learned from the single hole when starting the measurement. If there is no single hole, (very rare) do the best you can. When measuring for World Record measurement, you can use a hole from the same rifle on another target to get your reference, assuming there wasn't a caliber change.

Scribe Line

The line on the measuring tool is used in the proper line up of the tool. To properly measure a group, start by aligning the tool scribe line with the direction of travel. Center the reticle over the starting hole. The scribe line should go through the middle of the bullet hole where you'll end the measurement. If you don't properly line up the measuring tool, you can have substantial errors.

Set Pin

After lining up the measuring tool over the starting hole, with the line passing through the center of the finishing hole, the set pin is pressed to hold the measuring tool in place. There will be an error if the tool moves when its opened to conduct the measurement. In fact, this set pin is often the cause of measurement errors. If the pin is sloppy it allows the tool to slip sideways, the target will measure small. When comparing tools and using proper technique, the tool which measures the group the biggest is correct, sorry.

Figure 7. Scoring and data entry at the World Championships 2005.

Errors

When there is a measurement error, they're typically of a couple of types. The three most common measurement errors are having a loose set pin, mis-reading the tool face, and double measuring. If the tool is substandard (lose set pin) all of the targets will be off slightly (measure small). Normally at the end of the day, this will not normally effect the outcome of the match. This can be very disappointing to any shooter that has targets sent for world record measurement, only to have the record denied because the targets were measured to small. This happens with great regularity.

Analog tools have the potential to be mis-read. No tool has an automatic reset. After every measurement, you must return the tool to zero. Double reading happens when the tool is not reset to zero after measuring a group, then measuring the next group. The result is the combination of two groups, usually WAY bigger than the actual size. It's very easy for the shooter to recognize.

Remeasurement

Don't be afraid to bring gross errors to the attention of a referee. You must pay a fee to have a target remeasured. The fee will be returned if the new measurement is in error more than .009 for the NBRSA.

I caution competitors measuring their targets with a calipers and arguing about ten thousandths. While serving as a head referee at a National Championship tournament I was approached by a competitor wanting a target remeasured. I inquired about the competitor number, target number and inquired about the problem (I wouldn't tell the scorer). I cautioned the shooter about measuring with calipers. I collected the fee, removed the target from the wailing wall, covered the competitor number and previous measurement, and returned the target to the official scorer for re-measurement.

I've scored thousands of targets, I looked over the scorers shoulder while the target was re-measured. After the re-measurement the dial is uncovered, and the reading taken. This is repeated three times. *(The three readings are averaged. If the new measure is not more than .009 different nothing is changed and the competitor loses the fee. If the re-measurement is more than .009 in error the measurement will be changed and the fee returned to the competitor.)*

The target was measured wrong, the bad news was it measured small and was actually bigger than originally measured. The new measurement was recorded on the target and in the official score sheet. Remember my warning about measuring with calipers. I returned to the loading area with the news. I found the competitor and said "I have good and bad news." The good news was "I am returning the protest fee." This meant the score was in error. The bad news was "the target measured bigger." As you can imagine, the shooter was unhappy, I warned him. The moral of this story is "When you know the targets are being measured small, keep quiet."

Wailing Wall

Targets are displayed after they're scored. They are hung in a place on the range called the wailing wall. It's affectionately named after all of the crying which takes place immediately after the targets are displayed. Sounds such as "My last shot added..." and "That darned middle flag just picked up when..." I could go on for hours.

Figure 8. Wailing wall at Kelbly's at the World Championships 2005.

Competitors have an opportunity to inspect the targets. Although rare, errors do happen. Don't be afraid to question major errors. At Raton, NM., an error was brought to my attention. The problem was easy to see; the previous group measurement was added to the target. This was caused by not resetting the tool to zero before measuring the next group. It's a unique feeling. You make your way to the wailing wall expecting to find a .260 you fired in the previous relay, only to find your target measured a nice .601. In horror you look at the group, but there are no bullets out of the group and realize there was an obvious error. No problem, after your heart rate goes back to normal find a referee. These problems are easily corrected. Before you make preparations to throw the first stone, I have a job for you.

Awards Ceremony

Stay for the awards, especially at the smaller local tournaments. At home I can calculate the results before most shooters can pack their equipment. Be gracious in defeat. Show your respect for those shooters who finish in the awards, especially for those who win infrequently. It's important to show good sportsmanship. Kind words and actions will go a long way and are remembered.

I still remember the first time I received a visit from Tony Boyer. He went out of his way to congratulate me. I do my best to follow his example.

Figure 9. Trophys for the 2006 NBRSA Nationals.

Figure 10. Awards ceremony at 2006 IBS Nationals,

Wind Flags,
What are these for?

Wind flags are used to gauge wind direction and intensity. They're used to accurately determine where to hold on a target to impact a desired spot. Flags, and the ability to use them, have been the most important improvement in modern Benchrest competition since the advent of the internally adjusted rifle scope, and the action glued into a fiberglass stock in the early 1980s.

Centerfire Benchrest competition is conducted with the most accurate rifles in the world, built with attention to every detail and capable of delivering bullets with unparalleled accuracy. All of this would be an exercise in futility without the use of wind flags. Flags are the most important equipment used in competitive Benchrest today. Wind flags are required when shooting in the atmospheric conditions that exist on earth, wind and mirage.

Figure 1. St. Louis NBRSA Nationals September 2005.

The accurate Benchrest rifle will only carry you so far in competition, and when wind conditions are very light, could be considered the most important factor. However, conditions in most parts of the world are seldom light, and the worse the conditions, the more important the flags become. The difference between an aggregate of .350 and .250 is much more than one tenth of an inch. It's the difference between night and day. In comparison the difference between an aggregate of .250 and .150 is equal to the distance between the earth and sun. In my opinion, a good Benchrest rifle capable of competitive accuracy won't shoot any worse than about .380 with good components, simply being out of tune.

Knowledge of how to use flags is much more important than a rifle tuned to peak performance. Shooting two inch groups at two hundred yards with a finely tuned rifle is easy when shooting at the wrong time. Shooting Benchrest rifles or any accurate rifles without flags, is a waste of time, money, barrels, bullets, powder, and primers.

Air is a substance which has mass and is in motion most of the time. We are surrounded by a sea of air which to us is colorless, weightless, and normally tasteless. I often hear people say bullets are traveling too fast to be effected by wind. This could not be farther from the truth. Our atmosphere effects everything within it. Air in motion effects supersonic jets, falling asteroids, and yes, bullets. The weight of air can be measured and has mass, and when in motion exerts forces on everything that passes through it. Physics explains the actions of things in flight. Absolute pressure, temperature, and the amount of water vapor in the air determine its mass and the effects it will have on the bullets during their flight.

I don't need flags.

My rifle shoots too fast to be effected by the wind!

Anonymous

Flag Construction

In this chapter we will consider many factors used to design wind flags, from the choice of style, vane shape, tail material, weight, pivot types, color, and poles or stands. After everything has been considered, I'll explain how to evaluate whether or not you have the correct flag for you.

Figure 1. Smiley Hensley putting a tail on one of his flags at the WBC8.

Flag Styles

Flag style is very important and should be considered carefully before building something new. DON'T reinvent the wheel. Look at what's being used successfully and buy or copy them. Simplistic flag design is important when looking at five or more flags at the same time. <u>Complicated flags slow the shooting process</u>. A compromise of characteristics will be needed to give usable and timely information.

The perfect flag would say "Shoot, stupid, shoot!"

Flags must be easy to see and give useable data that reflects direction and intensity of wind at any given time. Using your peripheral vision, you should be able to quickly identify if a condition is stable, increasing, or decreasing in intensity (same, more or less).

There are three basic types of flags.

1. The daisy wheel with single vane, or Smiley Flags shown in figure 1.
2. The single vane.
3. The double vein.

Each of these basic styles have pros and cons.

Daisy Wheel

The primary function of a daisy wheel when used in flag construction is to aid in determining the angle. Daisy wheels are NOT used to indicate wind speed. If this were true, there would be no need for the tail. The daisy wheel does not respond instantly to increase in wind speed or a "pickup," and will coast in winds which are decreasing in intensity or a "letup." In either case, the daisy wheel will not give timely speed info even if you could tell the velocity using them.

Velocity will be determined using a piece surveyor's ribbon. I'll cover this in detail later. Typically one pedal of the daisy is painted brown or black which would possibly be used to tell velocity, but the only time the daisy could be used to measure velocity would be in a light and stable head to tail wind. I have only seen one tournament which had stable winds, and will probably not live long enough to see that again.

Figure 2. Smiley Hensley flag.

Figure 3.   Vane hidden behind the daisy wheel, hard to see when wheel is turning.

Head and tail wind angles are difficult to see with the daisy wheel flag. This can be seen in figure 3. As you can see in the left row of flags, the vane is covered by the daisy wheel. The vane becomes lost or camouflaged behind the daisy wheel. In a head and tail wind you must be able to see the angle of the vane. Minor angle changes shooting in head or tail winds make dramatic changes to the impact point on the target, "angle is everything." In other words, if you shoot one shot in a head wind from right to left, and the next in a left to right (with an angle change of only a few degrees), you'll have major vertical changes in your impact point.

Single Vane
The single vane flag, as seen in figure 4, is great for shooting in a cross wind. They don't take up so much of the visual space in front of the shooter as do the bigger flags. This flag style, when set in the correct place, is good for seeing head and tail wind angles. In order to properly see head and tail wind angles, the flags must be set in a line from the shooter to the middle of the target.

A disadvantage of the single vane flag is the inability to see changes in the cross wind angle. I personally don't care to see minor angle changes in a direct crosswind, for example, wind from 2:30 to 3:30 on the clock.

Figure 4.   Single vane flags during practice.

The single vane is a good indicator of angling winds when the vanes are the correct shape. The correct shape will be covered in more detail later. The single vane will appear to get shorter when the wind turns in or out. In a 90 degree crosswind, say from 9 or 3 O'clock, they are rectangle shaped, in a crosswind from 45 degrees, or wind from 10:30 or 7:30 (and 1:30 and 4:30) they are shorter and almost appear as a square and disappear in the head or tail wind.

Figure 5.   Double vane on left, single vane on right.

Double Vane

The double vane flag is arguably the best indicator of angling conditions. You will find out in the chapter about "How to use the flags" that 45 degree angles are some of the hardest conditions to shoot successfully.   Double vane flags usually have stripes on the inside of each vane that helps gauge the angle. You can see from the photo in figure 5 that the wind is coming from left to right from about 10:30, and at about a 45 degree angle, and that the inside stripes are visible. Remember KISS, "keep it simple S@*^#d."   If you elect to shoot quartering winds, you must be able to integrate both the angle and velocity instantly. For me, this is extremely difficult. Many consistently good shooters prefer a cross wind or a head and tail wind.

Figure 6. Wind Probe

Wind Probe

The wind probe is a relative newcomer. I remember seeing an early prototype at the Buffalo Shoot in 1998. The original probes moved in two axes, side to side and front to back. I remember commenting to Arnold Jewell that I needed medication for motion sickness. They were very unique indeed.

In my opinion, the wind probe is much like the double vane flag. You are required to look directly at them. For me this narrows my field of view, slows my decision making process, and causes tunnel vision.

How Do Other Shooters Feel About Your Flags?

When sharing a bench with others, (30-35 at the Super Shoot and 15-25 at the Nationals), you'll have an advantage if you're familiar with flags that are popular. I'm not on a crusade to convert anyone to any flag style by any stretch of the imagination.

Like the old adage "you can lead a horse to water but cannot make em drink." It would be to every shooter's advantage to have all the flags the same while on the firing line at major tournaments. This can be seen in figure 4 in the chapter "How to Use Flags" from the World Benchrest Championships.

I recommend purchasing flags from Smiley Hensley or copying them. This style is not my personal favorite, but is very popular, and I can use them successfully. If you would decide to copy the daisy wheel design, also copy the vane colors of both sides. This way, come major tournament time, your copies will be the same as the others. Wind right to left shows fluorescent orange on the tail, wind from left to right shows fluorescent green. I've seen flags in the same row with opposite color vanes, which is very confusing and distracting.

Shape of Vane

The flag vane shape must provide usable angle information. Different methods are used to determine angle with the three basic types of designs: Daisy wheel, single vane, and double vane. I will explain how the different styles are used to determine wind angle.

Daisy Wheel Flag

The daisy wheel on the daisy wheel flag is used to give the angle information. Daisy wheel flags with wind at 90 degrees will leave almost no view of the daisy wheel, and the farther in or out the wind turns, the more of the daisy you'll see, thus giving the angle. The front of the Daisy wheel is painted brown. the back is yellow. It's easy to tell if the condition is coming in or going out.

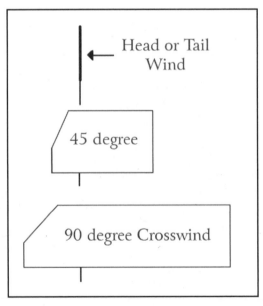

Figure 7.   My single vanes at different angles and get narrower.

Single Vane

The single vane flag must also show the angle. This is accomplished by using a rectangular shaped vane with the long side horizontal, as seen in figure 7. This flag is its longest when in wind at 90 degrees, and gets shorter when the wind turns in toward the bench or out to the targets. This flag vane should be the proper proportion in order to provide useable angle information. Colors from one side to the other should have good contrast, which will help with acute angling head and tail winds. You should be able to see the different colors when switching from right to left and back again.

Visually Similar

I would like all of my flags to be visually similar at different distances. Normally when sitting at the bench the flags at the longer distances look smaller, even though they are the same size, making the vanes harder to see. Using a larger vane at the longer distances helps make them look similar. It would be nice to be able to apply this to the tails, but DON'T do it! The tails would be of different weights and give different information making their reading extremely difficult.

The perfect set of flag vanes would look the same size regardless of distance. In order to accomplish this you would need to have a different size for each flag which would border on ridiculous when considering making a full set of flags for the Nationals or Super Shoot bench rotation.

I just wanted to give you an idea of what perfect would be. The idea of visually similar would be difficult to apply to daisy wheels and double vanes. Just try finding daisy wheels of different sizes, making the stripes different thicknesses on the double vanes. The idea of visual similarity is only practical for the single vane style.

I have settled on dimensions of 4 inches high by 16.5 inches long for the flags out to 100 yards. Past 100 yards I like a bit larger vane that is 5 inches by 19 inches. This is not exactly the same ratio, but seems to look okay at the longer distances.

Odd shaped flags, which are as tall, or taller than they are long, should be avoided. This type flag looks like an up and down rectangle when at 90 degrees. They still look like a rectangle oriented up and down when at a 45 degree angle, just a bit thinner. Odd shapes do nothing to add to the angle indication and make what you see more confusing.

One final note about the vane and the two basic schools of thought on flag construction: Tony Boyer prefers the Smiley Hensley Flag style and says, "You can't tell minor angle changes when shooting in a cross wind with a single vane." I agree, but I don't watch the vane angle in a 90 degree cross wind, just the tail.

With a Smiley flag, you cannot see changes in tail wind angle because of the vane being hidden by the daisy wheel.

Choice of Tail

The tail is the most important part of the flag. Most of our attention will be focused on the tail. The tail must indicate wind speed without being to heavy and it must be visible in low light conditions. The most popular tail material is surveyors ribbon about 1.187 to 1.250 wide and about 3 mils or .003 inches thick. Most of the long term successful shooters use this type of material. The reason is simple. They don't attenuate or dampen the effects of the wind. This type of tail looks "alive," or moving all of the time. just like the wind.

Other tail materials include super light Mylar, cloth, yarn, Sail Tails, Christmas tree tensile, foam, or chain.

Be consistent with your selection of tail material. Do not change tail weights from day to day. Doing so will make your decisions of where to hold dependent on the tail weight. In other words, your tail readings from the different weight tails will give you different absolute values of drift. Changing tail weights is a strategy mistake. Get comfortable with one tail (single surveyor's ribbon), and you will quickly learn what they are trying to tell you about how much drift a tail reading is worth. You're probably thinking, "he has lost his mind, my Sail Tails are easier too read." Write down my recommendation about using a single surveyor's ribbon for your tail choice. This way, after several years of limited success, only in the steadiest of conditions, you'll remember you've been told.

I made one of the most important observations at my first match was while standing on the range at Okie Shooters in Luther, OK. While watching the flags and comparing one style to another, I saw the tails (single surveyor's ribbon) on Don Creach's flags go straight into the air and stay there for about 10 seconds. My immediate thought was "WOW, I need to be able to see that." I'd been using a bit heavier tail, (three pieces of surveyor's ribbon stapled together). I made the correct choice by going to the single surveyor's ribbon and have had no regrets.

Tony Boyer uses a single surveyor's ribbon for the same reason. It's the best all around choice. Most of the "Top Guns" of Benchrest use surveyor's ribbon. I can tell you with 100% certainty, none use an inferior tail to give the competition an advantage, (food for thought). If there's something better than the single ribbon that could help shrink aggregates, it would be used.

In my opinion, the best choice is a single surveyor's ribbon. I know what you're thinking, when the wind blows more than 5 mile per hour they are maxed out. I live in a VERY WINDY part of the country and still believe the single surveyor's ribbon is your best choice.

Surveyor's Ribbon Will Show;
   Light wind conditions by tail angle,
   Heavy wind conditions by tail movement or oscillation,
   "Suckout" (instant reverse, more in the chapter of how to use wind flags),
   Up draft.

Use New Tail Material

Every time you set your flags, install new surveyor's ribbon. As discussed earlier when watching the tails, you want to see the movement or oscillation. You don't want to see wrinkles or folds in the material. New material will do away with this problem. This ribbon is inexpensive and affordable by anyone interested in shooting sports of all types, be it Benchrest or just for fun.

Adding new material every time allows you to use longer lengths (up to about 5-6 feet) when the flag height allows. You don't want the tail touching the ground. A tail tangled in the grass or weeds isn't very good at indicating intensity.

Fluorescent colors fade quickly. Using new tail material solves this problem.

Sail Tails and Foam

Sail tails appeared on the Benchrest scene in about 1996-1997. This type of tail is a piece of material used in the making of boat sails which have been starched into a semi circle. This removes the fluttering of the lighter ribbon. Rain will wash out the starch.

Several shooters have used thin pieces of foam which act like the sail tail but are a bit heavier, but don't lose their rigidity when rained on. You can see the sail tail on the flag in the front on the left side in figure 8. (Larry Scharnhorst's flags.)

When I look at sail tails, I get the feeling the conditions are stable no matter how unstable they actually are. This feeling is artificial. It's caused by removing the flutter of the tail. I want to see the flutter, it helps judge the stability and intensity.

Figure 8.   Sail Tails.

Color

Flag color is used to enable the user to see the flag. Your choice of colors should provide good contrast from side to side without either color being too dark. White or bright green is almost always a good choice for one side. The most popular color in use today is fluorescent orange (or safety orange). It's very important that your choice of colors be easily seen in a heavy overcast condition. In bright sunshine you will have little problems. Whatever your choice of colors, you should be able to see your flags and get usable data from them when given less than one second to look at them.

New US Federal research has shown fluorescent pink is more predominant with normal vision than safety orange. (I've known this for some time. Think of the money I could have saved the US on that research.)

IF YOU CAN'T SEE YOUR FLAGS THEY ARE USELESS. The vane of the flag must be of one solid color. Any stripes or spots take away from the main color making them harder to see at longer distances. I have seen flags which use the same colors of stripes on both sides oriented differently. In the heat of competition, when time is running out, is the wrong time to look at your flags for the right reading only to discover you shot in a complete reverse, and didn't notice the last two flag's showed stripes up and down instead of sideways. But hey, they were the right color!

You can see in figure 5 (photo of the double vane) the stripes in the last two flags seem faded, blended, or camouflaged. The resolution ability of your eye is not good enough to see the stripes at longer distances. You would have to make the flags and stripes bigger at the longer distances to have the ability to see them the same as the closer flags (visually similar).

Tail color should be selected so you can see them in a heavy overcast low light day, with contrast to the background. Settle on a color which can easily be seen in your peripheral vision. Blaze orange is the most popular color, followed by pink and white. I carry pink and white ribbon and use whichever color looks best at the time.

Difference in eyesight will determine your final color selection. If you are color blind and plan to build a set of flags for the major tournaments, seek the advice of other shooters about what colors to use. Talk to others who are not color blind about you choices. They can help you determine what colors you are looking at. When you are trying to buy paint, tape or surveyor's ribbon you'll need to know what color you need. If you guess and you're color blind, this won't be the first time to make the wrong choice of color. Ask someone to help you figure out what colors you see well.

Dull or Flat Finish

If you have a choice, use a dull or flat finish on the vanes. This is important when shooting in almost straight head and tail winds, where very small changes expose the different sides of your tail. In very acute angles you'll see the reflection from the glossy finish. If you have a gloss finish on both sides you will have more trouble seeing the small changes in angle and color. Using the dull finish will minimize this effect.

Black

Black is defined as *opposite of white* and *although we speak of black as a color, it is the <u>absence of color</u>* and *a surface which absorbs all light and reflects none back* and *the achromatic object color of least lightness characteristically perceived to belong to objects that neither reflect or transmit light* and *total or nearly total absence of light*.

You are probably thinking, where is this going?

Well, light must enter your eye and strike the optic nerve in the back portion of your eye in order for it to be seen. When light strikes a black object all the light is absorbed by the object and NONE is reflected. White reflects all visible light, black reflects none. This means <u>YOU CANNOT SEE THAT WHICH IS BLACK</u>! This is a physical fact and not up for argument or discussion. I have been told so many times "I can see black," that I hate to even say anything. The intention of this text is to help educate. I'm sure this will spark a couple of good debates by including this information, but it's VERY important. I was encouraged by a friend of mine who is a Doctor and PhD chemist to include this information. He argued that I would not be available for debate. If you want to debate I will be happy to give you his number.

What does this mean to us?

Well, no part of a flag should be black. Black seems visible when it covers up the background which is visible, or a background that has light being reflected or transmitted from it. For gosh sakes, pick a color you can see, or to rephrase, pick a color that reflects light from it. I want to see my vane and tail, not depend on the background to make my vane and tail visible. I'm sure I will be sorry for bringing this up again, just thought you should know about this simple property of physics.

Physical Properties
Balance

To balance or not to balance? That is the question.

Balancing a flag requires equal weight on opposing sides of the pivot. The static balance in your living room is all about the weight. When considering air pressure on the flag this becomes a more involved process. The air applies forces on the outside of the flag pulling and pushing in many directions. The finest balanced flags will be tail-heavy when in a nice 10 mph wind, as the aerodynamic drag pulls on the tail and pushes on the front of the flag.

I prefer to use the lightest flag possible made of coroplast or corrugated plastic. The corrugated plastic is about 30% lighter than balsa wood. The only attachment to my flag is a paper clip and surveyor's ribbon.

Over Rotation

Flags should be kept as light as possible. As you make the flag heavier you will observe a condition called over rotation even when the flag pole is plumb. When the flag changes direction, the mass of the flag is set into motion. Once this mass is in motion you'll need a force to stop it. The lighter the flag weight, the less force will be needed to stop the flag at the appropriate spot. The heavier the flag, the more it will overshoot or over-rotate in order to get enough force from the wind to stop its movement. When you have two flags with the same surface area of vane, the heavier flag will rotate farther past the current wind vector. If the flag is heavy enough, it will oscillate back and forth until finally coming to rest at the proper wind vector.

Autorotation

Autorotation is the movement of the heavy end of the flag down hill. A flag which has its center of gravity off center of its pivot point will auto rotate if the flag pole is out of plumb. Almost every pole is out of plumb, and setting them perfectly plumb is hard to do. If the weight of the flag can overcome the friction necessary to make it move, the heavy end will rotate to the downhill side. This can be distracting in light conditions when the flags lie about the wind vector. My personal flags are tail-heavy but extremely light. The weight of my flags is not heavy enough to overcome the friction forces of the pivot to auto rotate.

Basic Pivot Types

There are two basic styles of pivots, pin up and pin down. Figure's 9 & 10 show the pivot pin attached to the flag pole which points up. This type of pivot is great for keeping out the rain, dirt, and grit. One drop of high viscosity oil on the pin in figure 9 will keep out almost everything, and lubricates the pivot point. A single ball (bearing) is hidden inside the socket in figure 9. The pivot pin touches just the one contact point, which provides an almost friction free movement. The only downside of this type of pivot is that the pin is exposed when transporting. They must be protected somehow, either by taking them off or storing the pole in something like a gun case which will get very heavy (experience picking up a friends).

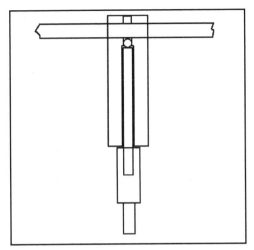

Figure 9.   Ed Adams' style pivot.

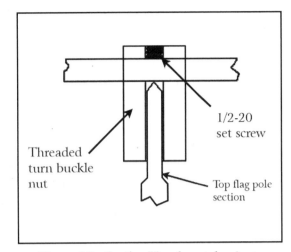

Figure 10. Smiley Hensley style pivot.

The Smiley Hensley flag style is shown in figure 10. The pivot pin fit is not as close as Ed Adams' setup in figure 9. The pins of the Smiley flags are actually the inner-most pole of the flag pole and are stored upside down in the flag pole itself. I believe Smiley has gone to a threaded turn buckle nut, which is already threaded and has the correct hole size for the pivot pin. Easy, just drill the cross hole for the flag shaft and use a stock 1/4-20 set screw to stop the flag fron rotating. Smiley turns down the top of the 1/4 inch pole section to fit inside the turn buckle nut.

My setup is a basic copy of the first pivot but is upside down. The pivot pin goes into the vane of the flag, the socket is in the pole. This is represented in figure 11. The advantage of my setup is there are smaller and fewer pieces. Nothing special to interface to the vane, just drive the pin into the bottom of the vane. The main disadvantage is that rain and dirt can infiltrate the socket, but after all the years of competitive experience, it seems to work just fine. I leave my water proof flags in the poles over night which helps keep stuff out of the sockets.

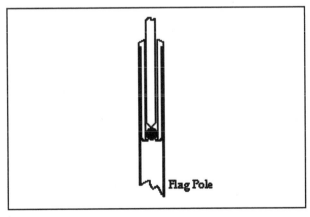

Figure 11.   Ratigan style pivot diagram.

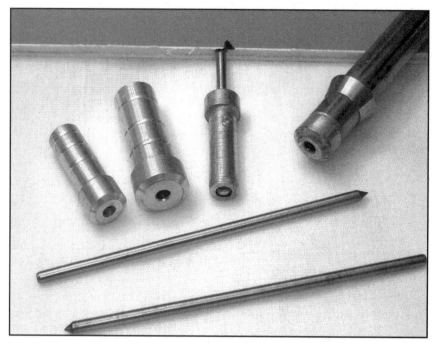

Figure 12.   Photo of Ratigan's pivot and pin in flag pole.

Figure 13.   Pivot using two bearings (Aussie style).

Flags In Your Scope?

Unless you use a modified cross hair (7 minutes high), as seen in figure 14, you'll not be able to see flags in the first 80% of the field at 100 yards, and then only a couple inches of the last flag will be visible. If you can see your flags, they will be to high and illegal. At 200 yards you'll be able to see the top of a flag at 100 yards and most of a flag at 166-170 yards when shooting the record target. It will be difficult to see the tails of any of the flags seen in the scope. Ignoring the tails in the last half of the range will not give you consistent competitive results.

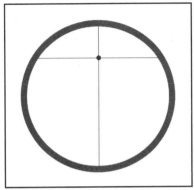

Figure 14. Crosshair installed 7 MOA high.
Skip Otto used this crosshair to shoot .099 at 200 yards.

Flags must be lower than a line from the top of the bench on which you are shooting to the bottom of your target card. I prefer to be below the bottom of the board. Flags higher that are too high and could be laid down by the referees after the match starts. This is a bad time to learn the rule. Practice setting your flags as per the rule book and you'll not have any trouble come match time. You will also have experience looking at them while they are set at the legal height.

Figure 15. Aiming at record with 36   Figure 16. Aiming at record with 45

The photos in figures 15 & 16 were taken through a scope aiming at the record portion of a target at 100 yards. You can see, no flags are visible in the scope at 100 yards. My flags are there, set at the level of the bottom of the board just below the legal height, but you can't see them. You might just see the top 2-3 inches or so if the last flag was exactly at the legal height, but you will not see flags any closer. Even if you can see the top of the flag, you'll not be able to see the tail.

Looking at flags in your scope should only be done when you cannot see them any other way. Looking at flags placed in your scope gives you an incredible amount of tunnel vision. You'll not see changes coming.

Flag Poles

There are two basic types of flag poles or stands being used by most shooters. They are music stands, as shown in figure 17, and stainless steel telescoping poles, as seen in figure 18. Whichever type of stand you decide on should be variable in height. Most ranges were built on uneven ground and require different height poles depending on what bench you shoot on. Many ranges also have slopes between the benches and the targets requiring poles of different heights.

I've been to most of the rifle ranges in the US which host the major tournaments. A couple of ranges require short stands or poles. The St. Louis range requires a bit shorter pole. The range is very flat, most poles are similar in height. The top of the flags will be about 24 to 30 inches high. The right side of Phoenix requires shorter poles. The overall height needs to be about 24 inches. The left side of Kelbly's range require extremely short flag poles, some as short as about 10 inches.

Several ranges need tall poles. Between 100 and 200 yards at Kelbly's, 15' poles are required. Fairchance, PA., requires tall poles when shooting 200 yards.

Some shooters use telescopic music stands. This type of flag stand is well suited for ranges which are flat without much slope. When used in areas of the country with high winds, you will need to hold them down with tent stakes, weights, or both.

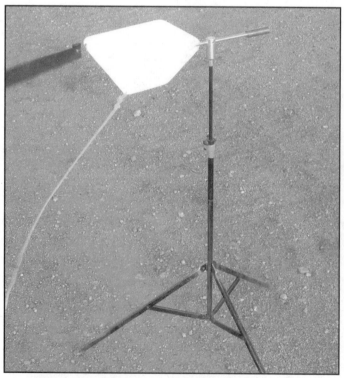

Figure 17. Music style flag stands, Adams flags.

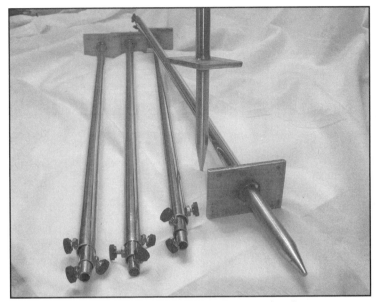

Figure 18.   Ratigan stainless steel poles.

Many shooters who travel seem to prefer stainless steel telescoping poles with a point on the end. The stainless poles can be purchased in many different heights.

I copied a stainless pole I saw at the first match I attended at Okie Shooters in Luther OK, and have used this type ever since.

Do I Have the Right Flag?

Having flags that work for you is very important. How to make this decision is easy. The right flag style and flag setup is one that allows you to instantly get information from the flags without having to study them for a few seconds, or having to look at each flag one at a time. It's called pattern recognition.

To determine whether you have the right flags, sit at your bench, look out onto the range toward your target, and have a friend put a hand in front of your eyes while you continue to keep your eyes pointed downrange. Have your friend give you one (1) second to look at your flags. If you can tell what is happening in front of you and whether it's time to shoot or not, you have the right flags. If you're unable to tell what's happening, it's time to get different flags. If you can tell when there's a letup, pickup or angle change in the given time you are on the right track.

Having to look at each flag one at a time is too slow. Just as having flags which are too complicated with such things as numbers, different colors to line up, and stripes. While looking at one flag the others will be changing. Peripheral vision is used to look at the whole range and get a feel of "same, more or less." Again, you should be able to INSTANTLY decide whether or not it is time to shoot.

Do I have the right flag?

Six hand signals
to flag setting success.

Learning six hand signals will enable anyone to set flags without yelling or radios. When using hand signals, batteries rarely die and your vocal cords never get sore. Many shooters have aspirations of getting a nice set of radios, GPS and compass to aid in setting flags. With very little training you can learn to set flags without any of this and faster. Before going down range, decide what line to set your flags in, and about where on the range yardage wise. Take the flags out, put them about at the correct yardages. Start the flag setting process with the back flag or the flag closest to the target and work towards the bench.

Plant   Tilt
the Pole   the Pole   That's Good

Whoever will be setting the flags on the range must be able to see 160 to 180 yards without a rifle scope or binoculars. You will also need to convince whoever will be setting the flags on the range, that they are NOT transparent. Many shooters turned flag setters do not realize they're not invisible. They need to stand to the side when setting the flags The person giving the directions won't be able to see through the flag setter. As the flag setter you must stand to one side or the other, preferably outside of the line you'll be using is preferable. This allows the person at the bench a clear view of the target when trying to decide where to put the flag.

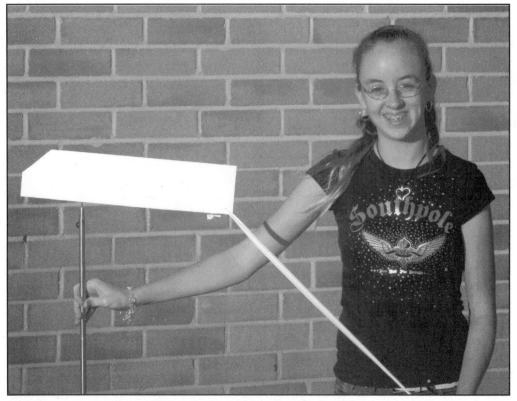

Figure 2. Lacey standing to the side.
If I can teach a teenager to do this, there's hope for everyone!

Again, start the flag setting process with the last flag, or flag closest to the target. By setting them in reverse order you'll set the flags closer to the shooter so they don't interfere with the farther flags. If you start with the close flag you must try to imagine where the farther flags will be, as to not cover up their potential place.

The person at the bench will give directions or "drive." I will refer to them as the "driver" for purposes of this chapter.

Start by raising the flag high enough so it can be seen by the driver. The flag setter should set the flag down on the ground and stand to the side. Then look to the bench and get directions. If you're driving, you must wait to give instructions until the person handling the flag looks towards the bench. Arm signals for right and left are simple, extend your whole arm in the direction the flag needs to be moved. Use your whole arm, not just your hand, or the movement of a finger. Arm movement will help the flag setter locate you on the line at longer ranges. Some ranges will have large numbers on the bench fronts. The sole purpose is so you can find your bench when setting flags. This can be seen in the photo of the Mooreland Public Range in figure 3. Even as big as they look I would make them bigger next time, and use a font or numbering style that more bold.

Figure 3. Numbers painted on bench fronts at the Mooreland Public Range

Figure 4. Dani, move the flag that way!   FIgure 5. "I'm still waiting, go that way".

It's pointless to give directions when the flag setter isn't looking. Also, if you're driving and giving directions and see no reaction from the flag setter, there's a good chance they cannot see you. There are several reasons they might not be able to see you on the firing line, the most prevalent is that you blend into the background behind the firing line. The second most popular is you're wearing dark clothes and in the bright sunshine you're in the shade of the firing line roof. The third is the person on the range is blind and can't see from one flag to the next. In any case, once you discover there's a problem, step out of the shade of the firing line roof. When the flag setter looks in your direction, give the signals again. If light conditions are making your arm signals hard to see, grab something to make your signals more pronounced. I use a flag vane and use whichever side has good contrast to the background. Butch demonstrates this in figure 6. You may use anything for a visual aid, like a brightly colored hat. The closer the flag setter gets to the firing line the easier it will be to see the directions.

Figure 6. Use any aid to help flag setter see your instructions

The flag setter once armed with which way to move, should move the flag some distance then STOP. Move the flag using a quick motion "up, over then down." This will be easy for the person doing the driving to see from the bench. Move some distance, then stop.

If you keep moving the flag sideways, you'll pass over the spot and by the time you see the driver tells you when to stop, it will be too late. This can be an endless cycle. There's no good way to signal STOP! Just move some, then stop. If the driver tells you to go back the other way, just go about half the distance you moved. When you get the flag to the correct spot, the driver will give you the touchdown sign for American football, both arms up. Set the flag or plant the pole in that spot.

Figure 7. That's good, plant the pole.

Once the right and left location has been found, lower the flag tap the end of the pole into the ground. You lower the flag because many poles will fall down when hammering on them. If you're using a Tripod, they will stay up while you hammer in the nails.

If the flag pole or stand is not perpendicular (straight up) with the world after the final location has been determined, correct it at this time. After the flag setter finishes putting the pole in the ground you might see the signal to straighten the pole at this time as shown in figure 8.

Chapter 20: 6 Hand Signals to Flag Setting Success

If you are just beginning your Benchrest career, start out right by setting your flags below the height requirement of the rule book. No flag is allowed higher than a line from the bench top to the bottom of the target card, and I would recommend no higher than the bottom of the target board. Many frames are white and if you have your flags too high, say over the board below the target it can be hard to tell if you're looking at the flag vane or the board. Hey, it's just a suggestion.

Figure 8. **Straighten the pole, tilt the pole that way.**

By lowering the flags after setting them in the correct place, the driver will need to give the up signal. The up hand signal is easy to see. The driver will need to have their head down at bench top level to set the flags below the legal height. The driver will make minor corrections so what the shooter in the shooting position will see what was ordered.

Instructions to lower the flag are hard for the flag setter to see. If you're raising the flag and see some unusual instruction lower the flag about half of the amount it was raised. Go up just like right and left. Move the flag quickly then stop, say 6 inches or 2 feet if you are way low. Make a quick adjustment so the driver will see it move. If you go too far or overshoot go back half way. Chuck Nelson demonstrates the signal to raise the flag in figure 9.

When the correct height is reached the driver will wave arms above head. Walla (Alabama technical term, learned from Col. Billy Stevens (Ret)) you're done setting one flag. Repeat, working toward the bench.

Watching the flag setting process at the Super Shoot is quite a spectator sport. Many have radios, and believe it or not, many shooters use the same frequency. One driver will tell a flag setter to move to the east 6 inches and almost instantly you hear "no not you" by six others. What ends up happening is just what I've tried to described above; lots of screaming and yelling. Learn these techniques and you'll thank me; you can set flags in complete silence. Butch Fjoser and I can set five sets of flags in the same amount of time the average shooter takes to do one or two sets.

Figure 9. "Go up Please"

Once you learn these simple hand signals, share them with your friends who like to walk back and forth many times while setting one row of flags. Help someone, two shooters can do two rows much faster than each can do there own. Butch and I set several flag sets at our local matches, along with moving frames, cleaning and reloading, scoring targets and overseeing the data entry. After all of this, we still must wait 15 to 20 minutes for several shooters to finish up setting flags.

Figure 10. That's good.

Also when setting two rows of flags at benches that are relatively close, say bench 5 and bench 10, the driver can do both rows at once. Move back and forth between the benches. This save the person out on the range from walking back out again to set another row of flags. Butch and I have done as many as four at one time. When I set three rows of flags for myself it takes just one trip out on the range.

Wind Flag Use

Wind flags are the most important equipment used to obtain extreme rifle accuracy in competitive benchrest today. Proper use of Wind Flags is what separates the hobbyist from the champion. If you don't believe a bullet is effected by the wind, I can save you some time. Skip this chapter.

Fact: *Bullets Drift in the Wind!*

The quicker you come to terms with this fact, the sooner the process of learning to read the flags can start. You'll be an interpreter, translating what the flags are trying to tell you into the proper hold on the target to make the bullets hit where you want. This allows your bullets to hit the same spot on the target during your few minutes of glory on the firing line.

Figure 1. Flags

The methodology and concepts to read flags at a competitive level are among the hardest things to teach and what separates the causal shooter from the champion. I will do my best to convey the concepts for successful use of your wind flags. HOLD ON! ... I hope you enjoy the ride.

I have a couple analogies to help express this principle. We all know a balloonist is completely dependent upon the wind current to carry them aloft, they are blown downwind and effected by up and down drafts. Similarly, a submerged submarine is effected by water currents. I want to leave you with one final image of a fish in a toilet bowl. That poor thing is going with the flow whether or not it wants to. I tried to warn you.

Figure 2.

Air has mass and is in motion and anything in it will be effected by it, even a supersonic plane and, yes, a bullet.

To learn to read flags you'll need a rifle which is accurate, very accurate. If the rifle is responsible for errant shots it can be hard to tell why the shot was out because of a flag reading or because of some problem with the rifle, components or shooter. When you become proficient reading flags you'll be able to evaluate your rifle's performance. You'll know the bullet should impact at a specific spot on the target. That's the goal.

Flag Setting

Where to put the flags between bench and target is important. Be flexible setting your flags; include local knowledge of the prevailing wind. Your flags should be placed up wind or on the side of the bench the wind will most likely be coming from. Using a flag reading which reflects what's already gone by is pointless. In other words if you are in the middle of the firing line with 60 benches and the wind is blowing from right to left, watching the flags to your left would not be your best choice. Watch the upwind flags.

If you're likely to have wind coming from left put your flags on the left. If the wind is likely to be coming from the right, put your flags on the right. A prevailing head or tail wind calls for flags directly in line from you to your target. If the range will normally have wind from any direction, two sets of flags might be called for, one set on the right and left. The point of this is to be flexible about where you put your flags. Avoid getting into the habit of having to have your flags in any specific spot or line, such as 20, 40, 60 and 80 yards. For example, if there's a hell of a gap in the trees protecting the range at 30 yards, you might be better served to setting a flag about thirty yards. There's no magic formula for where to set them.

How high you can set your flags isn't up to the shooter. The rule book explains how high your flags can be. They must be no higher than a line from the bench top to the bottom of the target card. My preference is -- no higher than the target board, so, no flag is visually over the board. I think it's too hard to see the flags when they are higher than the bottom of the board. It slows my flag reading straining to see them. Set your flags at or below the legal height, come match time you'll be familiar looking at them that way. When shooting on the left side at Kelbly's range in Ohio, come time for the Super Shoot you will have your flags as high as legally possible because of how low the targets are on the left side. The flags are limited to about 10 inches high on several benches on the left at Kelbly's.

Figure 3. The authors flags for practice, note flags upwind to see changes coming.

You can see from the photo in figure 3 above, the flags were set at about the bottom of the board just a bit higher than I like. I'd rather shoot than go back and lower them all. This photo was taken while the camera sat on the bench top.

It's a common question about how many flags to use. Different shooters use different numbers of flags out to 100 and 200 yards. Jerry Johnson (deceased) would use nine out to 100, most shooters use less. Jerry was one of the best 100 yard shooters we've had to date. Four flags when shooting 100 yards and six while shooting 200 yards is very common.

I like two and sometimes three sets of flags, one set to the right, one set to the left, one down the middle for ranges like Raton. If I'm on an end bench, I'll use one set out in the empty space to see a condition coming. I also like to have an extra set between frames, especially if there's lots of room between the frames and there's no readable flags on that side. You might be thinking, "you can't watch that many flags," but you would only be half right. I use my peripheral vision to look at the up wind flags. For example, when the wind is from the right, I look right, using my peripheral vision. My only interest in the other flags is to make sure that the wind isn't trying to backup or let up. Wind from the left look left and with a head or tail wind look straight ahead.

"When looking onto the range, look at the whole field using what is called pattern recognition in a global sense to get the big picture."

Dr. Jack E. Jackson

When setting your flags, make sure they are far enough away from the flags of other shooters so the tails won't get tangled in the others flags, or get caught on the poles. It's bad manners to set your flags directly in front of another shooters flags obscuring them. Set your flags so they won't interfere with another shooter. Yep, there's no rule against putting your flags wherever you want. There's also no rule in the shooting rule book to keep the others from burying non-cooperative shooters behind the firing line with one leg sticking out of the ground.

At the 2005 World Championships in Ohio, there were several heated discussions about setting the US flags at Kelbly's. We set our flags directly in line with the shooter to the target. I suggested we might have a crosswind which would require us to look at our neighbors' flags. When all was said and done, we didn't have any head or tail winds. I watched flags that belonged to our neighbors'. Our neighbors used the same flags with the same colors, we had the best setup you could have, flags left, right and straight.

If you can't see your flags, they are useless.... no matter how much care was taken in setting them in the correct spot. When sharing a bench at bigger match's, compromise must be reached. It's common to <u>request a bench rotation with flags you can read</u>. At the first Super Shoot, there will be thirty to forty people sharing your bench; and even if you come with four other shooters and you're on the same rotation you'll still face 25-30 other shooters who might not like your flags. This isn't the time to try to learn a new flag. Picking a popular flag will help if you have plans to travel to the major tournaments.

Look up wind!

When shooting in a cross wind don't sit at the bench staring out in front of you. Look up wind scanning the field for a condition coming that you could shoot in. If you see a condition which looks like it will last long enough to get off more than three shots get ready to shoot. When the condition moves in front of you and stabilizes, fire a sighter. If the shot prints about where you think it should, time to start your group on the record, if it's holding of course.

Basics

You must use your flags every time you shoot. Eventually you'll get used to looking at them. The more time you spend watching them, the better. Pretty soon you'll feel naked and not be able to shoot without them. It only takes one or two trips to the range without your flags to learn to get them out first. I've set up all of my stuff only to discover I left my flags at home. Had to put everything away and travel back to get the flags.

Popular flags used by the top shooters are very simple for a reason. You must be able to tell instantly what you are looking at in terms of same, more or less.

SAME, MORE or LESS

The process of looking at the flags MUST be kept as simple as possible. I've had many discussions around the proverbial campfire about wind reading without a single memory of anyone referring to the wind in mph. The reason is simple; we want to know how much the bullet will move on the target and don't care about any mph number. This eliminates the step of trying to calculate drift from mph. If the first shot hits where it should, reload, look at the flags and if everything's the same, then shoot again. Don't waste half a second trying to convert mph to drift. The more complicated your flags, the slower the shooting process, unless of course you're not watching or looking at the flags (not the key to long term success).

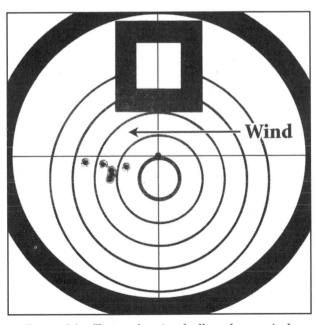

Figure 3A. Target showing bullets down wind.

I have assumed your impact point is down wind of your crosshair. Let's expand on my example above. If, after the first shot, the condition picks up (increases in intensity), we only care about how much farther the bullet will drift, and change our hold upwind or away from the first bullet hole. If the wind has slowed, hold closer to the first hole.

I would advise against having your impact point upwind of your crosshair. It's too confusing. You WILL get caught holding the wrong way.

Fundamentals;

1. Wind from right to left causes the bullet to drift left and up a bit.

2. Wind from left to right causes the bullet to drift right and down a bit.

3. Read up wind flags. Using a flag reading which reflects what is already gone, is absolutely POINTLESS.

4. Flags need to be set so you can see them while in the shooting position, with your head down behind scope. For most, using your off eye takes practice and if you can't see with your left eye (right handed) you'll need to do something different, which will slow the shooting process.

5. When shooting in a cross wind, watch only the tails on the upwind flags.

6. When shooting a head or tail wind, watch the vane (direction indicator) on the flags in a line from you to the target.

7. When shooting any 45 degree angle you must watch everything, vane and tail. To shoot this condition correctly you would use the vanes on the flags right in front of you and the tails upwind. Obviously, this is more complicated, harder to read, and why you rarely hear any great shooter say "boy, I sure love that angling stuff."

8. Learn to shoot fast, especially when shooting at longer distances. The longer you wait, the more conditions change, the more you will have to hold, the more you will get hurt under holding.

9. I left calm, or what looks like a calm for last. Most top competitors hate this; an absence of flag movement will often cause stupid shots that go places for no apparent reason. Calm, or what looks calm, can be one of the trickiest conditions to shoot because of slow moving mirage. Mirage causes apparent displacement of the target, or the target is not where you see it through your scope. The mirage effect can be so slow the target will appear to be stable when it's actually moving. Don't be fooled, when the flag tails are hanging, air is in motion, you just can't see it. The calm causes so many troubles, At home we warn visitors to our local matches, "DON'T SHOOT THE CALM." Of course many think it's some ploy to save any good conditions for ourselves. This myth dies a fast death if there's ever a calm, the temptation is too great. After a couple bad groups your quickly converted to a believer.

Figure 4. Dwight Scott practicing at the 2005 World Benchrest Championships in Ohio

The photo in figure 4 shows a stable 90 degree crosswind. In this situation you should be looking right. The flags in front of Dwight indicate what has already passed; the row or two on the right are stable. With this flag reading you ignore the angle and focus on the tails to the right. Notice about how long it will last and if it's stable. Watching Dwight, I was thinking "WHAT ARE YOU WAITING FOR? SHOOT! SHOOT! SHOOT!" You can see in the flag setup how consistent things look, except where wind probes cover the tails to the left of Dwight. The left side of this picture shows how sometimes more is just more, not necessarily better.

The row of flags left of Dwight have two sets of velocity indicators in the same row of flags. The probes break up the sight picture making things more confusing. When looking at that row of flags you must make a conscious effort to find the velocity indicators.

With about any change in wind direction or intensity, there will be vertical to compensate for. In a crosswind, when the bullet goes left, it should also go up a bit, right, it should go down. In head or tail wind which change from one direction to the other, you can have major vertical shifts. If you think there's no vertical component I suggest you don't shoot any head or tail winds. In the head or tail wind straight in or out, a couple of degrees in angle will cause MAJOR vertical impact shifts. Now there can also be extra vertical components to a crosswind in the form of up drafts and down drafts. If this happens, you'll not be the only shooter having problems. Time to go look at the wailing wall. Others will be having the same problems with the unexplained vertical.

Large Tournament Considerations

I talked to many shooters wanting to have a flag rotation for the Nationals. The common theme is to have only one set of flags per bench. It's a great idea, but when you host large tournaments, you must use all of the available benches. Other shooters will be sharing your bench rotation, unless it's full. If you want a rotation to yourself, you must have enough shooters to fill up all of the benches on your rotation. At the nationals in 2006, with three relays, you must have provided a list of 15 shooters (5 shooters per relay, remember we move 1/5 of the range to the right after every group).

When rotating benches, there's often shooters assigned to every bench for every relay. Three relays you'll share your bench with 15 shooters. Four relays gives you 20 shooters on your flag rotation. I've had many fun hours squadding relays, especially when more than one flag rotation owner puts the same shooter on their list for flag rotations. To make things worse, when the actual shooter sends in their entry form, many times they request something completely different. Makes for some great fun.

Many who request a flag rotation, have three or four other shooters who would cooperate and use one set of flags. I try to explain, I can't leave the unused benches unoccupied.

This problem only gets worse when the number of relays increases. When having seven (7) relays at the Super Shoot, you have 35 shooters that shoot on every bench. Every relay puts five more shooters on every bench. This reinforces the issue of picking a popular flag style. Maybe one day this won't be an issue; wishful thinking, I know. Hey, if you don't plan to travel, this is a non issue.

Advance Flag Reading Concepts

Holding in the same place, and waiting for a condition to repeat is relatively easy when conditions are steady. But when conditions are normal, holding every shot at the same place for every shot is harder to accomplish. I'll attempt to explain some things which are well know to the best shooters in the game.

Using the sighter target for a prediction of bullet impact puts you behind when the conditions are changing. The condition you test on the sighter often changes while you're going back to the record. Good predictive skills will help you recognize how much more or less you'll need to hold on the record target.

Major Misconception

There have been several articles on the subject of flag reading. The common theme is that the first flag is the most important. The idea is that if the bullet is pushed closer to the muzzle, the bullet will spend more time on this new trajectory. This is expressed in the following diagram.

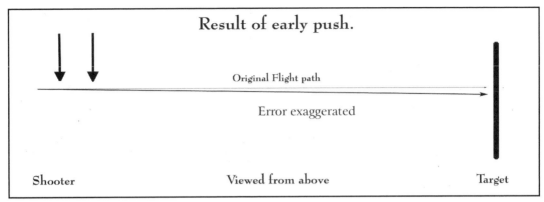

Figure 5.

Figure 5 shows a bullet's flight that's had a push from the wind close to the muzzle and then continues to the target without any further influence. If the wind force is constant during the bullets flight in the same direction, the bullet moves to the side in a logarithmic arc, not a straight line. In figure 6 I have tried to show the bullet flight when a constant force is applied from the side during it's entire flight to the target. My drawings of the deflection in these drawings are exaggerated for the purpose of this discussion.

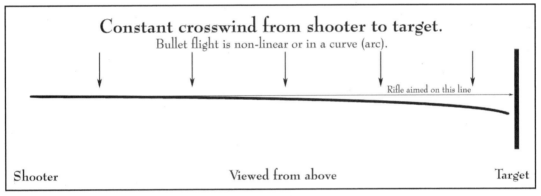

Figure 6
Even and stable left to right wind over the whole range, looking from above.

There's several important things about figure 6. The bullet slows down as it flies to the target in an exponential curve. The farther down range the longer it takes to fly each section. For this discussion, I will break up the range in three equal portions, 0-100 yards, 100-200 yards and 200-300 yards. The amount of drift is dependent on many things. Remember my comment about not trying to associate mph to bullet impact, because you can't. The same 10mph wind at 200 feet elevation and 7000ft will cause significantly different amounts of drift because of the the differences in the weight of the air in motion and the applied force.

There's many different ballistics programs on the market that help with the math. I had input a starting speed of about 3250 at 2200 foot altitude. The flight time between 0-100 yards is about 99 milliseconds (.099 sec.). From 100-200 yards it's

113ms or 15% longer, a significant change. The flight time from 200-300 is 130ms or again about 15% longer than from 200-300 but is 30% longer than the first section flight time of 99ms.

The following shows my data for a 10 mph crosswind.

Range (yrds)	Velocity (fps)	Time of Flight (ms)	Incremental Time	Drift(in) Absolute
0	3250	0	0	0
100	2835	98.64	98.64	1.2
200	2486	211.96	113.3(+14.8%)	4.8
300	2168	341.19	130.0(+14.7%)	11.3

What's all this mean? Well, without trying to write a doctoral thesis about bullet flight, in short it means you better watch your downrange flags. If you buy into the old adage that "The first flag is the most important", and ignore the rest, you'll have lots of company in the middle of the pack come match time. It's almost unanimous amongst the best shooters in the game, "The back 2/3' of the field is the most important. If you must ignore something, ignore the front."

The sooner you embrace this, the smaller you aggs will become, especially at the longer yardages. You might also surmise that watching one flag, any one flag, might not be enough data, especially in changing conditions. In my short example I have broken the range into 3 sections. Data about the wind should be sampled more often with flags. It's common to use 3-4 flags out to 100 yards and about 6 out to 200 yards.

If the wind were constant in direction and velocity over the whole range in front of the shooter, one flag would work nicely. I remember only one match where I have observed this rare phenomenon. When this happens, you don't need any flags, just aim at the same place for every shot and carefully squeeze the trigger. The last time I saw this was one afternoon during the Heavy Varmint 100 yards at the Nationals in 2003. I prefer bad conditions, takes care of some of the guy's with great guns that hold in the same spot for every shot. This game or sport is equipment dependent, but is more about the quality of the shooters than the equipment. This is why we take photos of the shooters and not the rifles when it's time to hand out the trophies. I'd rather take the whopping I deserve by a great shooting display than a hot shootin rifle.

Most of the best shooters in the game don't ignore the front flags but keep very close watch on the flags in the back. If I was forced to either remove my 25 yard flag or my 165-175 yard flag, it would be an easy choice. Get rid of that 25 yard flag. I can get some feedback about wind close to the bench by the feel of the wind on my body, face, arms and legs when wearing shorts. I've never taken a poll of successful shooters, but would make a substantial bet about making the choice of which flag to remove. The overwhelming choice would be to remove the first flag. This should just give you an idea of how I value the first flag.

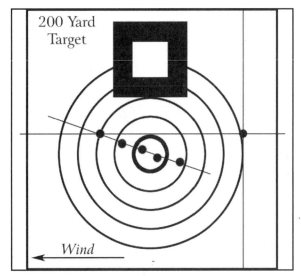

Figure 7. Target showing rifle in perfect tune.

Consistency leads to predictability. Use the same flag vane type and tail weight; soon you will be able to predict the bullet deflection based on the flag reading.

Learning an absolute flag reading is complicated by the fact that on any given day the atmospheric conditions change, which change the weight of the air and change the absolute amount of push on the bullet for any given flag reading. But that being said, experience reading flags is the single biggest factor to improving your performance and shrinking your aggregates. Ignoring flags will not provide consistent competitive success.

At the 8th World Benchrest Championships in Ohio, we had a very peculiar situation for wind flags. The US shooters provided Smiley style flags for any team wanting them. The United States team members set all but two sets of teams flags (that's a bunch of flags). The Aussies borrowed a set of flags similar to the style they use at home, the French team had a set of Smiley flags stored at the range. The French flags were the Smiley style but different vane colors and with almost no tail. The remainder of the flags were Smiley flags with the same tail material and color. This was a very impressive sight. It was so nice to look over the range and have almost all the flags the same. You could easily see a condition increasing, decreasing and any whirl wind; you could look across the range and tell how long you could expect a condition to stay.

My only regret from the World Championships is the lack of video of the range showing what this looked like. I would like to play the video back continuously at our Nationals and Super Shoot, where we have all out wars over flags. I've been on flag rotations that had five sets of flags on one bench rotation. Shooting on that bench rotation was like looking at a bad finger painting from a four year old child. You could tell nothing about what the wind was doing. Sometimes more is just more, not better. When there are too many flags, the vanes overlap making the angle information hard to see. Also the tails are all hidden in a forest of poles and vanes making them almost impossible to see.

In the following picture taken at the WBC8 it's easy to see what I have described. With the exception of the wind probes on the far left which are in the way, there are five rows of flags side by side and exactly the same. It was an impressive sight, these flags aren't even my favorite, but it was very nice indeed!

Figure 8. Flags at the World Championships 2005.

You must become comfortable shooting in different conditions with different flag readings. During your 7 minutes on the firing line and the subsequent time pressure, you will shoot in whatever wind conditions are present. You'll shoot in different conditions from one target to another; conditions are rarely the same throughout the day.

Tournaments which have similar conditions from match to match, where you can aim at the same place and impact the same point on the target are few and far between. The last time at a major, was the NBRSA Nationals in 2003 in Phoenix, during the heavy varmint. The conditions on Friday were such that teen aggregates filled the top 20 plus spots on the leader board. Saturday was not much different with 5 teen grand aggregates. Having just one teen grand aggregate is a pretty rare thing, outside of Visalia, CA., when you're west of the Mississippi.

After you gain experience and confidence reading your flags, you'll need and use the sighter target less and less and start to hold on the record without going down stairs to the sighter. I hold off, without returning to the sighter, and know exactly where the shots will hit, most of the time anyway. This is learned by repeating many times in practice.

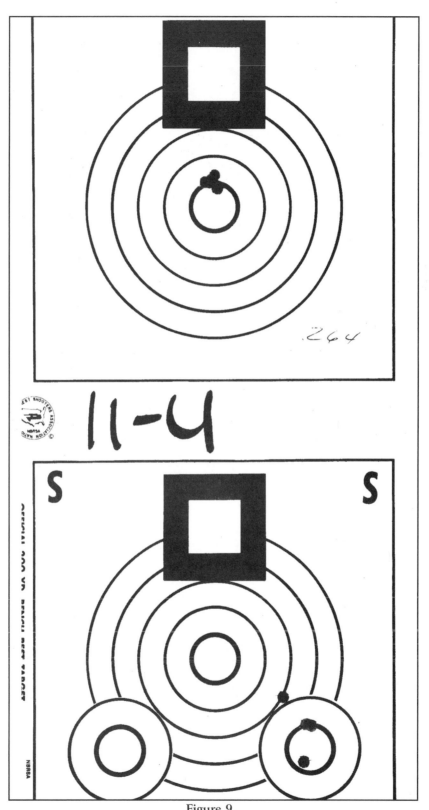

Figure 9.
200 yard target, no shots in the middle of the sighter.

Don't Hold for the vertical

If you shoot in a head wind or tail wind with the standard tune-up don't hold for any vertical you might get in your groups. If you fire the first shot and it impacts about right, the second shot hits a bullet hole low, don't hold up for the third. If you do, you'll stand a good chance the next shot will be out the top of your group.

It's normal to get a bit of vertical in your groups if you shoot in slightly different wind angles without compensating for the changes in vertical.

It's also possible to have vertical from the range even when shooting in a crosswind. Normally this is caused by some unseen condition. I say unseen because your flags cannot indicate range induced vertical in a crosswind. The up draft or down draft might show on a flag, the condition might be between your flags. If you are confident of your rifle's performance, the outcome will be the same as holding for the vertical in a head or tail wind. I'm not talking about the first shot problems but unexplained things you don't see. The unexplained vertical is akin to the section on "Its okay to hit the second hole." If you shoot a couple of shots that impact okay, then hit high. If you hold down for the next shot, you stand a good chance of shooting out the bottom of your group. If you don't change, you might hit the second hole. If you don't see the reason why the shot went astray, don't hold.

Suck Out ?

I wish to express you a warm welcome to my favorite range, Okie Shooters range at Luther, Oklahoma. Benchrest Hell is northeast of Oklahoma City, Oklahoma, and has the toughest average conditions on earth. Don't take my word for it, look at the aggs in the NBRSA news, and if that's not enough to convince you... come on down, but you've been warned.

Luther has a condition that there's no description for. I call it a "Suck Out". Our normal conditions are wind in every direction about 15 to 35 mph, almost ALL of the time. The "Suck Out" is simple; the flag tails are straight out in a hard blow, with no decrease in the intensity. The tail draws up like an accordion, then extends out in the other direction. The tail actually pulls the vane around, the tail never lets down during the reversal, there's no let up.

This is why we don't have very many daisy wheel flags at Luther; they end up with the tail wound up in the daisy wheel. Welcome to the condition known as the "Suck Out". It does similar things to your group if you shoot during the condition.

La-Di-Da Condition

Another condition common at Luther: flag tails sticking straight out, but the movement of the tails, or oscillation, is minimal. If you take the angle of the tail on it's face you would think that it's a nice 25 to 35 mph blow. But upon further inspection and looking at the tail movement you can see they are just hanging there. This is one of my favorite conditions to shoot, especially at 200 yards, flags in every direction and straight out, but it's hardly pushing at all. Oops, better stop, giving up too many secrets! Luther has humbled many a shooter big and small. If you plan a visit, keep FUN in mind.

At home I had been teasing a local Texas shooter about his flags which he places about 20 feet in front of the bench and another under the target, so as to be in the focal plane of his scope. I rarely missed an opportunity to comment about his choice. My friend decided to come and try Luther. After the fourth target at 100 yards, I had a chance to visit and asked how things were going. He said "OH ..., I DON'T HAVE THE RIGHT FLAGS FOR HERE!" I could not help myself and said, "You don't have the right flags for ANYWHERE!" We have had several talks about flags since then.

The shooters who frequent Luther love to talk about it. There's only one rule, tell the truth! Tell the truth, without embellishing. The true stories sound so unbeliev-able that the listener thinks you're exaggerating. I remember one friend, after a couple years of listening to the stories, had made plans to come and show us how to shoot this range. I had a front row seat. He was assigned the bench on my left. During the first match at 100 yards, my friend started with a nice .752 at 100 yards, Yep, that's right. Don't laugh, its easy at Luther. Needless to say he was upset when heading back to the loading area. For the second group, he laid down a .943 and to add insult to injury, the computer entry error was made. It was entered into the computer as a .543. You might be thinking that's great, but think about it for a minute. When's the last time they took off four tenths (.400) of an inch at 100 yards and it was still bad, getting the idea!

Luther is my favorite place to shoot. At Luther you MUST watch all of your flags all of the time. Come and join the fun. You'll have memories which will last a life-time, even with expensive psychotherapy.

Jack Snyder has been to visit. He's the maker of Edgewood Shooting Bags. While at Luther, his first time, he shot a group at 100 yards which was a modest .850. Jack tells the story very well. He said he held each shot about a bullet hole farther to the left and the shots kept going farther to the right and so on.

Lest We Forget!

Jack's five shot group looked like his rifle was perfectly tuned, the bullets were in a diagonal line. No two bullets were touching. Jack was so impressed he carefully cut out the target and glued it inside the lid of his loading box, after writing these words on it, "Lest we Forget!" to remind him to watch the flags. Memories fade, at least Jack's does. About a year and a half later he shot another group at Phoenix in a 40mph crosswind that was about an inch (1.000). Jack glued that target right beside his other with the inscription, "We Forgot."

Shoot Through Condition

Every once in a while you will come across what is referred to as "a Shoot through condition." This idea is simple. With relatively light flag movement, once in a while you will shoot several sighters and find no apparent effect from the different flag readings. I have seen this twice since I've been shooting. Once in July of 1995 at the NBRSA Nationals in Kansas City, the flag tails were not showing much for velocity but the vanes were turning all over the place, with no prevailing condition. The vanes were meandering, for lack of a better word. I fired nine sighter shots on my sighter with no change in the hold. All the shots were into about a .130, and my thought was "what am I waiting for!" I went to the top and shot 5 shots into a .092, which was not small group of that relay. I saw this condition again, several years later, while on the firing line at the Cactus in Phoenix during the month of April 2002 while shooting 200 yards. Early in the relay, while I was sitting at the bench with my arms crossed, watching the conditions, and thinking of the last time I had seen this condition, and that I should be shooting. The firing line was almost completely quiet except for one shooter three benches to my right. It was Skip Otto shooting his record breaking .099 and first ever zero at 200 yards. That's just what I was thinking would happen, why wasn't I shooting? I'm not saying I could have shot a small group, just that I was wondering why I wasn't shooting.

Watch Good Shooters, whose rifles are shooting!

Learn from the mistakes of others and by watching. You will see many top shooters gathered behind the firing line looking through spotting scopes. They are not there for the drama but to learn from the other shooters they are watching. You must watch from directly behind any shooter which you hope to learn from. You must be able to see the flags when they are shooting. To properly watch you will not look through the scope until after each shot, you operate the spotting scope like the rifle. Watch the flags, then look to see where the shot goes, and repeat. If you watch a shooter take a shot in changing conditions and hit the previous hole, you know they were holding (or they have a superhuman rifle). Likewise, if they fired and missed, you know they held the same hold and did not see the change. You can learn more by watching the top guns. You will also notice many things they have in common and about how they shoot the sighter in preparation to go to the record. You might also notice many good shooters prefer the same type conditions on any given day.

Make a watch list, which contains the competitor number of the shooters you wish too watch. You will not watch the shooters on your relay. However, you might look at targets of shooters who are on your relay after the targets are posted on the wailing wall, looking for stupid shots. Assemble the list by relay number, then competitor number, and then note who the shooter is. When you are trying to find a shooter on a relay with your spotting scope, you will scan for their competitor number on the target. I carry my hit list in my pocket, some shooters have theirs hanging from their spotting scopes. Having the list in my pocket allows the use of anyone's scope, and it's handy while at the wailing wall.

Goals

Everyone who buys or borrows a rifle has some goal in mind. Whether shooting a cape buffalo, going on the prairie dog hunt of a lifetime or shooting some groups on paper, there is some underlying goal; the biggest, longest shot, most or smallest. Most rifle owners aspire to improve the accuracy of their prized shooting iron. Benchrest is the be-all and end-all of rifle accuracy. Benchrest leads the way in the shooting sports to lay claim to being the ultimate in accuracy, which is the goal. Many newcomers arrive on the scene at their first benchrest tournament with completely unreasonable goals.

Figure 1. Some accomplishments in 2002.

To get started, you need to decide how committed you are to the sport. Whether you're joining in just for fun, or have decided this will be a lifetime dedication to achievement and excellence. Set your goals to help achieve your level of commitment. After deciding on your commitment, you must determine what needs to be learned. Identify the needed skill set to reach the level which you've decided upon earlier. Many successful shooters have some natural talent which contributes to their level of achievement. You must also consider other factors in your life to aid in setting reasonable goals in your extra curricular activities. Other factors in your life which need consideration are your family, career, education, personal businesses and the time requirements, just to name a few.

Set Performance Goals, not Outcome Based.

Base your goals on performance instead of winning or finishing place. If you set your goals to win, you will often fail to reach them because of factors beyond your control such as the performance of others, weather, and other personal things in your life. Performance based goals can be achieved without influence from other shooters. You can shoot well and better any previous performance, yet finish poorly. This example happens with great regularity. Shooters will have their personal best ever performance, which is not good enough to finish in the money or trophies. This example is one of success, but is often seen as negative. I often overhear shooters comments like, "What do I have to do to win?" You should be thinking about how good your performance actually was. Conversely, it is also possible to shoot poorly and come out on top. When this happens and the specific performance goals are not reached, this should be considered as a failure, even with a good finishing place.

Many shooters are put off by winners telling stories of falling short of performance expectations and or making mistakes along the way which could have been avoided. This is common among successful shooters and athletes who regularly look at their relative performance in respect to making mistakes along the way. These comments are often perceived as being arrogant, however, it's important when evaluating the performance. The top guns in Benchrest focus on reducing mistakes in strategy, gun handling, and wind flag reading to name just a few. Shooters at the peak of their ability will not be satisfied with winning a tournament while making avoidable mistakes along the way.

Another problem setting finishing place goals are the prizes themselves. Whether monetary or recognition based, these outcomes are highly motivating in the beginning. Most shooters remember winning their first trophy. After you reach the higher levels of accomplishment, the winning of another award at the same level is not as important and becomes progressively less motivating. Spectators often simply base their opinion of the capability of the shooter on the frequency of winning. Shooters able to ride out the storms of good and bad and perform at an elevated level over a long period of time are what make the real top gun, not one bunch of great bullets or one good barrel combination.

Figure 2.
One of my most prized trophy's. A hand made trophy from Red Cornelison's estate.

I remember a 200-300 yard match at Raton in 05 where I finished a close 2nd in the 2-Gun to Pat Byrne. My performance was great for me, just so happened Pat had broken one of the 300 yard records by a MILE, I couldn't have shot any better than I did. I consider this tournament a success when looking at what happened and not where I finished. These are the some of the things which should be considered when evaluating your performance.

Specific Goals

Set specific measurable goals when starting your pursuit of the elusive .000 group. Fun should be one of these goals and should be attainable every time you attend a tournament. After you are able to reach all of the conditions set forth in your goals in a consistent manner, you're ready to set new, more difficult goals. If you consistently fall short, reassess your goals for reasonability. Adjust your goals after trying to figure out why you have failed to reach them. You might be able to take specific action to improve your skill level. Ask an accomplished shooter in your area to help improve your methods or techniques. They can help with equipment evaluation when needed. Spending the weekend with a good shooter will increase your knowledge base faster than anything else you can do.

Long term success will be reinforced by physical training. Physical training helps prepare your mind and will help you compete longer and at a higher level.

Be Reasonable

Setting goals which are attainable, but not too easy, is important. Setting goals too high will result in no serious effort towards achieving of the unrealistic goal, or worse, getting frustrated by them, which often causes the shooter to quit the sport.

Goals should be reasonable. Expecting benchrest performance out of a Savage 110 is an unreasonable expectation of your equipment. The end result will be disappointing no matter how capable the shooter.

On Benchrest.com, there is a never ending stream of folks who tell tales of factory rifles which shoot less than ¼ inch every time they shoot them. Also none (or few) of the shooters ever seem to have any use for wind flags. Almost instantly the few competitors who read and post on the forum will call their bluff. What frequently seems to happen is that some feelings are hurt. I'm not mentioning these follies to embarrass anyone. I just feel the need to mention that the Super Shoot, an annual event held at Kelbly's Rifle Range in Ohio the week before Memorial day, gives away money. These shooters should consider coming, they would walk away with LOT's of money. By the end of the Super Shoot week very few of the more than 350 benchrest competitors will have bettered the magic mark of less than .250 (1/4 inch) in the two gun.

One thing the new shooter should realize when stepping up to the firing line at their first ever registered tournament is that they will be participating in the most difficult shooting sport on the planet. Many spectators and newcomers to Benchrest with little or no exposure to this demanding sport often enter it with aspirations of becoming the next Tony Boyer during their first match. This will lead to certain disappointment. In Benchrest, there's no separation between shooters of different skill levels, as so many sports have. The first timers' performance will be judged along side some of the best shooters in the game, no matter where you go to attend your first registered match. This very thing attracts many who like being thrown right into the mix with the best in the sport.

In many sports, there is segregation between the ranks of the pros and the amateurs. For instance, the weekend basketball player won't be sharing a locker room with Michael Jordan. Just as the segregation in the professional sports, benchrest has some very accomplished and dedicated shooters who would be in the professional ranks if there were such a thing.

Your First Match

Stepping up to the line with some of the best in the business should help the new shooter set easy goals for their first match. If I may suggest some early goals:

1. Be safe and have fun.
2. Talk to the shooters in attendance, most of these folks are very friendly.
3. Develop an equipment list after talking to the experienced competitors.

As I have already covered, expectations of new shooters are often far from practical and why many do not return. I do my best to explain how difficult this sport is when you step up to the firing line the first time. Every active competitor will encourage and help almost anyone to the line for the first time. I think it's mainly because misery loves company.

My First Match

After spending a couple years with my new benchrest equipment, I finally made my way to the Okie Shooters range at Luther, Oklahoma. I clearly remember my first match. I was armed with directions from Jack Dever, instructed to find and talk to Rex Reneau (I had to write his name down on my hand). I arrived at the range the night before to find three shooters testing their equipment. I was welcomed and introduced myself. I said I was looking for "Rex..." He quickly said, "That would be me," before I could finish butchering his last name. I learned many things by watching, subtleties you can't read about. Rex ushered me to the firing line to meet the other two shooters, Dennis Wagner and Larry Scharnhorst, also known as Scharny. I am still in therapy from meeting Scharny. They inquired about my interest in the sport, how I found out about the range, and many things I can't remember. I was shown some of the groups at 200 yards just before dark, they were pretty good. Rex asked if I would be shooting the next day. I conveyed my intention to watch. All three encouraged me to shoot. They had enough equipment between the three of them to accommodate at least two shooters. I had my stuff but explained my intention to only watch my first match, sure glad I did.

My first goal was to make sure I had the equipment needed to participate, look at some of the different flags, poles, and tail styles. In college I learned to "NOT reinvent the wheel," which was why I came. I learned many more things than I could remember. It took approximately 27 seconds to realize it was necessary to have two cleaning rods as one is way too slow. Time is better spent visiting rather than standing over one's cleaning stuff changing from the jag to brush and back again.

Everyone was very nice and encouraging. There was one character, JT Powell from Meade, Kansas, who consequently drives right by my home traveling to and from the range. Rex introduced me to JT, and we became instant friends. We would ride together many times back and forth to the range at Okie Shooters.

I learned several things about flags while watching my first tournament. One vivid memory which lives today was of watching Don Creach's tails stick straight up in the air. My tails were way too HEAVY and too short. I had been using three pieces of ribbon stapled together, which were trimmed to all the same length. I realized the longer tail is nice, if not touching the ground. I copied a stainless steel flag pole design from Larry Scharnhorst. I still use this same design today. Rex's flags (Sherwin Williams paint sticks) drove home the idea that simple will work. Rex is a United States Benchrest Hall of Fame member, and if simple worked for him, it would work for me. I also still use the same basic flag vane design today. Traveling to this local match was one of the best experiences of my life, MORE would be needed. I thanked everyone for the learning experience and I quote Rex when he said, "we haven't done you any favors." I now understand what he was trying to say. Benchrest shooters are a bunch of proverbial drug dealers, pushing the elusive hope of a small group or agg, which is still legal, for now.

This is still great advice: Visit a good competitor in your area. You'll receive advice from equipment to shooting styles to strategy. You will save a fortune with the advice. Many new shooters attempt to save a little money by equipment purchases which only delay the inevitable, then spend more hard earned cash by purchasing stuff they will never use in a tournament. This is repeated in about every aspect of our life. In benchrest there's almost no room for any compromise. A rifle which will not perform will not only disappoint the shooter come match time, you'll never learn to read your flags with a sub-standard rifle.

First Year Goals, Suggested

1. Read as much as you can about the sport of benchrest.
2. Have fun, most new shooters love the feeling and the thrill of the one hole group.
3. Meet and get to know some of the experienced shooters in your area.
4. Attempt to stabilize your performance. New shooters should have few problems agging in the middle 3's, by eliminating wild swings in your grand aggregate ability. This makes your equipment evaluation easier. This usually will indicate your rifle handling ability is moving from sporadic to predictable and repeatable. By getting help from a nearby competitor, you can shorten your learning curve on equipment and methods, help identify flinching etc…
5. Learn the methods and techniques required to be successful.
6. Try to shoot a couple of small groups in registered matches.
7. Learn how to eliminate common mistakes.
8. Have fun.

Many new shooters set goals to beat up on one of the good experienced shooters from their area. This is an unreasonable goal, to better the performance of some of the best shooters in our game, at least on a consistent basis. Many of the top guns attending small matches treat them as a social event and are not trying to set the world a blaze. If they shoot good or bad they don't care. Many test bullets, barrels, powder, scopes, rifles, and many things during the heat of competition at the smaller matches. If a new rifle won't cut it at local match, you'll not see that combo at the Super Shoot. Any shooter can be beat at any time, but if you keep in mind the consistent meeting or exceeding of the goal, it's more of a stretch and unreasonable. It's not unusual to better the performance of the top guns in benchrest at the small tournaments with nothing at stake. But during state, regional, national, and world team qualifying tournaments, it's usually a different story.

There's somewhat of a consensus among experienced shooters. Most believe it takes about five years to make a benchrest competitor. I can't argue with this too much. Once in a blue moon a shooter will blow the curve, but not often. There are many things that contribute to the continued success on the firing line, some of which just take a little time to learn.

Fifth Year Goals, Suggested:

1. Have fun.
2. Better your performance by reducing mistakes along the way, by refining and improving strategy.
3. Bettering your agging capability into the .2xx's consistently in poor weather. I mean multi guns here. Shooters who live in the east and shoot ranges with lighter conditions should have performance expectations or agging capability smaller. Shooters who live out west and in areas with tougher conditions your average aggregates goals will be larger.
4. Consistently finish in the top half of the field, especially in bad weather. Remember weather is our friend.
5. Should be able to solve any equipment problems by this time.
6. Finish in the top five in the multi gun at a local tournament or two.
7. Be encouraging to new shooters thinking about our sport and help when you can.
8. Western shooters; try to shoot a teen yardage aggregate or small two for a yardage. Eastern shooters might be a grand agg in low twos or even a teen.
9. Win a top 20 patch at the Nationals and Super Shoot.

Unreasonable Goal Setting

After you have some experience you should consider setting a goal or two which is a bit more unreasonable or over the top. Don't go crazy, or you won't put any effort into the goal if you believe there's no way of reaching it. Winning a yardage at a major tournament would be a good choice. Reaching 200 hall of fame points would be unreasonable for anyone and would border on insanity.

My Personal Past Goals

My main goal for 2004 was to qualify for the United States World Benchrest Team, make the first team and qualify #1 if possible. Goal accomplished!

My Future Goals

Have fun.
Help others in our sport, whenever possible.
Help at our smaller tournaments however I can.
Get to know experienced shooters, personally, not just by name.
Improve the function, performance and operation of my equipment.
Find more superman bullets (hard to do).
Find a 45 power scope that will not move.
Be a good sportsman, in defeat and victory.
Be one of the best benchrest shooters on the planet, long term.
Improve my strategy.
Make no strategy or handling mistakes.
Shoot as good as I can, instead of just good enough to win.
Continually work on my bench techniques.
Obtain a Rail gun which shoots competitively.
Qualify for future US World Benchrest Teams.
Qualify for the United States Benchrest Hall of Fame.
Write a book on rifle accuracy, including strategy.
Have fun.

Figure 3. Rail Gun.

United States World Team Goals

Goal setting is a part of building the US team for the World Benchrest Championships. The US Team Director plans the qualifying tournaments with one goal in mind.

To field the best twelve shooters from the United States who will act as a team and who want to represent the United States at the World Benchrest Championships.

To meet this goal, the qualifying process is scrutinized to pick the best shooters available who will be able to perform when traveling to another country. This requires a certain amount of adaptability when shooting at a range where none of our shooters have been before. We use powder we're not comfortable with and many other things. After the team is selected, then the goal setting is refocused on building the team to act as one unit with a common goal of performing at such a high level to win every team medal.

Figure 4. Vest, Hat and some Gold Medals from World Benchrest Championships 1999 in Italy.

Right Thinking

Sports Psychology applied to Benchrest

Success = Desire, coupled with some natural talent+ Determination +
Commitment + Knowledge + Good Equipment + Practice

Sports psychology is an important part of many sports, benchrest is no exception. The power of the positive attitude has a place in Benchrest. Every shooter has thoughts about their coming performance called self talk. Some examples are "I hope I shoot a good group" or "please God let me shoot a nice group." A little training about the powers of positive thinking can improve your aggs and your overall performance and your experience.

"Self Talk" is a reflection of how we think. This is what you say when you talk to yourself. It is the words you say out loud or think silently in your head, everybody does this. These thoughts help set you up for success or failure.

It's a well documented fact that 75% of self-talk is negative which causes you to worry and lack confidence. I would like to give you the tools and insight to overcome the obstacles on your way to success. In our sport, the self talk will often be things like, "if I just don't screw this up," "why does relay x get all the good stuff," "nobody ever wins from the last relay," I wish _____ would shoot a bad group and give us a chance", "oh, no, look who's here, we're just shooting for second place" and so on. Positive self talk might include things like, "I can't wait to get back to the line to shoot another group," or "I have been shooting superhuman today." These are just a few of the things we think or say to ourselves. The top guns of our sport say things like, "the harder the conditions the better," "lets go shoot a group," and "I can't wait to try that condition again." The process of learning to keep your thoughts positive lasts a lifetime. As we age, there's new challenges which will need to be addressed. But, as we gain experience, our powers of positive thinking will become more natural and will help us to overcome these new challenges.

During Friday morning practice for the 2004 Cactus in Phoenix, we had a hard early morning rain. I was on the line by myself and eager to get started in the rain, which continued for about 30 minutes. Then came Walt Berger and Tony Boyer, two hall of fame members; they too were ready to shoot in the rain with a positive attitude. We shoot in the rain during competition, and often a good group can be had during rain. I like the unique challenges of rain and they're best addressed before you NEED to. I asked Tony and Walt where they had been. Many shooters who were at the range to practice were hiding under cover like they were made of sugar or salt. To quote a friend of mine "enjoy yourself, you _are_ waterproof."

What follows are some examples of positive self talk. These simple thoughts help us to achieve consistent good performance over the long term. Every successful athlete will tell stories about their career ups and downs. It's unreasonable to assume you'll have nothing but success. The times of our biggest struggles give us our character and our ability to know we can weather any poor performance.

1.   Give yourself a chance.
2.   I can handle it.
3.   Never Quit.
4.   Keep positive attitude even when struggling.
5.   Agg them to death, be around for the long run.
6.   Everything will be OK.

Example "Give Yourself a Chance"
While watching Aaron Segura (Ed Adams step son), Ed and I were amazed that Aaron shot on the record target after a three minute pause without going to the sighter. He should have gone down and fired at least one or two shots on the sighter. This would have given him some idea about where the condition would impact on the target. Ed explained "Give yourself a chance to hit the group," go down and check on the sighter when you don't know what to do.

Example "I Can Handle It"
At the 2005 long range Nationals the conditions began to pickup dramatically on the last target at 300 yards. There was a strong crosswind from the left. I was on the left side of a frame. I thought early on when the relay was started that I knew how to shoot this condition. If I could shoot any kind of group that looked like a group I would be in good shape. I lined up my crosshair with the left hand edge of the target frame (not the paper target, the wood board) and expected to hit about one ring to the right of the center of the sighter target. I fired and hit within about ¼ inch where I thought it should (about 24 inches from my aiming point). The condition looked like it would hold. I went immediately to the record and let-em-rip. I had a group about .700 at 300 yards, plenty good enough. Many shooters completely missed the target to the right.

Example of "Never Quit"

At the Mid-Continent Light Varmint Regional at Luther in April of 2004, I started the match with the largest group I have ever shot at 100 yards, a nice .668, which is proudly displayed over my fireplace. I had four shots on the record target into a group which measured about .240 inside the mothball. I reloaded and shot again after checking the flags, gun handling was perfect, the last shot hit about ½ inch high and left.

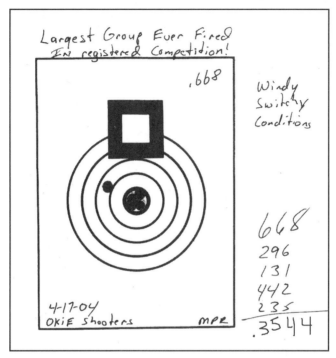

Figure 1. Largest group ever fired in competition from Luther

I knew I had fired at the correct time and handled the gun properly. My first thoughts were of an equipment failure, but after working on the sighter I proved the gun and loads were ok. While cleaning my rifle my thoughts turned to that of having a bad bullet or some condition on the range I could not see and/or was unexplainable. This was my "Welcome to Luther Oklahoma."

While walking back to the loading area, not particularly pleased with my unexplainable group, I mumbled sarcastically, "I'm going to quit!" Rex Reneau, our match director, overheard me and commented "You can't quit." I responded "I know, you're right, but I want to." I didn't dwell on my unexplained bad luck. I refocused on reloading and returning to the firing line. I forgot all about the previous group and continued on with the task at hand. My next four groups were good enough to climb back up to 7th in the yardage, not very far out of first. I managed to shoot a pretty good aggregate at 200 yards, winning the yardage and subsequently finished 1st in the grand aggregate. This was the first tournament of the Mid-Continent 3 Gun which is contested at three ranges in the Mid-Continent Region of the NBRSA.

Example of Keeping a Positive Attitude
Charles Huckeba shot a group over an inch at 100 yards during the first yardage of the 6th World Benchrest Championships in Nelson, New Zealand. After traveling half way around the world, Charles continued on instead of throwing in the towel. At the end of the Championships Charles helped his 4 man team capture the Team Gold Medal in the 6th World Benchrest Championships. Charles continued as only a champion knows how, and finished second in the individual 2-Gun.

Example of Agg'em to Death
This simply means, don't pass up the ability to shoot a group that's ok. Many shooters try and shoot too small, only to have one shot which ruins their group. That one shot hurt the group worse than just making an educated guess on where to hold, holding there and shooting. By applying this, you can shoot many groups which are ok. Yes they might have been really small, but who cares, shoot for the grand agg, or two gun, three gun, etc..

Example of "Everything will be OK."
Dwelling on an early performance which was not what you had hoped can negatively affect your future performance. Once you've completed a group or agg, it's over. Learn what you can and focus on the next event. Ed Adams was very unhappy with his performance at the start of the qualifying for the eighth World Benchrest Championships at the Cactus in Phoenix, Arizona in 2004. Ed was concerned about his start at the Cactus, he was afraid of not being able to qualify for the world team. Ed is a friend of mine and I immediately went to work on his psyche. Ed's a very good shooter but needed just a bit of encouragement. I insisted that he would be ok. His ability is steady, which is what was required on the long road to qualify. The second qualifier was the 2004 Super Shoot. Ed did not shoot this match as well as he had hoped. I insisted he would be ok and should keep a positive attitude. Ed was afraid of not being able to qualify for any team. He shot well in the last qualifying tournament. I calculated the points while on my way home. After I was sure I had not made any major mistakes, I informed Ed that he had qualified in the number 5 spot (of 12). You should have seen the look on his face when we meet at a rest stop on the way home, mission accomplished.

Visualization, Imagery and Match Simulation

Visualization and Imagery
The goal of visualization, imagery and simulation is to make you more familiar with the skills you'll need in a low stress environment. You will be more confident of the effectiveness of your skills when the time comes to put them to the test.

Imagery can be used in benchrest to rehearse and perfect strategies that will be used during match time. Use imagery when you're unable to get to the range and practice because of time constraints, bad weather (cold), injury, etc. You can visualize yourself at the Super Shoot while 100 or more shooters and spectators are watching through spotting scopes; these techniques can help reduce your anxiety levels.

Match Simulation

Practice with everything as in match conditions. Use your flags. Practice under the pressure of your clock. Shoot a 5 or 10 group aggregate and measure the targets. Often a good looking target through your scope will measure much larger. This will give honest feedback of your performance of the day.

In many ways match simulation is better than using visualization and/or imagery. You'll have real feelings of anxiety and stress because it's real. However match simulation requires greater resources of time and effort. The range of possible eventualities which can be practiced is less. You'll not be able to apply all of the different strategy and shooting techniques in practice because of environmental limitations. However, over the long term you will be able to practice in many different conditions and will be able to apply the proper techniques and strategy. For example, it's hard to practice shooting in a head wind when you have a cross wind. It's hard to practice in the rain while the sun is shining. Imagery techniques can be used in conjunction with match simulation to improve your mental preparedness. In my rain example, "I look forward to my next opportunity to shoot in the rain during a match!"

Practicing in the worst conditions possible will give you many physical and psychological advantages:

1. Confidence you can handle any condition, including driving rain.
2. Confidence in your application of proper techniques when needed.
3. Confidence in your ability to handle the stress and distractions of poor weather or spectators.

Focus

Our attention should be completely focused on our shooting and the task at hand; proper finishing of a group to the exclusion of everything or almost everything else. This includes spectators and your shooting neighbors. While on the firing line your attention should be focused on the mental input from the range, flags, and any other relevant information needed. You shouldn't be thinking about, or concerned with, any distractions. Keep your eye on the ball (stay in the moment). You can think of doing your taxes when you get home and reorganize your loading area after you are finished shooting. Any thoughts outside of the scope of the task at hand can be distracting and destructive to your concentration and performance on the firing line.

Benchrest shooting requires your attention to be focused on what needs to be done and when. This is unlike many sports where success requires a physical skill to be learned to become successful. Our attention and focus will be on our flag reading skills, applied strategy, equipment, load development, and gun handling. By understanding what to look for, you'll be able to separate the important from the unimportant stimulation in the competitive environment. For example, look at the upwind flags and tune out the downwind stuff.

<u>Exercise to improve focus ability:</u>   Study an object intentl. Get completely involved with it, study the shape, finish, color, texture, smell, cleanliness, function, etc., then switch your attention or focus to another object with the same intensity, focusing only on it. This is a small exercise from any first year psychology course.

Improving skill levels can cause a loss of focus as you get better, your physical actions or how you operate your rifle becomes second nature. As your shooting improves and you shoot better, you're not as challenged by the other competitors. As you learned in the chapter on goals, when setting outcome based goals such as winning and when the winning becomes easier, focus problems often follow. This is one reason many of the better shooters don't attend the smaller tournaments- the lack of challenge. Performance based goals which aren't dependent on the level of the competition will help you maintain your motivation and concentration on the goal. If winning becomes easy, you will become bored and disinterested and often unchallenged.

Figure 2. Jack Neary focusing on the flags and shooters target during a relay.

Example of refocusing

On a Saturday afternoon at Raton following two 100 yard aggregates, I was visiting with Ed Adams. I conveyed disgust with my performance during the day's shooting in which I made 4 strategy mistakes. Ed and I were leading after the 100 yard aggregates, but neither Ed nor I were happy with our performance. We talked about our performance and focused on the mistakes that were made that day. We both realized that our performance was inadequate and should be improved the following day. When considering the mistakes that were made which could have been avoided, this day's shooting would be considered a failure even with the good finishing places. This is a good example of poor shooting with good finishing places, and should clarify why outcome based goals are not near as important as performance evaluation.

I mentioned to Ed, "If we can't shoot any better than this, nobody wins." Ed reminded me to keep that type of thinking to myself; many of the other shooters would interpret that as being arrogant, although it was true. This is the type of thinking which is required to compete at a National and World level and is popular amongst the Top Pros of any sport. An honest evaluation of daily performance goes to the heart of knowing what you are and aren't capable of doing on the firing line.

State of Mind or Your Mood

Your state of mind or mood is completely under your control. Being in a bad mood hurts your motivation and tends to make you susceptible to negative thinking. Through the power of positive thinking you can alter your mood. Another simple exercise; SMILE, by making yourself smile for only a few seconds you'll feel better and more positive, TRY it – smiling works!

Figure 3. Wayne Campbell and Jack Neary, proving a serious match can be fun. Actually, this is what you look like when you've had too much fun.

Positive Attitude

Attitude is very important when shooting during match conditions. Complaining about starting the relay late, bad conditions, a previous bad group etc. is something that only helps your fellow competitor.

Happens like this, it starts raining just before your relay. Many negative comments will be heard around the firing line, and many of those shooters have already decided that they are going to shoot a bad group because of the rain. They have already failed without firing a shot. Those few who are focused on what's going on and what they're doing will find a way to shoot a good group. Give yourself a chance and you too can shoot a good group. Often what is perceived to be adverse can yield some incredibly good groups. When conditions are bad it's the time to put some distance between you and the rest of the field.

Immediately following registration at the 2004 Super Shoot, I overheard a well know shooter thinking out loud. He expressed concern about being on the last relay saying, "Nobody ever wins from the seventh relay." I was also on the last relay and I exclaimed, "how can you say that, you're already thinking of an excuse for shooting bad and we've not even fired the first shot and don't start for another two days. Not only do I want to be on the seventh relay…. I want to be the only one on the seventh relay!" He asked why I wanted to be the only shooter on the seventh relay. I explained, if I were the only shooter on the seventh relay there would be no question who everyone was watching through the spotting scopes, and, they could watch while I was whopping up on them. Six days later I won the 32nd Super Shoot. Besting one of the largest ever number of competitors.

Winning the Super Shoot never entered my mind that week. I also never thought being on any particular relay would stop me from winning. Just go to the firing line and do your best and forget about anything which might negatively affect your performance. You must try and focus on where you are and what you are doing, i.e. stay in the moment.

Figure 4. It's a rare thing, The Super Shoot Trophy

Jim Borden relayed a story to me about a group he shot during a heavy rain with high wind during relay 1 match number 5 at 200 yards during Light Varmint at the 2005 Super Shoot. Jim told me about what he was thinking when he sat down to shoot, "I can handle this, just aim about there." Jim's first shot on the sighter was about where he thought it should be. He waited for the strong wind to stabilize and fired the first shot on the record, about right, then let'er rip. He shot a good group when many shot off to the left of the target. 'Jim's neighbor asked, "How did you do that?" Jim replied, "I sat down and said to myself, 'I know how to shoot this,' then held on the right border and ran with it."

Jim Borden

Distractions

There are many things that can disrupt our focus, they are known as distractions. If you're distracted while shooting, it will be harder for you to think about applying proper strategy, good gun handling techniques, and looking at the flags.

Common Distractions:

> Choice words for your neighbors
> Video taping and cameras
> Spectators
> Spotting Scopes
> Other shooting around you
> Family or relationship problems
> Other competitor's good performance (anxiety)
> Past mistakes
> Unjust criticism or comments from others you did not deserve
> Bad Refereeing decisions

Many of these things are only minor irritations. Accept them and move on. During the course of our tournaments, some of which are quite long, wasting energy worrying about these minor things can negatively affect your performance. If you make a mistake after being distracted, remember you haven't lost your skills. You've just temporarily lost your focus. The larger tournaments will have more distractions: spotting scopes, vendors, and new benchrest toys or "dodads", just to name a few.

Many shooters are bothered by others standing behind them looking through a spotting scope. I tell the new shooters not to worry. At the major shoots no one will be watching them shoot. This helps settle their mind about all of those people watching. This is a true statement. Most shooters are watching someone specific and if you don't know who they are, they're not watching you. When the top shooters go to the firing line at the major tournaments most of the people watching through the spotting scopes will be watching them. You must be focused on what you're about to do and not worry about someone watching. In fact, if another good shooter is watching, you can get good feedback about your rifle tune, the conditions you shot in, and any strategy mistakes you might have made. Many shooters are fearful of shooting a bad group while people watch. Just the opposite should be true. If you have a bad group you can get valuable feedback. Hopefully you will learn something about any strategy mistakes you have made or maybe feedback about a rifle being out of tune. Both are valuable and should be considered positive.

Self-confidence and Over-confidence

As in any sport, self-confidence can be either helpful or destructive. Effective goal setting can build self-confidence. Honest evaluation of your capabilities will help eliminate over-confidence. As discussed in the chapter on goals, you must decide on your level of commitment to the sport. Effective goal setting is setting measurable goals and achieving them, setting new measurable goals and achieving them, and so on. You'll have a reasonably accurate assessment of your ability, which has not been inflated by your ego, pride in yourself, or your ability. By consistently meeting or exceeding your measurable goals, you'll gain and build up your self-confidence, which is an important attribute of consistent performers.

Over-Confidence Example

During a tournament at home, I was approached by a shooter after we finished our first record group of the weekend. The competitor let me know, "I beat the pants off of you." I thought he was just teasing. As it turned out, the shooter was serious. I was set back a bit when I realized the shooter was not trying to have a little fun. I thought to myself, "How could you say that?" We have a long way to go I said "yep, but it doesn't look too good for you, we have 19 more groups to shoot."

I never judge the quality of a shooter by any single group, good or bad. Serious competitors compete for the long run. I often shoot my smallest group at the end of the day, not because I try harder, but because I am getting more comfortable with the conditions that we've been shooting throughout the day.

Be self-confident, know what you can and cannot do, be honest: You,

> Can shoot good aggs
> Can read flags very well
> Can keep a positive attitude
> Can act gracious if defeat
> Can not make a rifle which shoots .300 shoot .200
> Can not affect anyone's performance but your own

One of the largest margins of victory I have ever had was two weeks before the Nationals in 2002 at Midland. I just happened to be looking toward the lunch room at Midland when a shooter friend of mine who was just arriving saw me in the road. He exited the vehicle and came right over to visit. I was a fair distance away and could tell something was up, looking at the big smile. We said hello and he went right into the trash talk by saying, "it's hell to peak the week before the Nationals". He heard about the shoot at Kansas City the week before. I replied, "You haven't seen peak just yet" and went on win the 3 Gun.

He was attempting to affect my performance by psychological warfare, hoping I would not shoot as well by over thinking the task at hand. Many shooters who shoot a small group often shoot a big group on the very next target. As if another small group is some form of entitlement, "I shot a small group so I will do it again." You must focus on the moment and not dwell on the past.

Example of Sports Psychology applied to Benchrest
Many of the topics discussed in this chapter were used in this story from the 2003 Super Shoot. I applied positive self talk, imagery, focus, positive state of mind, positive attitude, proper techniques to minimize distractions, discussions of self-confidence and shooting ability and equipment evaluation.

After the Heavy Varmint 100 yard event on the second day of shooting, Pat Byrne and I engaged in a discussion outside the loading barn at Kelbly's. We talked about our poor relative performance; our running aggregates were a dismal .3000. My 100 yard place finishes were 79 and 77th respectively. We both felt our equipment was performing to the best of its ability, but felt the cause of our poor performance was ourselves. My most frequently used troubleshooting tool is a small thing you look into. It's called a mirror.

We discussed the upcoming 200 yard events, specifically the Heavy Varmint 200 the following day. The evening time is used by competitors to practice, make any equipment and tune adjustments, and just test conditions. I conveyed my desire to improve MY performance by eliminating the mistakes of the two previous days. We talked about goals for the next two days; I went so far as to set aggregate goals of "20-20" or .200 for the Heavy Varmint 200 yard and .200 for the Light Varmint 200 yard events. When my equipment is shooting well, I am capable of shooting aggregates in the teens providing I make no strategy mistakes. Just having the desire is not enough. For example, if you are 30 years old and 4'6" tall you will not be playing professional basketball in the NBA no matter how strong your desire.

I added by shooting 20-20 my 2 Gun aggregate would be about .2600 which would be competitive, probably not win, but would be competitive. We visited more about the equipment and the agging potential of our rifles. My rifle was easily capable of shooting 20-20 or a pair of .200 aggs. When coming to the line for the first match of the Heavy Varmint I was focused on the goals from the evening before. After the last shot had been fired in the Heavy Varmint 200 on Friday, I managed to shoot a .1877 aggregate, good enough for 4th place in the Heavy Varmint 200. In tougher conditions on Saturday I managed a .2255 which was good enough for the Light Varmint 200 yard aggregate win.

If you add up the two yardage aggs from the 200 yard events you end up with an average of .2066 and pretty close to the goal. I ultimately finished with a .2547 2-Gun aggregate which was good enough for a seventh place finish at the Super Shoot, a competitive success, given the first two days of mediocrity.

Don't **EVER** Give Up

Benchrest Strategy

I'll attempt to cover the one of the most difficult aspects of of extreme rifle accuracy in competitive Benchrest Shooting; knowing what to do and when or Strategy.

Outside of flag reading skills, you must develop skills concerning what to do and when. The equipment (rifle and loading tools) is relatively easy to setup and once properly setup will occupy little of your time, 90% or more of the balance will be used in an attempt to learn what to do, and when.

I've heard many comments from spectators after seeing our equipment for the first time *"Anyone can shoot small groups with that stuff,"* I say *"**Show me!**"* Let's address this type of thinking right away, "Just having the right equipment will not make you a consistently good performer on the firing line." No shooter will have continued success without learning and applying this information. These are relatively simple factual principles you <u>must</u> learn to be a consistent performer in about any type of competitive rifle shooting that requires accuracy.

LUCK IS NOT A FACTOR!

Success, as far as I'm concerned, is measured over the long run. Considering how many groups you must shoot in multi gun aggregates, (the goal of most consistent competitive shooters) luck is hardly a factor, except to say, it would be nice to avoid any bad luck. You might get lucky in shooting one single 5 shot group, but the laws of probability exclude luck as any factor past two groups. The skill and preparedness of the shooter is much more of a factor. Preparing by practicing, studying and mastering all of theses strategy aspects will put you in a position to succeed.

As we've learned in the chapter on goals, focus on performance goals, not outcome based goals. It's easy to better your best ever performance and still not win, that's great and should be looked upon as a success.

I will be covering what is required to be competitive when the weather is normal or worse. Many shooters travel to the range only on calm sunny days (picnic weather) to shoot. Tournaments are scheduled months in advance and are shot in whatever conditions are present at the time. Tournaments are conducted in every imaginable condition: rain, hurricane force wind, bright sunshine, etc. Often when the weather is very nice you'll find out which shooters have the best rifles and not learn much about their skills.

I have only two memories of tournaments being postponed or cancelled. One was a tournament which was in a hurricane on the Gulf Coast of the United States, the other was the NBRSA Nationals in 2005, we had a break in the action due to a malfunctioning moving backer motor. My point is, you'll shoot in conditions which are far from a "trigger pulling contest," or aiming at the same spot on the record target and carefully squeezing the trigger. Normal weather has many characteristics which you must learn to deal with. Even if you have no intention of ever stepping to the firing line at a benchrest tournament you'll find this chapter full of many things which effect your shooting, be it for fun or competition.

Major Benchrest Strategy Rules

During a layover in Frankfurt Germany, Skip Otto and I had a lengthy discussion about strategy; I expressed a desire to attempt to write a paper on the subject. We spent the next couple fun filled hours talking about what I like to call "Major Benchrest Strategy Rules."

Major BR Strategy rules are the things you must learn, some of which are common things that can, and will go wrong. Consistently successful Benchrest competitors have many things in common, including experience. There are two ways to gain experience, from your mistakes or from the mistakes of others. Most shooters will not live long enough to make all of the possible mistakes and learn from them. This writing is an attempt to speed the learning process. I'll focus on simple, but important things to help minimize mistakes, common problems and how to reduce or completely eliminate them.

You must learn these Major BR Strategy Rules if you plan on being a force on the firing line at a Benchrest tournament over the long term.

1. Watch your Flags.
2. Be Flexible.
3. Never fire the first shot to see where it will go.
4. Don't shoot a big group in the first thirty seconds
5. It is OK to hit the second hole.
6. Learn to shoot fast.
7. Never use an intermediate starting hold.

Watch your flags!

When considering any type of rifle shooting sport, you will (or should) quickly learn the importance of wind flags. Wind Flags are the most important equipment a competitor has in their repertoire. Knowing how to interpret information from wind flags is what normally separates the average competitor from the Champion.

Figure 1. Flags at the 8th World Championships at Kelbly's

One common mistake, when shooting a group is, getting to the end of the group and everything is going according to plan through shot three or four. Then having the thought that everything is going so good that the last shot will go without looking at the flags, which are changing. This seldom works in the shooters favor.

"YOU CANNOT WISH THE LAST SHOT IN!"

Tony Boyer

Keep your eye on the flags while reloading between shots. If you look down, you will loose your reference and be less able to see subtle changes in the flags. When you look up, you will be required to try and remember what the flag reading looked like. Practice reloading your rifle while keeping your attention on the flags.

Shooting without flags, or ignoring them, will not provide consistent competitive results. In other words,

"A very good rifle may get you a match win or two, but good flag reading skills will take you much farther."

Ratigan

Be Flexible

As we age it's common to favor a structured life and this can be bad if applied to benchrest. Remain flexible and apply whatever is needed when it's needed. Flexibility extends to every aspect of BR including flags, such as where to set them, what color of tail to use, when to shoot, shooting style, which condition to shoot and even loading. Most shooters settle on one shooting style and setup and become so inflexible as to have little or no chance of winning an agg with the style they've adopted. Sorry for being so windy here, this Major BR strategy rule needs a few examples to help in the explanation.

Shooting Style for...

Calm Weather

Calm is the condition I am most afraid of. What often looks good to the newcomer often times will prove less than desirable to shoot in and produce some ugly looking groups for no apparent reason. During a trigger pull I would favor shooting free recoil and be very careful with my gun handling and trigger control.

New shooters tend to visit the range when the wind is calm and everything looks nice. Calm morning conditions, which would be considered a trigger pulling contest, may be good for testing your equipment but will do little to improve the skills you will need to shoot in normal weather conditions. Trigger pulling conditions will of course help the shooter learn some "table manners" or how to operate the rifle without jerking and flinching. I've only seen good conditions which would be considered a trigger pull a few times since I have been shooting: two days in Phoenix at the NBRSA Nationals in 2003, about two hours in 1995 at the NBRSA Nationals in Kansas City, and about 3 minutes at the Cactus in 2002 when Skip Otto shot his world record group at 200 yards. Focusing on shooting in good conditions can be a waste of time.

It's common for newer shooters to shoot some good groups while applying careful gun handling shooting free recoil. This will work fine when the conditions are nice. The problems start when the flags begin moving and the mirage makes aiming more difficult, then, the aiming at the same place and pulling the trigger strategy will often prove less effective.

After you've mastered your table manners you should practice improving your different gun handling techniques. Practice shooting faster when shooting free recoil, different types of holding techniques and pinning your rifle. You should be able to shoot pretty good groups while shooting faster and using the different techniques, if not, time for more practice. You'll become comfortable shooting faster with the different techniques and will have no trouble using a style of hold when needed during match time.

Direction stable, changing intensity (pickups & letups)

When shooting in a wind condition which is stable in direction but changing in intensity I'd suggest a change to your approach. If you can find a condition that is stable in intensity you might get away with holding in the same place from shot to shot. This style of shooting might be best for the trigger pulling contest but might not yield the best results. Timing becomes more of an issue when shooting in intensity changes. Just changing intensity will often yield some good aggregates and you must not be too sloppy when pulling the trigger, but you should speed up. Shooting faster becomes more important. If you can find a condition which will hold where you could shoot five shots, get on with the business of shooting a group.

Jack Jackson tells a story of shooting next to Jeff Fowler while attending his second Super Shoot. They were shooting one of the 200 yard aggregates with conditions that were varying in intensity, the wind was coming from the right and would pickup then hold for a bit and then letup. Jeff started shooting during one of the pickups and shot a nice group at 200 yards. Jack asked about his decision of when to start shooting. Jeff replied "I do that frequently, hold into a pickup (farther away from your bullet holes)". Jeff had been shooting well and won that 200 yard aggregate. Jeff added, "I never like to hold against a letup."

Jack inquired "But, why"?

Jeff added "I have never found the letups to be very honest (predictable)."

I often do the same when shooting in a crosswind. Wait for the intensity to start to increase then start my group. I start holding away from the first bullet holes or into the wind, when the wind increases. You must have your impact point be downwind of your crosshair when you hold away from the group in a pick up.

Direction Reversals

Raton

Timing becomes even more critical when the conditions are more variable. Your ability to shoot fast becomes even more important. Some ranges have conditions on occasion where the wind over the entire range changes both in the direction and intensity. Every now and then at Raton, N.M., the conditions will change 180 degrees in direction and vary in intensity from 5 to 35 mph. The whole range can run from right to left at 25mph, then switch from left to right at 25mph. It's easy to see that shooting one shot in the right to left, and then next in the left to right, using the same aiming point won't work very well. These are times when you should favor the "look last" style of shooting as covered in the chapter on shooting styles. No matter how fine your aim and your trigger control, shooting at the wrong time will yield unacceptable results.

When shooting when the wind has wild reversals, survival is the name of the game. Try to avoid any big groups. Shooting at the correct time is absolutely essential. Fine aim and finesse on the trigger is out the window. If I can find any type of condition which looks like it might remain reasonably stable for 15 seconds, I let-em rip and run my group, holding for the changes as I go. You must get the big picture when looking out onto the range so you don't get caught in a major change.

Continuously Variable Direction and Intensity - <u>Luther, Oklahoma</u>

It can be hard, if not impossible, to describe how to shoot some types of variable conditions. Extremely difficult conditions are my favorite, and are the norm at Okie Shooters in Luther, Oklahoma, affectionately known as Benchrest Hell. I use my peripheral vision to get the big picture or a global view of the flags on the range. Looking at one flag at a time is way too slow and will not work consistently. Knowing when to start your group, is almost impossible for me to describe. It's more of a feeling than anything else. I've started many groups in a condition that I thought was "the right time" only to find the condition vanish after the first shot. I've shot many groups where I have shot a couple shots using one shooting technique, then switched to another. When approaching the firing line, I keep an open mind.

I've shot a couple shots on the record target shooting free recoil, then stopped because things really changed and I felt like I didn't know where to hold. I sat there watching flags, running out of time, then with about 15 seconds remaining I decided where to hold without returning to the sighter, fired the last three shots pinning the rifle as fast as I could, holding three different places for the each of the last three shots. When the conditions change faster than you can shoot a sighter, then return to the record, you need to make quick decisions while looking at the flags and based on where the previous shot impacted. This is where your practice time in switchy conditions will pay off. The tougher the conditions, the more important your flag reading skills become.

Figure 2. Firing line at Luther, Oklahoma.

100 finesse, 200 aggressive

You'll find shooters who use different shooting styles when shooting 100, 200 and 300 yards. I will usually be more careful on my aim and more particular on the flag readings when shooting at 100 yards. I'm more aggressive and put less emphasis on a fine aim and more on when to shoot while shooting the longer distances.

"I'm so used to shooting aggressive at 200 and putting more weight into the back half of the range, I often ignore the front end when shooting at 100 yards. With the ultra small aggs at 100 yards often seen today, you must also keep an eye on the first flags when shooting, at least at 100 yards".

Jim Borden

Flexible flag setup

For example; if the range always has wind from the right, put your flags on the right. If the wind is always from the left, put your flags on the left. If the prevailing conditions are a head or tail wind, consider setting them straight in line from you to the target. Your flag reading should be taken from the upwind flags. Reading a condition which is long gone is not only a disadvantage, it's pointless.

Our National championships are a good example of inflexibility. All you have to do is come and shoot it once. You'll quickly realize how many people have flags that are completely unwelcome by the other shooters sharing their bench, sometimes as many as 24. These competitors insist on setting their 6 flags after requesting a flag rotation (on a relay full of flags). This is done to the detriment of everyone, including themselves. You can actually make it harder for yourself even when you believe you're helping. This situation happens at every major tournament every year. Your only hope is to have a full rotation which doesn't include one of these type A personalities. I attempt to get on a flag rotation I can read. All that's needed is a positive attitude.

Figure 2A. Too many Flags on one bench at the Nationals at St.Louis.

Never fire the first shot to see where it will go.

This Major BR Strategy rule has to do simply with the title, "good competitors never fire the first record (top portion) shot on the record target to see where it will go." Impact point management is very important in reducing the amount of confusion during your 7 minutes to glory on the firing line.

The first shot on the record target **MUST** hit a specific spot on the record target. If not, you must correct before firing the second shot. It happens like this: after a relay has finished shooting, you'll hear throughout the loading area, tales of the first two shots making the group. In fact, after more consideration, it's usually the first shot which caused the problem, not the second. In this situation, the shooter didn't notice that the first shot didn't impact where it should have, or they just thought the impact point would be different on the top target.

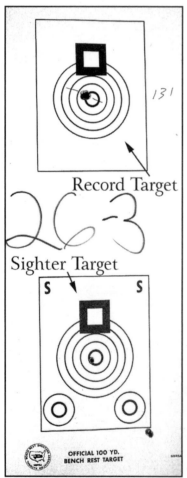

Figure 3. Impact point shift.

It's common for the first shot on the record target to be high and a bit left, just as in figure 3. The impact of all of the sighters are below my aiming point. You should notice the record group is higher. The first shot was high and if I had not held up after the first shot, the group would have been much larger. Many hours have been spent trying to figure out what causes this problem and how to stop this from happening. The problem seems related to changing how the gun sits in the bags from the sighter to the record. Many say they haven't seen this problem, but let's dispel this myth right away. There are two kinds of shooters, those who have this problem, and those who have this problem and don't realize it. What's important is your ability to recognize when this happens and what to do when it happens. This first shot trouble can be as common as two or three targets in every ten.

Proper scope setup will help recognize this when it happens. All that's required is your impact point being below your horizontal cross hair. After firing the first shot, reload and return the rifle to battery. Re-aim and look at your first shot, and now you notice it's much closer to your aiming point than it should be. If your normal impact point is above your aiming point this problem is harder to recognize. With your normal impact above your aiming point, and your first shot hits high, say 3/4 of a bullet hole at 100 yards, it just goes a bit farther away from your cross hair and nothing seems out of the ordinary until you fire the second shot, and it cuts out of the bottom of the first shot by almost a bullet hole. Upon further examination it's discovered the second shot impacted where it should be, the first shot was the offending shot. Now you have a .200 group (or bigger at 100 yards) and still need to fire three more shots.

When you recognize the first shot is high and a bit left, you can hold up and left the amount needed assuming the flags are still ok and continue shooting. I've shot several official screamer groups in registered tournaments doing this very thing, without going back to the sighter to confirm.

The first bullet hitting low is abnormal and the above technique shouldn't be applied. A first shot being low will give more trouble than the first shot high and left. A first bullet low should be chased very carefully after trying to figure out why it's low on the sighter target. A word of caution: just holding low and continuing to shoot will almost never work. One common technique is to hold half of the distance when having a shot go low and to continue to shoot. Option two is go back to the sighter and figure out where to hold, and then hold the full value you need then continue shooting. Option three would be to borrow a neighbors gun that shoots better than yours, figure out where it shoots then finish your group. Whichever method you choose, I wish you luck. This first shot being low will cause trouble. Faye Boyer, she is the only exception to this rule. She has more first shots low than any other shooter I know, and she makes it work, but cannot explain it. It's so frequent with Faye we've teased her about holding up about two rings on her first record shot so the record group will be about where the sighters impact.

I was alone among the forrest of spotting scopes watching Wayne Campbell at the 2002 Super Shoot. After fouling his barrel, he shot one sighter to see what it should look like, then went to the record target. His first shot was 3/4 of a bullet hole high. He stopped, and I could see him pull the joystick down on the Farley to go back to the sighter. I thought I was alone and spoke to myself out loud (softly) "what are you DOING, hold up and keep on shooting!" Wayne finished his group just fine after shooting a sighter; he held up and finished his group, Good Job! I turned to go back to the loading area to find Tony Boyer about 10 inches behind me and to the left. I didn't see him approach. Tony gave me quite a complement, saying "Not many would know to do that". Needless to say that made my day.

While watching a US World Team member during the Super Shoot at 200 yards, the first shot on the record had impacted more than an inch from where the sighters were, in the same wind condition. He was in trouble and should have stopped! I looked away, he shot again; my thought "wow that was fast." Looking through the spotting scope, he shot another on the record. You guessed it; he hit right where the sighters were more than an inch away. Now he had 1.1 inches AND three more to shoot.

I returned to the loading area and I must have looked frightened. My neighbor asked what was wrong. I explained, I'd witnessed a US world team member make a major strategy mistake and explained what I saw. After the shooter was finished with the relay, I talked to him, a good friend of mine, about what had happened so as to learn from it and not have a repeat of the situation. He explained what he was thinking when shooting the group and sure enough he had the thought after the first shot "Oh, there it is" and fired the second shot without thinking about the first one and why he had a different impact point.

Don't Shoot a Big Group in the First Thirty Seconds

This Major BR Strategy Rule is simple. If you're not comfortable, DON'T shoot. I see many competitors shoot their record group in the first minute regardless of how bad conditions are. Remember; be flexible. If you have better shooting conditions at the start of a relay than you've seen all day it might be a good idea to shoot early. At other times, this might be a bad thing to do. Wait for a condition you're comfortable with before you shoot. If that never comes, you can shoot as big a group as you want in the last thirty seconds.

This strategy rule emphasizes the importance of knowing how fast you can comfortably shoot five shots on the record target. Most shooters can easily shoot five shots in 30 seconds and; therefore, should not have any problem waiting until there is a minute or so left. It should also be apparent that every shooter must have a timer. It's the shooters responsibility to keep track of time. There's no provision for any shooter for any reason to shoot after the relay is over, NONE. Range officers occasionally miss calling the time commands which reinforces the need for you to be aware of the time remaining.

During a local tournament at Kansas City, in 1996, during match one (1) at 200 yards, the mirage was so bad I couldn't see the rings on the target let alone bullet holes. Competitors up and down the line were shooting while not being able to see. Rex Reneau and I sat there just looking out on the range, and after five minutes of the ten minute match, the flags started to move on the left side of the range, moving across the range to the right. Rex and I were side by side in the middle of the firing line. As the flag movement made its way across the firing line, the whining got louder as the competitors were able to see what they were doing. As soon as flag movement reached our benches, the mirage cleared up making the targets visible, we could see. Rex and I shot a group in less than 15 seconds, both were ½ inch groups at 200 yards which was less than half of any other competitor during match one. It's nice to get off to a good start by simply knowing what not to do. This was one of the first things I learned from Rex about strategy.

If you want to shoot in a popular condition but would like to wait out your neighbors to reduce your chance of doubling (shooting at the same time) with them, WAIT! The condition will return, almost always. Then shoot.

Don't shoot if you're uncomfortable, or you cannot see. Even if the condition seems popular where many of the others start shooting!

You're trying to shoot smaller than the others on the line. Shooting in a popular condition you're uncomfortable with can quickly normalize you to the middle of the pack on the stat sheet. It's not a democracy while on the firing line. However, don't ignore fellow competitors, saying bad words around you while shooting, especially if you know they are good consistent competitors.

The following situation reinforces the need to know how fast you can comfortably shoot five shots. Just like the major BR strategy rule says "Don't shoot a big group in the first thirty seconds". At the 1998 NBRSA Nationals on my relay during match four of the sporter 100 yard stage; it began to rain just before my relay started. By the time the relay was started (in the middle of the day), it was raining so hard and the light was so dim you could hardly see your target at 100 yards. The wind was blowing harder than we had seen all week, it was a pretty hard thunderstorm but with no lightning, so the match went on (as it should). I had my rifle under a tarp and after 5 minutes into our relay, Perry Morton noticed that a target had blown out of the frame, which caused a cease fire.

We started back up after adding two minutes to our remaining time which was about 2 minutes for a total of "You have four minutes to complete your firing....ready on the right, ready on the left....commence firing". I still had yet to fire a shot, even to foul the barrel. About another two minutes had lapsed the conditions let up to about half of what it was. I pulled the tarp back and proceeded to shoot, a .604 at 100 yards. I sat there knowing my hopes to win the yardage and one hall of fame point was gone. You see, I was shooting very well. I watched the conditions while my clock was counting down. When my timer reached 30 seconds the rain had almost stopped, the wind went to calm with heavy overcast and no mirage.

What a mistake I had made. I can shoot five carefully aimed shots in ten seconds. Any kind of a normal group in match four would have given me the yardage win. My last group was a nice .158, and I finished in the top bunch with a .600 in my set of targets. Out of the fifty shooters on the line during the rain storm at Fairchance PA., best I remember, Faye Boyer was the only shooter who shot anything that resembled a group. Now I look forward to getting even with the rain and look forward to trying that again, next time with a positive frame of mind.

Figure 4. Flags at Luther Oklahoma on a relatively nice day.

It's OK to Hit the Second Hole.

This Major BR Strategy rule covers a very common mistake made by most competitors. During the middle of the group you shoot a shot that doesn't go were it should. The mistake then comes when you hold for that impact change with no apparent change in the conditions. Then you will have doubled the error by shooting a shot that is opposite of the first shot out.

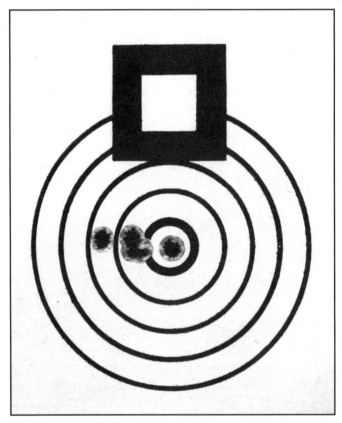

Figure 5. It's OK to hit the second hole.

The situation happens like this: you fire three shots and with no apparent change in the condition, then fire the fourth and miss to the left. You look at the flags after the shot. There's no apparent change in the flags to indicate why the shot went left. Then, without any reason, you hold to the right and fire the next shot and it goes right where you held it, out of the group to the right. The morale of the story is if you don't see what caused the problem <u>don't hold for it.</u> By all means if you look and see what caused the bullet to go where it went, hold for it. Thus "it's OK to hit the second hole."

This mistake is one of the most common mistakes made on the firing line.

Learn to Shoot Fast.

This Major Benchrest Strategy Rule is simple. When conditions dictate, the shooter with the ability to shoot fast has an advantage. Benchrest shooting, done properly, is waiting for the right condition, and then fire your five shots off before the condition changes, Sounds easy, rarely done!

Most shooters can shoot five shots in 20-30 seconds. This isn't terribly fast even with a gun without an ejector. My setup takes this BR strategy rule to every possible extreme to speed up the process, action design, bag setup, preferred shooting style, where I put my cases, etc. I've been unknowingly independently timed shooting five aimed shoots on the record target in less than ten seconds. This type of speed is impractical for most shooters.

Reload before looking. One major waste of valuable time is looking where the shot went before reloading. By switching the order and reloading first you can easily cut your cycle time in half between shots. I don't think I've even watched a new shooter reload first. I believe the thought is "the bullet's moving on the target until I look." Correct this one thing and you'll be able to shoot a group much quicker.

One key to becoming quicker is doing the same thing every time you shoot, not only when you need to shoot faster. The skill needed to shoot faster will become second nature. After a while you'll not notice your shooting speed has increased.

When I ordered my first ejector action, I considered the problem very carefully before ordering. I was shooting a right bolt left port action, and was already using both hands when reloading. I just needed a way to speed the process by getting the fired case out of the action without taking the time to remove it myself. For this, I ordered a left port left eject action. Since then I have tried every conceivable combination of port type and location. I'm still using the right bolt, left port, left eject.

One final thought on this subject. Your action must perform flawlessly and eject every time. An action that ejects four of five will be a detriment to your confidence. When letting your clock run down, you'll be thinking about if your action will eject or not, instead of watching your flags and the other things in this writing.

I remember a spectator asking "What was that all about" when I was leaving the firing line after a relay. Like you, I did not know what "that" was. I was running the tournament, firing line, shooting and initially thought he might have seen something downrange, a safety problem? I asked the spectator what he had seen. He said "Why did you shoot like that". I then understood the question. I found a condition that would hold so I ran my group. I explained "What you witnessed was five (5) carefully aimed shots on the record target". You should have seen the look of disbelief then. I invited the spectator to look through my scope since the relay had ended, there were only three holes, two shots on the sighter and a nice group on the record. He was really at a loss for words after that.

Never Use an Intermediate Starting Hold

Be consistent on your starting hold. Many shooters hold someplace different for the first shot of every group. The goal is to build proper strategy and reduce different starting holds you will simplify the things you need to remember when the heat is on. This reduces the chance of forgetting where you were aiming.

It's important to be able to tell where you started holding without having to think about it. Many of you reading or hearing this will be guilty of violating this rule. Remember, this isn't a debate, just, just an opportunity to hear about the strategy used by many successful competitors.

Eliminate intermediate starting holds and minimize mistakes made by holding errors is very important.

I recommend a center hold (12 o'clock) until the bullets blow out to about the second to last ring on either side. Once the bullets are being blown out to about the second to last ring, I will change my hold to the upwind outside ring (figure 6) to start my group and as usual try to find a condition that allows as many shots in the same condition as possible.

In the heat of the moment it's easy to forget where you started holding. By using the outside ring as your starting hold, your change in impact on the target will be obvious. After awhile, recognizing where you were holding will be very easy. If the last ring is not enough hold to keep your bullets somewhere in the middle of the target, your next hold should be somewhere easy to remember and repeatable like the edge of the target holder. Then farther out you should find something on the board to make your hold repeatable; maybe the start of the mirage stripes, etc. I have held on the end of the target frame when shooting 300 yards.

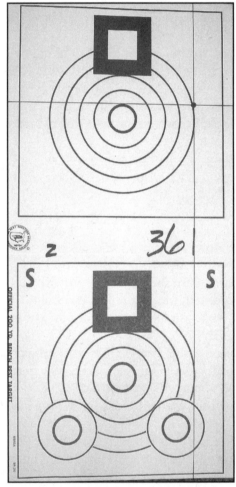

Figure 6. My first point to hold off.

By employing this simple BR strategy rule you'll be able to think more about the flags, first shot impact problems and many other things which will require your attention. You can forget about where you were holding. You'll know simply by looking at the target. After you make this change in how you approach your starting hold, you'll be glad you did, I promise.

Strategy Extras

Think You Fired Five?   Stop!

It won't take long after starting your competitive endeavors to hear someone telling about shooting six shots on their record target. Competitors will shoot their group and then, while picking up the empty cases, will have second thoughts. This only happens when you shoot a good group where you cannot see every shot. What happens next is avoidable. The shooter is convinced they have fired less than the required shots. Then without thinking, the shooter reinserts their bolt and fires another shot on the sighter in preparation for another shot on the record. Then he takes careful aim and shoots the sixth shot on the record, sometimes not hurting their group, but usually causing damage to the group and aggregate score. After damaging their group, the shooter often discovers the lost case, laying on the ground, under their towel, etc.. Now comes the feeling of being a _____! With the resurgence of the ejector guns this mistake becoming more frequent.

I've had this happen to me, many times. With my left eject rifle, I know losing a case is easy to do and I don't have a single thought of shooting another shot. I've never had less than the required number of shots on any target.

If you think you have fired the correct number of shots STOP!

Take Full Loading Block to the Firing Line

Go to the line with full block even for the last target. Never go to the line with less than 15 loaded rounds. If you have any cases you wouldn't shoot on the record target throw them away. Don't start segregating the cases as sighter shots and record shots. You cannot get good data from loaded rounds that are not accurate on the sighter. During the heat of battle isn't the time to find you shot a bad group because you mixed up your cases. Anything which takes your attention away from watching our flags should be removed. Watch the flags, not pretty colored case rims.

If there's a cease fire for any reason and you came to the firing line with only six cases you'll wish you had a few more rounds. You will need a couple to warm up your barrel back at the very least. You will really be having second thoughts about the time you saved by putting away your loading tools early.

Leave Rifle Sitting on Rest

Leave your rifle setting on the rest and rear bag and pointed at the target until the end of your relay. Just before the cease fire, take one last look at your target for any shoots which aren't yours. The reason is simple; if someone crossfires on your target after you finish your group you'll see the bullet hole(s).

If someone crossfires on your target, you must inform the range officer immediately following the completion of your relay. The referees will need to look over the target and stationary backer before anything is changed by the target crew.

The stationary backer is a target board 3 feet behind your target. When someone crossfires on a target, the record target and the stationary backer will look different. The bullets which came from another bench will have been shot at an angle and is easily seen by comparing the record target to the stationary. The amount of displacement can indicate from how far away the stray bullet(s) came from.

After your target is scored, it's too late to complain about a crossfire.

How Do You Know When to Start Shooting?

A very compelling and popular question, one which is almost impossible to express in words, is "How do you know when to start your group"? When to start shooting is often a feeling when looking out on the range. One thing is very clear, just shooting when the firing line gets busy isn't always the best time. Following others is <u>almost</u> always the recipe for failure. If you start when your neighbor starts, you're counting on who you're following to know what they are doing. Just starting to shoot when everyone starts will often put you solidly in the middle of the pack, assuming, you make no mistakes. Just as bad is waiting to start shooting when your well known neighbor starts. Shooting when they shoot assumes they don't hold. This is a big mistake. Many of the consistently good competitors will hold off during their group. If you don't learn when and where to hold, you will not recognize when they are holding, when the conditions are changing. If you follow shot for shot you'll not hold when the other shooter does, bad idea. It happens often when the new shooter plans on shooting when their neighbor starts. After the good shooter starts, the new comer often never notices the better shooter has moved to the sighter. The new shooter fires their shot on the record when the other shooter has shot a sighter, OOPS.

Stupid Shots

This is a benchrest slang term for "unexplained shots". If the condition you're shooting is causing stupid shots which are not being caused by your rifle, tune, powder, bullets, or the like, SHOOT ANOTHER CONDITION! If you have unexplained shots which are caused by something on the range which is unseen or unexplained, other competitors will have them also. Go and check the Wailing Wall where the targets are displayed. Look for other competitors who are experiencing stupid shots, going the same direction. Only look at the targets of shooters who you know are shooting ok.

This is another good reason to have a watch list of shooters by what relay they are on for the major tournaments, and why I carry my watch list in my pocket and don't leave it on my spotting scope. When I go to the Wailing Wall I have a quick reference of who's who and their competitor number in my pocket. What a time saver when wanting to know someone's competitor number at the Super Shoot when there are 360 or more competitors.

Watch Your Neighbors

Most new shooters never hold off of center on the sighter target. If your neighbor has a good rifle, you can get good usable data from their sighter target. If your neighbor is one of the top guns of benchrest, proceed with caution. Many of them will hold when using the sighter to gauge where to hold to hit where desired, especially when they have already started the record group.

Watch for Cloud Cover

During partly cloudy days be aware of pending cloud cover. Bright sun often causes mirage which can make aiming more difficult by displacing the image of the target. This means the target is not where you see it.

Many partly cloudy days offer some relief be means of cloud cover which can obscure the sun and completely clear up the sight picture.

In this sport (and/or game) of .0001 (one hundred millionths of an inch), any advantage can be big. During partly cloudy days, take notice where the clouds are, which direction they are traveling, and if there's any possibility of cloud cover during your relay.

Look at the surrounding lay of the land for the shade and take notice of the direction it is traveling on the ground and of impending shade over the firing line. If it has been sunny with lots of heavy mirage and you notice, when arriving to the line, you have cloud cover, don't pass up the chance. You might want to shoot early before the cloud cover ceases, if the wind conditions allow.

Agg'em to Death

This Benchrest Strategy Rule is simple; you don't have to shoot any little bitty groups, just don't shoot any BIG groups. Successful shooters never lose sight of the big picture. There are 10 groups in a grand aggregate, 20 groups in a 2-Gun aggregate, 30 groups in a 3-Gun and 40-48 groups in a 4-Gun.

Shooting one sloppy group will not ruin your weekend. As mentioned earlier, Charles Huckeba shot a group over an inch at 100 yards during the first yardage of the 6th World Benchrest Championships in Nelson, New Zealand. After traveling half way around the world, Charles continued on instead of throwing in the towel. At the end of the Championships, Charles helped his 4 man team capture the Team Gold Medal in World Benchrest Championships and was second in the individual 2-Gun.

Many shooters become overconfident after shooting a good group early in an aggregate, and often shoot a large group following their exemplary performance. The top guns of benchrest will return to the firing line and shoot the next group with the same focus and intensity as the first group.

Trying to "shoot small" often ends in failure (having four shots in a hole and then stopping). Aggregates are made of many groups which are acceptable, while being able to avoid the large ones. Many of the top guns of benchrest love to shoot small groups but would never pass up a chance to shoot one which would be ok and not hurt their aggregate. Never pass up a chance at .220, to shoot a .375. Many shooters will shoot four into a nice hole, then stop shooting to admire their unfinished group when the conditions are changing just a bit. They don't want to hurt the group. Many times this shooter would go back to the sighter target and shoot a few shots in conditions which are now completely different than the first four shots.

Agg-em to death with groups which will not hurt your agg, the recipe for success.

Give Yourself a Chance

This should be engraved on everyone's front rest. If you must stop in the middle of a group with plenty of time remaining, give yourself a chance to finish your group. If you have the feeling of being lost, return to the sighter and make an attempt to salvage your group. Just guessing where to hold on the record, is not the best choice. Don't be anxious to finish your group especially when there is plenty of time left on the clock. Even experienced competitors have the feeling of being lost from time to time in the middle of a group. The difference is, experienced shooters stop, and do not ruin a group by just firing another shot knowing it is a guess. If the conditions were bad enough to get you to stop and then after a time your condition seems to return, it's almost always different than what you shot before. Return downstairs to confirm your hold.

Stay in the Moment

Learn from any mistakes you make, don't dwell on them, and refocus on the task at hand. At home I run the tournaments, score, and oversee the target crews and shoot. Frequently I am asked about how I do that. Well, I stay in the moment. I focus on what I'm doing at the time. When the targets come in, I score. If there's a problem, I take care of that. When it's time to shoot, I shoot.

How to shoot your target

Proper use of the target is essential for long term success. There are specific rules which describe how to shoot your target. Apply these during your practice. Don't shoot at or above the top line of your sighter target during practice. During match time, you won't shoot at that area of your target. Avoid using that area.

Tournament Procedure, Record Target:

Any competitor whose first shot of any match strikes the record portion of the target shall report at once to the range officer before firing another shot. (This also includes shots outside the target and above the top line of the sighter target that would be a penalty). The range officer shall satisfy himself/herself that no other shots have been fired, and shall make a note to the official scorer that the target not be penalized, and the shot not be scored.

Any shot higher than the top line of sighter target (this line extends between targets) and outside record target is a record shot, and if not touching the border of the record target shall be a penalty. This means if you fire a shot and it's blown three inches to the left of the record portion of the target, and not touching the target card, you'll have a penalty, and should shoot four more times at your record target. If you fire five on the target with one out to the left, you'll be disqualified for technically having attempted to conceal a crossfire. There's no shots allowed anywhere on the board between the targets above the top line of the sighter target.

Using a target of mine in figure 7, let's shoot a group at 100 yards. I fire my barrel fouling shots at the lower right corner of the sighter target. Then when I find a stable condition I fire a shot or two on one of the lower sighter bulls. If they hit where I want and are together, I'll go right to work on the record target. Often I like to shoot a shot at one of the lower sighter bulls just to see what the condition should look like on the target. Assuming the conditions will hold long enough to shoot a group, go to the record. This target might have been better by taking more time and being more careful with my gun handling. I pulled back too quickly on one shot on the record target giving me a bit of vertical. However, I never complain about groups smaller than .200. This one measure .170 something. I would take this size target all day and never fire a shot. I would just take my chances, if someone shoots smaller that's ok.

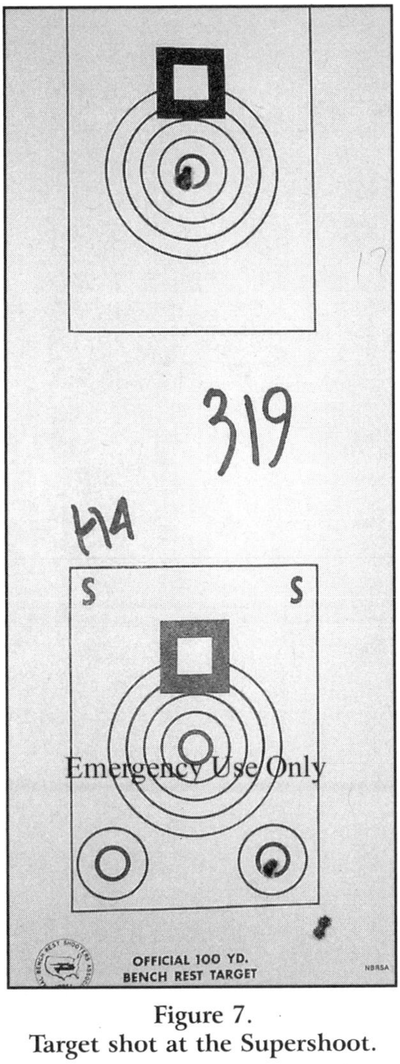

Emergency Use Only!

Save the center of the sighter target for when you are in trouble (emergency use only). When you get into trouble, you will need somewhere to shoot where you can see what you are doing. By shooting the target the same every time you will have space when needed. When shooting at 200 yards, you can use the space between the lower bulls to foul your barrel, and the lower circles for your first sighter shots.

Figure 7.
Target shot at the Supershoot.

Democracy is NOT Used in Benchrest.

World Benchrest Championships

Walt Berger began dreaming of benchrest competition on a world stage in the 1970's. Walt endured much frustration attempting to strike up interest in international competition. Skip Gordon (originator of the Super Shoot and Hall of Fame director from 80-87) traveled to Australia several times from 1975 to 1979. Walt and Skip made several trips to Europe beginning in 1985, to Bisley, England, then Sweden and France. Walt was invited by Dr. Lou Palmisano to Sweden for the 1986 300 meter World Championships, where they would be testing the Berger 105 grain 6mm bullets. This would be the first time 6mm bullets were used in these Championships. Lou and Walt stayed for two weeks of practice, the week long tournament, and for the awards banquet.

Walt Berger at the 2006 Cactus Classic

It was at the awards banquet where Walt conceived of a World Championships for the sport of Benchrest. In 1989 Walt meet with the Monsieur Michel Ternisien, the President of the Federation Francaise de Tir during a trip to Versailles, France. The French Federation agreed to host the 1st World Benchrest Championship in 1991. The ground work had been laid for benchrest competition on a world stage.

In 1989, during Super Shoot week in Ohio, there was a gathering of international shooters in a secluded motel. In attendance were Walt Berger and Skip Gordon from the USA, Carlos Pacheco and Herve du Plessis from France and Peter Hammerich from Germany. They worked out many of the details about the format for the first World Benchrest Championships which would be held in Frejus, France in October of 1991. Dream fulfilled!

Skip Gordon

Herve Du Plessis

Carlos Pacheco

Peter Hammerich

World Benchrest Shooting Federation

World Benchrest Shooting Federation

The World Benchrest Shooting Federation (WBSF) was formed for the purpose of assisting with the establishment of Competitive Benchrest Target Shooting in any country and to help member countries when hosting a championships, to be contested every other year.

The goals and objectives of the World Benchrest Shooting Federation are simple.

1) Promote and expand the sport of benchrest to the world by bringing together shooters from around the world to exchange ideas for the betterment and advancement of the sport.

2) Standardize rules so participating countries would compete on an equal basis.

3) To encourage camaraderie and fellowship amongst the Benchrest shooting community for the benefit of all (One of the Author's favorite objectives).

4) Provides a forum for the exchange of information associated with the sport of Benchrest at an international level.

5) Last but not least establish a set of World Records which will only be contested at the World Benchrest Championships.

Walt Berger once told me he wanted to spread our passion or addiction to the rest of the world, just like the proverbial drug dealer, Success! The sport is growing throughout the world. In 2005 there were 23 member countries in the World Benchrest Shooting Federation (WBSF), the sanctioning body for the World Benchrest Championships.

The World Benchrest Shooting Federation adopted the rules of the National Benchrest Shooters Association (NBRSA) of the United States for the basis and establishment of the World Championship rules concerning equipment and tournament procedures.

Everyone felt it was important that the existing equipment in use throughout the world qualify for use in the Championships which made the adoption of the NBRSA rules as it's starting point only common sense.

**Graeme Smith of New Zealand.
President of the WBSF**

The National Benchrest Shooters Association (NBRSA) is the shooting organization which first sanctioned the sport of Benchrest Shooting in the USA, and with the long standing history and over 50 years of competition, the rules, by-laws and methods used by the NBRSA were the logical starting point to establish the World Benchrest Championships and the WBSF.

It is the honor of a lifetime when representing your country at a World Benchrest Championship. The pressure is intense and at the same time I've had some of the best times in my shooting career while attending these Championships. I've had opportunities to visit with shooters from around the world who share our passion, and who just happen to live in another country. Our fine sport truly transcends distance and cultures, bringing shooters from around the world who gather together as friends. I've made friends from around the globe; what a great sport we share.

For several countries, the membership in the World Benchrest Shooting Federation helps to legitimize rifle competitions in their home countries. There are several countries, who, without membership in the WBSF, wouldn't be allowed rifle ownership outside of the military.

World Benchrest Championship Format

Every two years the best Benchrest shooters from many countries around the world gather for the World Benchrest Championships. The World Benchrest Championships is a 4 person team competition. The format for the championships is a 2-Gun, Light and Heavy varmint.

Preceding the championships are two official practice days. Then comes the competition, six targets a day, format like the Super Shoot. Each day of the competition is started with a warm up target, then five targets for the yardage aggregate.

After the end of the team 2-Gun event there is a fun day, either a 300 yard aggregate or a 10 shot 200 yard event, depending on whether the range has 300 yards available. By the time the last shot, is fired we'll have spent seven days at the range practicing and shooting the tournament. In the evening of the final day of competition, there's an awards banquet, the crowning event of the championships. The awards banquet is the final social event of the championships where we say our goodbye's to our international friends and wish them the best until we meet again.

United States Qualifying

Walt and Skip spent many hours discussing how the qualifying should be done for the United States in the late 1980's. Skip Gordan devised the qualifying system which remains to this day. It's amazing how thorough he was, Good Job Skip!

The qualifying system used by the US is held in high esteem by the international competitors, some of which must endure many requirements of organizations which know nothing about our sport. There are several countries who must wait to within a couple of months of the tournament before team members are chosen.

This requires some hasty travel arrangements, planning is out the window, grab your passport and run to the airport.

Qualifying for the United States takes place the year preceding the championships. Top Guns of the United States gather together in elbow-to-elbow competition to earn one of the twelve coveted spots to represent the United States on a US World Benchrest Team. Our qualifying takes place at different venues where shooters prove their ability when traveling out of their "element". Our qualifying eliminates any one tournament wonder or any shooter having an elevated performance that was, for lack or a better word, a fluke.

At the United States qualifying tournaments, shooters earn one point of every shooter they finish ahead of in the Light Varmint and Heavy Varmint Grand Aggs. The qualifying tournaments are selected well before qualifying begins. In years past, the best three points totals from up to as many as five shoots were used to select the team members. Some years have had only three points matches, then all three were used. No matter whether having three or five shoots, the biggest three matches have always been the matches which were used to determine the teams. This means the shooters must attend the three largest matches and shoot consistently at them. Although our present qualifying system may not be perfect, our system is considered by most all of the participating countries to be as close to perfect as is practical. In future years, your membership will also be based on your demonstrated ability to act as a team member. The change will be simple, just qualifying won't be enough if you've demonstrated an unwillingness or inability to work as a member of a team in the past. Make no mistake, this IS a team event.

Our qualifying process ends sometimes a year in advance, giving team members time to prepare physically and mentally. Shooters prevailing in the qualifying process are expected to perform well when traveling to another country while acting as a team. This is much different than our standard individual competition.

Of the many US competitors who would change our qualifying process for one reason or another, almost none have participated in a previous Championship. Almost all of the previous United States World Team qualifiers will tell you the current selection process and our (United States) ability to pick members is up to the task.

Whatever your opinion on the US qualifying, we must have everyone who wishes to qualify at the same range at the same time, in elbow to elbow competition. Any other selection system would have to take into account the difference in ranges, conditions, quantity of people in attendance, quality of people in attendance and many other factors. In order to be as fair as possible you just have everyone together and shoot it out.

Every member country to the World Benchrest Shooting Federation can only have one affiliated organization. This is to limit each country to 12 team members. Without this restriction, anyone could join the WBSF and send anyone they wanted to the World Championships. At this time, the NBRSA of the United States is the member organization to the WBSF.

One downfall of the United States Qualify system is the requirement in the United States that the qualifying tournaments to select the World Team be NBRSA Registered to be a qualifier.

The U.S. is headed into uncharted waters, so to speak, with our qualifying. I hope we can rectify this oversight come next time.

Historically the Super Shoot would be a qualifying tournament. In 2006 the Super Shoot would not be one of our qualifying tournaments; George Kelbly Sr. refused to register the Shoot. For now, our qualifying system will be skipping the largest shoot of the year and the single hardest test in benchrest anywhere.

Removing the requirement for the qualifiers to be a NBRSA registered tournament is what's needed. This would shift the power to decide the qualifiers from the range owner to the US Team Director who wants nothing more than to put together the strongest team possible to represent the United States, simple.

I hear many comments about the commitment of time and money required to make the qualifying tournaments. Let's dispel with this right away. Any shooter wanting to qualify will do whatever is required to attend the qualifiers. Think about the commitment you must have in order to pack up and travel to another country, for what is a minimum of two weeks of your life, the time commitment, paying many of your own expenses, obtaining rifle permits and passports, attend team meetings. If you cannot afford the gas or time to shoot some qualifying matches in your own country, you will not have what is required to be part of the team. It IS that simple. Several team members have quit high paying jobs to represent the United States on previous World Teams. The feeling of being a US World Team member and asked to represent the United States in a World Benchrest Championship is almost impossible for me to properly put into words. See you at the next qualifying tournament.

Preparations for the tournament

After qualifying ends, team members make preparations including building rifles, talking to the other members of the team to strengthen bonds and start the process of learning to work together in what's normally an individual sport. When planning to shoot abroad, you must have a passport and sometimes visas.

Team members acquire loading tools, make travel arrangements, plan for a formal awards banquet, order team uniforms, obtain rifle permits, arrange for powder, primers and solvent just to name a few. With the cost of the travel to another country and all of the trouble to get there, many shooters attending the World Championships abroad make arrangements for extended stays. Some shooters vacation in the area after the Championships. Others will make planned stops on their way home. It's common to spend 2-4 weeks or more after the championships. Just these few words should give you some insight about the commitment required.

I have some of the fondest memories associated with the World Benchrest Championships. I shared accommodations with Don Powell in Italy for two weeks; Powell being one of the "Boyer Bunch." It was like spending two weeks rooming with Tony Boyer. Many late nights were spent talking strategy and shooting stuff. It can't help but make you a better shooter, and he helped me. Thanks Don! When traveling, you spend endless hours talking about this thing called Benchrest. It certainly brings us together. What would a couple weeks be worth spent with some of the best shooters on the planet? I'll tell you, it's almost priceless. While attending these championships you have many opportunities to visit with the foreign shooters, of which I take particular enjoyment. The international shooters have the same passion but live in different parts of the world. This sport has truly transcended distance and cultures through the World Benchrest Championships. I hope to see you there. Once you've attended your first World Benchrest Championships you'll want to participate in another.

Dinner following the World Benchrest Championships in Sweden

I've included the match report from the 8th World Benchrest Championships in the next chapter to give you a sense of the camaraderie, teamwork, pressure and fun involved with the WBC. I hope you enjoy and feel like you're there, in the heat of competition.

1st World Benchest Championships

100/200 Meters in Frejus, France in October 1991

Representing the United States;

USA1	USA2	USA3
Tony Boyer	George Kelbly	Eunice Berger
Walt Berger	Brad Rosenthal	Don Nielson
Tim Cantwell	Lou Murdica	Stan Buchtel
Glenn Newick	Faye Boyer	Lou Palmisano

US Team Organizers Walt Berger & George Kelbly

2-Gun Team Medalists

Gold	*Silver*	*Bronze*
USA 2	USA 1	FRA 1
George Kelbly	Tony Boyer	Roger Serain
Brad Rosenthal	Walt Berger	Etienne Becker
Lou Murdica	Tim Cantwell	Carlos Pacheco
Faye Boyer	Glenn Newick	Herve Du Plessis

Individual Results

Light Varmint 100
Herve Du Plessis	FRA	.2289
Brad Rosenthal	USA	.2298
Barthelemy Cauvin	FRA	.2501
Tuomo Junttila	FIN	.2592
Albrecht Huf	GER	.2608

Small Group Scott Withey 2.71

Light Varmint 200
Roger Serain	FRA	.2614
Tony Boyer	USA	.2644
Faye Boyer	USA	.2683
Etienne Becker	FRA	.2687
Walt Berger	USA	.2711

Small Group Christian Balagna 6.85

Light Varmint Grand
Tony Boyer	USA	7.492
Walt Berger	USA	7.583
Brad Rosenthal	USA	7.697
Roger Serain	FRA	7.773
Etienne Becker	FRA	7.991
Faye Boyer	USA	8.159
Albrecht Huf	GER	8.200
Herve Du Plessis	FRA	8.353
Don Nielson	USA	8.376
Barthilimy Cauvin	FRA	8.493

Heavy Varmint 100
Jean-Pierre Troin	FRA	.2024
Carlos Pacheco	FRA	.2055
Martin Menke	GER	.2245
Tony Boyer	USA	.2258
Donald Anderson	SWE	.2372

Small Group Carlos Pacheco 2.59

Heavy Varmint 200
Faye Boyer	USA	.2512
Alan Peake	AUS	.2524
Jean-Pierre Troin	FRA	.2546
Carlos Pacheco	FRA	.2631
Stan Buchtel	USA	.2815

Heavy Varmint Grand
Jean-Pierre Troin	FRA	6.346
Carlos Pacheco	FRA	6.507
Alan Peake	AUS	6.800
Tony Boyer	USA	7.085
Bill Hallam	AUS	7.314
Werner Maggg	AUT	7.623
Peter Hammerich	GER	7.655
Faye Boyer	USA	7.725
Walter Burkhardt	GER	7.783
Martin Menke	GER	7.855

Two Gun
Tony Boyer	USA	.2625
Brad Rosenthal	USA	.2835
Faye Boyer	USA	.2860
Alan Peake	AUS	.2947
Jean-Pierre Troin	FRA	.2956
Peter Hammerich	GER	.2985
Roger Serain	FRA	.3092
Bill Hallam	AUS	.3128
Walt Berger	USA	.3129
Lou Murdica	USA	.3152
Christian Balgna	FRA	.3172
Herve Du Plessis	FRA	.3180
Herwing Falk	AUT	.3188
Martin Menke	GER	.3191
Carlos Pacheco	FRA	.3206
Barthelemy Cauvin	FRA	.3215
Don Nielson	USA	.3265
Robert Albrecht	GER	.3283
Tony Allison	AUS	.3297
Stan Buchtel	USA	.3306

Heavy Varmint 300
Brad Rosenthal	USA	.4054
Richard Rossel	GER	.4101
Paul Sulivan	AUS	.4253

Small Group Brad Rosenthal 14.58

Loading Tents

Wailing Wall - target display area.

Firing Line

2nd World Benchest Championships

100/200 Meters in Lohtaja, Finland in 1993

Representing the United States;

USA1	USA2	USA3
Faye Boyer	Skip Otto	Eunice Berger
Tony Boyer	George Kelbly	Manny Garcia
Don Powell	Glenn Newick	Gene Bukys
Walt Berger	Denny Andrews	Stan Buchtel

US Team Organizers Walt Berger & George Kelbly

2-Gun Team Medalists

Gold	*Silver*	*Bronze*
USA 1	USA 2	FRA 1
Faye Boyer	Skip Otto	Carlos Pacheco
Tony Boyer	George Kelby	Jean Claude Gros
Don Powell	Glenn Newick	Barthelemy Cauvin
Walt Berger	Denny Andrews	Jacky Gross

Individual Results

Light Varmint 100m
George Kelbly	USA	6.786
Enrico Arenzi	ITA	7.978
Denny Andrews	USA	8.018
Tony Boyer	USA	8.202
Bror Erikson		8.290

Small Group unknown

Light Varmint 200m
Eunice Berger	USA	8.392
Faye Boyer	USA	8.644
Donald Powell	USA	8.765
Tuomo Nissila	FIN	8.807
Paul Sullivan	AUS	8.812

Small Group Eunice Berger 7.500

Light Varmint Grand
Faye Boyer	USA	8.641
Tony Boyer	USA	9.000
Denny Andrews	USA	9.092
Rob Carnell	AUS	9.114
Paul Sullivan	AUS	9.220
Enrico Arenzi	ITA	9.287
Bror Erikson	FIN	9.410
Torsten Astrom	SWE	9.422
Antonio Negri	ITA	9.682
George Kelbly	USA	9.848

Heavy Varmint 100m
George Kelbly	USA	6.354
Glenn Newick	USA	7.530
Rune Fagerstrom	FIN	7.616
Don Powell	USA	7.800
Roger Serain	FRA	8.412

Small Group unknown

Heavy Varmint 200m
Walt Berger	USA	8.584
Carlos Pacheco	FRA	9.797
Ekehard Widman	AUT	10.840
Denny Andrews	USA	10.947
Glenn Newick	USA	11.033

Small Group Rolf Probst 8.380

Heavy Varmint Grand
Walt Berger	USA	9.254
Glenn Newick	USA	9.281
Carlos Pacheco	FRA	9.396
George Kelbly	USA	9.578
Denny Andrews	USA	10.250
Ekehard Widman	AUT	10.577
Don Powell	USA	10.608
Timo Juntunen	FIN	10.901
Herbert Mayer	AUT	11.010
Ralph Fisher	GER	11.119

Two Gun
Denny Andrews	USA	9.671
George Kelbly	USA	9.713
Carlos Pacheco	FRA	9.826
Tony Boyer	USA	10.096
Walt Berger	USA	10.185
Glenn Newick	USA	10.232
Enrico Arenzi	ITA	10.292
Don Powell	USA	10.662
Faye Boyer	USA	10.721
Ralph Fisher	GER	10.999
Ekehard Widman	AUT	11.054
Herve Du Plessis	FRA	11.219
Torsten Astrom	SWE	11.230
Matti Metsavaara	FIN	11.262
Paul Sullivan	AUS	11.300
Alan Peake	AUS	11.301
Timo Juntunen	FIN	11.348
Roger Serain	FRA	11.557
Rob Carnel	AUS	11.605
Bror Erikson	FIN	11.672

Stan Buchtel

Eunice Berger

Skip Otto

Dr. Manny Garcia

Walt Berger

3rd World Benchest Championships

100/200 yards in Brisbane, Australia in 1995

Representing the United States;

USA1	USA2	USA3
Faye Boyer	Dennis Thornbury	Tim Oltersdorf
Don Powell	Chuck Miller	Walt Berger
Lowell Frei	Gene Bukys	Glenn Newick
Tony Boyer	Dennis Wagner	Don Nielson

US Team Organizers Walt Berger & George Kelbly

2-Gun Team Medalists

Gold	Silver	Bronze
USA 1	USA 3	USA 2
Faye Boyer	Tim Oltersdorf	Dennis Thornbury
Don Powell	Walt Berger	Chuck Miller
Lowell Frei	Glenn Newick	Gene Bukys
Tony Boyer	Don Nielson	Dennis Wagner

Individual Results

Light Varmint 100
Tony Boyer	USA	.2638
Glenn Newick	USA	.2710
Alan Leake	AUS	.2780
Carlos Pacheco	FRA	.2810
Faye Boyer	USA	.2870

Small Group   Dennis Thornbury .145

Light Varmint 200
Don Nielson	USA	.2936
Glenn Newick	USA	.3432
Jean Louis Expinet	FRA	.3570
Brendan Atkinson	AUS	.3625
Tim Oltersdorf	USA	.3646

Small Group Stefan Karlsson .335

Light Varmint Grand
Glenn Newick	USA	7.492
Don Nielson	USA	7.583
Tony Boyer	USA	7.697
Brendan Atkinson	AUS	7.773
Tim Oltersdorf	USA	7.991
Jean Louis Espinet	FRA	8.159
Dennis thornbury	USA	8.200
Don Powell	USA	8.353
Dennis Wagner	USA	8.376
Stefan Karlsson	SWE	8.493

Heavy Varmint 100
Alan Peake	AUS	.2082
Tony Boyer	USA	.2468
Gene Bukys	USA	.2474
Stefan Karlsson	SWE	.2534
Tony Titheridge	NZ	.2654

Small Group Alan Peake .106

Heavy Varmint 200
Markku Ahlava	FIN	.4752
Ari Lopponen	FIN	.4951
Dennis Wagner	USA	.5296
Bo Peterson	SWE	.5425
Ralf Fischer	GER	.5662

Small Group Dennis Wagner .456

Heavy Varmint Grand
Markku Ahlava	FIN	.3930
Dennis Wagner	USA	.4148
Bo Peterson	SWE	.4190
Ari Lopponen	FIN	.4383
Tony Boyer	USA	.4427
John Dark	AUS	.4464
Gene Bukys	USA	.4524
Michel Dhalmann	FRA	.4631
Ralf Fischer	GER	.4681
Glenn Newick	USA	.4736

Two Gun
Tony Boyer	USA	.3789
Dennis Wagner	USA	.3830
Markku Ahlava	FIN	.3866
Glenn Newick	USA	.3904
Jean Louis Espinet	FRA	.4040
Brendan Atkinson	AUS	.4148
Gene Bukys	USA	.4169
Bo Peterson	SWE	.4290
Don Nielson	USA	.4309
Tuomo Junttila	FIN	.4371

Heavy Varmint 300
Stuart Elliott	AUS	.5807
Gene Bukys	USA	.6012
Antti Pallaspuro	FIN	.6367

Small Group Stefan Karlsson .893

Firing Line

Stuart & Annie Elliott

Australian Team

Club House

4th World Benchest Championships

100/200 yards in Phoenix, Arizona, USA in October 22-26, 1997

Representing the United States;

USA1	USA2	USA3
Faye Boyer	Ron Heohn	Glenn Newick
Gary Ocock	Tony Boyer	Jerry Hensler
Rex Reneau	Lester Bruno	Eunice Berger
Don Powell	Don Creach	Chet Whitebread

US Team Director - Walt Berger

2-Gun Team Medalists

Gold	Silver	Bronze
USA 2 .3075	USA 1 .3164	USA 3 .3722
Ron Heohn	Faye Boyer	Glenn Newick
Tony Boyer	Gary Ocock	Jerry Hensler
Lester Bruno	Rex Reneau	Eunice Berger
Don Creach	Don Powell	Chet Whitebread

Individual Results

Light Varmint 100

Eunice Berger	USA	.2142
Gary Ocock	USA	.2154
Manny Garcia	USA	.2222
Ron Hoehn	USA	.2364
Tony Boyer	USA	.2392

Small Group G. Turini .065

Light Varmint 200

Tony Boyer	USA	.3298
Ralph Garlich		.3379
Gary Ocock	USA	.3557
Ron Hoehn	USA	.3596
Tony Allison	AUS	.3668

Small Group T. Boyer .251

Light Varmint Grand

Tony Boyer	USA	.2845
Gary Ocock	USA	.2854
Ron Hoehn	USA	.2980
Jerry Hensler	USA	.3056
Rex Reneau	USA	.3097
Gary Hunt		.3211
Ralph Garlich		.3251
Don Powell	USA	.3255
Heikki Niemeka	FIN	.3312
Don Creach	USA	.3336

Heavy Varmint 100

Ron Hoehn	USA	.2088
Enrico Arenzi	ITA	.2180
Tony Boyer	USA	.2206
Rex Reneau	USA	.2314
Jerry Hensler	USA	.2330

Small Group Bo Peterson .098

Heavy Varmint 200

Don Powell	USA	.2647
Ron Hoehn	USA	.2920
Lester Bruno	USA	.3226
Don Creach	USA	.3287
Rex Reneau	USA	.3300

Small Group Bo Peterson .218

Heavy Varmint Grand

Ron Hoehn	USA	.2504
Rex Reneau	USA	.2807
Don Powell	USA	.2822
Tony Boyer	USA	.2836
Gary Ocock	USA	.2934
Lester Bruno	USA	.2950
Bill Gammon	CAN	.2995
Bill Hallam	AUS	.3009
Enrico Arenzi	ITA	.3029
Alan Peake	AUS	.3114

Two Gun

Ron Hoehn	USA	.2742
Tony Boyer	USA	.2841
Gary Ocock	USA	.2895
Rex Reneau	USA	.2952
Don Powell	USA	.3039
Enrico Arenzi	ITA	.3231
Jerry Hensler	USA	.3232
Don Creach	USA	.3265
Roger Serain	FRA	.3399
Jean-Louis Espinet	FRA	.3414
Lester Bruno	USA	.3453
Carlos Pacheco	FRA	.3485
Tony Allison	AUS	.3515
Hekki Niemela	FIN	.3520
Harry Mcdonald	AUS	.3553
Bo Peterson	SWE	.3624
Torsten Astrom	SWE	.3626
Bill Hallam	AUS	.3646
Nicole Pacheco	FRA	.3686
Glenn Newick	USA	.3689

Heavy Varmint 300

Enrico Arenzi	ITA	.2767
Jean-Marie Deletang	FRA	.3191
Tosten Astrom	SWE	.3227

Small Group Enrico Arenzi .482

Eunice Berger. Phoenix. AZ.

Phoenix 1997

5th World Benchest Championships

100/200 meters in Dobbicco, Italy September22-26, 1999

Representing the United States;

USA1	USA2	USA3
Tony Boyer	Skip Otto	Don Nielson
Faye Boyer	Bob White	Tim Oltersdorf
Ron Hoehn	Mike Ratigan	Manny Garcia
Don Powell	Glenn Newick	Paul Landell

US Team Director - Jim Kelbly

2-Gun Team Medalists

Gold	*Silver*	*Bronze*
USA 2 .2552	FRA 1 .2588	USA 1 .2612
Skip Otto	Paul Jung	Tony Boyer
Bob White	Philippe Octo	Faye Boyer
Mike Ratigan	Jean-Pierre Troin	Ron Hoehn
Glenn Newick	Carlos Pacheco	Don Powell

Individual Results

Light Varmint 100

Martin Menke	GER	.1632
Friedrich Gogg	AUT	.1755
Bo Peterson	FRA	.1925
Enrico Arenzi	ITA	.1981
Mike Ratigan	USA	.2000

Small Group   Paul Jung 2.02

Light Varmint 200

Mike Ratigan	USA	.2180
Stefan Schlichter	AUT	.2398
Chris Bosley	UK	.2450
Tony Boyer	USA	.2520
Phillpe Octo	FRA	.2563

Small Group   Kevin Duckworth 7.18

Light Varmint Grand

Mike Ratigan	USA	.2090
Friedrich Gogg	AUT	.2326
Tony Boyer	USA	.2355
Bob White	USA	.2362
Enrico Arenzi	ITA	.2403
Graham Southall	UK	.2448
Bo Leyon	SWE	.2483
Faye Boyer	USA	.2500
Phillippe Octo	FRA	.2525
Paul Jung	FRA	.2540

Heavy Varmint 100

Andrea Atzl	AUT	.1860
Paul Jung	FRA	.1860
Martin Menke	GER	.1861
Jean-Pierre Troin	FRA	.1963
Andrea Barbanti	ITA	.1997

Small Group   Joachim Schafer 1.35

Heavy Varmint 200

Paul Jung	FRA	.2161
Niko Katsikopoulos	GR	.2211
Faye Boyer	USA	.2240
Keijo Pulliainen	FIN	.2308
Carlos PAcheco	FRA	.2322

Small Group   Giuliano Turini 4.66

Heavy Varmint Grand

Paul Jung	FRA	.2193
Faye Boyer	USA	.2277
Enrico Arenzi	ITA	.2313
Markku Ahlava	FIN	.2344
Bob White	USA	.2353
Martin Menke	GER	.2357
Andreas Atzl	AUT	.2366
Risto Murisoja	FIN	.2379
Annie Elliott	AUS	.2382
Hubert Poussiere	FRA	.2438

Two Gun

Mike Ratigan	USA	.2317
Bob White	USA	.2357
Enrico Arenzi	ITA	.2358
Paul Jung	FRA	.2366
Faye Boyer	USA	.2389
Tony Boyer	USA	.2450
Andreas Atzl	AUT	.2472
Martin Menke	GER	.2474
Phillippe Octo	FRA	.2521
Hubert Poussiere	FRA	.2529
Annie Elliott	AUS	.2536
Barthelemy Cauvin	FRA	.2579
Friedrich Gogg	AUT	.2581
Carlos Pacheco	FRA	.2596
Markku Ahlava	FIN	.2611
Skip Otto	USA	.2703
Niko Katsikopoulos	GR	.2708
Joachim Schefer	GER	.2712
Bo Leyon	SWE	.2747
Donald Anderson	SWE	.2776

Heavy Varmint 10-200

Karl Dieter Kochendorfer	GER	.2924
Glenn Newick	USA	.3085
Bo Leyon	SWE	.3205

Small Group   Glenn Newick 10.47

From the Left, Mike Ratigan, Don Nielson, Glenn Newick, Manny Garcia, Paul Landell, Tony & Faye Boyer, Don Powell, Tim Oltersdorf, Skip Otto, Ron Hoehn and Bob White.

Medals

Awards Ceremony

Firing Line at Dobbiacco Italy

Dinner at Santer Hotel, seven cousre meals.

6th World Benchest Championships

100/200 yards in Nelson, New Zealand October, 2001

Representing the United States;

USA1	USA2	USA3
Wayne Cambell	Bob White	Charles Huckeba
Tony Boyer	Allen Arnette	Lowell Frei
Armond Pagliai	Gene Bukys	Glenn Newick
Lowell Hottenstein	Faye Boyer	Larry Scharnhorst

US Team Director - Don Powell

2-Gun Team Medalists

Gold	Silver	Bronze
USA 1	USA 3	USA 2
Wayne Cambell	Charles Huckeba	Bob White
Tony Boyer	Lowell Frei	Allen Arnette
Armond Pagliai	Glenn Newick	Gene Bukys
Lowell Hottenstein	Larry Scharnhorst	Faye Boyer

Individual Results

Light Varmint 100

Brendan Aktinson	AUS	.1588
Bob White	USA	.1846
Paul Jung	FRA	.1964
Lowell Hottenstein	USA	.2102
Allen Arnette	USA	.2278

Small Group   Alan Peake .091

Light Varmint 200

Tony Boyer	USA	.2188
Lowell Frei	USA	.2647
Charles Huckeba	USA	.2781
Wayne Campbell	USA	.2788
Brendan Atkinson	AUS	.2826

Small Group   Tony Boyer .214

Light Varmint Grand

Brendan Atkinson	AUS	.2207
Tony Boyer	USA	.2487
Wayne Campbell	USA	.2527
Bob White	USA	.2574
Paul Jung	FRA	.2666
Lowell Hottenstein	USA	.2784
Allen Arnette	USA	.2785
Gene Bukys	USA	.2897
Lowell Frei	USA	.2902
Larry Scharnhorst	USA	.2935

Heavy Varmint 100

Charles Huckeba	USA	.1870
John Wyatt	AUS	.2054
Gene Bukys	USA	.2250
Michael Peacock	NZ	.2250
Armond Pagliai	USA	.2278

Small Group   Charles Huckeba .107

Heavy Varmint 200

Lowell Frei	USA	.2791
Charles Huckeba	USA	.2909
Glenn Newick	USA	.3028
Armond Pagliai	USA	.3111
Paul Jung	FRA	.3360

Small Group Faye Boyer .279

Heavy Varmint Grand

Charles Huckeba	USA	.2390
Armond Pagliai	USA	.2695
John Wyatt	AUS	.2871
Lowell Frei	USA	.2873
Wayne Campbell	USA	.3005
Torsten Satrom	SWE	.3048
Faye Boyer	USA	.3057
Glenn Newick	USA	.3101
Paul Sulivan	AUS	.3115
Roger Serain	FRA	.3119

Two Gun

Brendan Atkinson	AUS	.2625
Wayne Campbell	USA	.2835
Charles Huckeba	USA	.2860
Tony Boyer	USA	.2947
Bob White	USA	.2956
Lowell Frei	USA	.2985
Paul Jung	FRA	.3092
John Wyatt	AUS	.3128
Armond Pagliai	USA	.3129
Allen Arnette	USA	.3152
Lowell Hottenstein	USA	.3172
Gene Bukys	USA	.3180
Roger Serain	FRA	.3188
Glenn Newick	USA	.3191
Faye Boyer	USA	.3206
Torsten Astrom	SWE	.3215
Larry Scharnhorst	USA	.3265
Paul Sullivan	AUS	.3283
Phil Jones	AUS	.3297
Ray Edwards	AUS	.3306

Heavy Varmint 10-200

Paul Jung	FRA	.3597
Gene Bukys	USA	.3701
Stuart Elliott	AUS	.3714

Small Group Paul Jung .430

Back Row, Allen Arnette, Gene Bukys and Armond Pagliai.
Middle, Don Powell, Glenn Newick, Lowell Hottenstein, Wayne Campbell and Charles Huckeba.
Front Row Bob White, Lowell Freim, Larry Scharnhorst, Faye Boyer and Tony Boyer.

Loading Tent

Paul Jung

Equipment
Inspection

7th World Benchest Championships

100/200 yards in Umea, Sweden July, 2003

Representing the United States;

USA1	USA2	USA3
Tony Boyer	Skip Otto	Faye Boyer
Wayne Campbell	Lowell Hottenstein	Darrel Loker
Ken Terrell	Gene Bukys	Bill Goad
Charles Huckeba	Mike Ratigan	Don Powell

US Team Director - Don Powell
Assistant Team Director - George Kelbly

2-Gun Team Medalists

Gold	Silver	Bronze
USA 1	AUS 1	USA 2
Tony Boyer	Annie Elliott	Skip Otto
Wayne Campbell	Stuart Elliott	Lowell Hottenstein
Ken Terrell	Ray Edwards	Gene Bukys
Charles Huckeba	Steve Brown	Mike Ratigan

Individual Results

Light Varmint 100

Sune Abrahamsson	FIN	6.49
Janne Juntunen	FIN	6.59
Gene Bukys	USA	6.59
Ken Terrell	USA	6.74
Annie Elliott	AUS	6.74

Small Group Janne Juntunen 3.05

Light Varmint 200

Darrel Loker	USA	14.10
Charles Huckeba	USA	15.72
Michael Heubner	AUS	16.62
Wayne Campbell	USA	17.06
Lowell Hottenstein	USA	17.14

Small Group Darrel Loker 7.36

Light Varmint Grand

Sune Abrahamsson	FIN	7.60
Charles Huckeba	USA	7.60
Janne Juntunen	FIN	7.70
Annie Elliott	AUS	7.84
Stuart Elliott	AUS	8.19
Darrel Loker	USA	8.20
Lowell Hottenstein	USA	8.22
Gene Bukys	USA	8.83
Wayne Cmapbell	USA	8.85
Tony Boyer	USA	9.01

Heavy Varmint 100

Darrel Loker	USA	4.63
Tony Boyer	USA	5.03
Jari Ollila	FIN	5.53
Bill Goad	USA	5.58
Bo Leijon	SWE	5.61

Small Group Tony Boyer 2.17

Heavy Varmint 200

Wayne Campbell	USA	12.56
Veikko Valioja	FIN	14.41
Stuart Elliott	AUS	14.71
Alfredo Alvarez	SPA	16.11
Seppo Desanen	FIN	16.26

Small Group Stuart Elliot 5.29

Heavy Varmint Grand

Wayne Campbell	USA	6.62
Seppo Kesanen	FIN	7.21
Stuart Elliott	AUS	7.30
Ian Dixon	UK	7.43
Gene Bukys	USA	7.54
Jean-Claude Gros	FRA	7.61
Annie Elliott	AUS	7.63
Jari Ollila	FIN	7.66
Bo Leijon	SWE	7.69
Mauri Mukari	FIN	7.70

Two Gun

Wayne Campbell	USA	7.74
Annie Elliott	AUS	7.74
Stuart Elliott	AUS	7.75
Charles Huckeba	USA	7.89
Sune Abrahamsson	FIN	8.10
Lowell Hottenstein	USA	8.16
Gene Bukys	USA	8.19
Darrel Loker	USA	8.29
Seppo Kesanen	FIN	8.37
Tony Boyer	USA	8.42
Mike Ratigan	USA	8.63
Janne Juntunen	FIN	8.70
Veikko Valioja	FIN	8.75
Ken Terrell	USA	8.95
Michael Heubner	AUS	8.96
Ian Dixon	UK	9.04
Herve Du Plessis	FRA	9.11
Faye Boyer	USA	9.19
Don Powell	USA	9.20
Steve Brown	AUS	9.21

Heavy Varmint 10-200

Wayne Campbell	USA	19.47
Jean-Louis Espinet	FRA	22.07
Annie Elliott	AUS	22.77

Small Group Wayne Campbell 13.75

Back Row, Doc Terrell, Don Powell. Middel from left, Lowell Hottenstein, Skip Otto, Charles Huckeba, Wayne Campbell, Mike Ratigan, Darrel Loker. Front from left, George Kelbly Sr., Tony Boyer, Faye Boyer, Bill Goad and Gene Bukys.

Opening Ceremony

Firing Line, Umea, Sweden.

8th World Benchest Championships

100/200 yards in North Lawrence Ohio, USA September, 2005

Representing the United States;

USA1	USA2	USA3
Mike Ratigan	Ed Adams	Billy Steven
Dwight Scott	Cecil Tucker	Jack Neary
Rex Reneau	Bill Goad	Larry Scharnhorst
Dale Boop	Lester Bruno	Allie Euber

US Team Director - Don Powell
US Tournament Operations - George Kelbly, Jim Kelbly, Hobie Bond

2-Gun Team Medalists

Gold	*Silver*	*Bronze*
USA 3 .2649	USA 2 .2794	USA 1 .2860
Billy Steven	Ed Adams	Mike Ratigan
Jack Neary	Cecil Tucker	Dwight Scott
Larry Scharnhorst	Bill Goad	Rex Reneau
Allie Euber	Lester Bruno	Dale Boop

Individual Results

Light Varmint 100
Charles Decanini	FRA	.1892
Paul Jung	FRA	.1982
Jean Louis Espinet	FRA	.2074
Lester Bruno	USA	.2090
Larry Scharnhorst	USA	.2112

Small Group   Chris Vanzijl .077

Light Varmint 200
Paul Jung	FRA	.2277
Billy Stevens	USA	.2278
Lester Bruno	USA	.2317
Bill Gammon	CAN	.2318
Bill Goad	USA	.2431

Small Group   Ivaldo Gabasio .184

Light Varmint Grand
Paul Jung	FRA	.2129
Lester Bruno	USA	.2253
Charles Decanini	USA	.2373
Jari Raudaskoski	FIN	.2394
Larry Scharnhorst	USA	.2442
Bill Goad	USA	.2443
Billy Stevens	USA	.2485
Vlad Lobaev	RUS	.2525
Allie Euber	USA	.2525
Dave Holmes	CAN	.2542

Heavy Varmint 100
Steve Williams	SAF	.2150
Jack Neary	USA	.2168
Billy Stevens	USA	.2210
Bill Goad	USA	.2230
Herve Du Plessis	FRA	.2298

Small Group   David Holmes .080

Heavy Varmint 200
Rex Reneau	USA	.2218
Jyrki Vuorjoki	FIN	.2247
Mike Ratigan	USA	.2354
Dave Holmes	CAN	.2418
Jari Raudaskoski	FIN	.2521

Small Group   Jyrki Vuorjoki .209

Heavy Varmint Grand
Jack Neary	USA	.2434
Andrey Komkov	RUS	.2467
Jyrki Vuojoki	FIN	.2482
Jari Raudaskoski	FIN	.2567
Jean Louis Espinet	FRA	.2597
Mike Ratigan	USA	.2622
Dwight Scott	USA	.2625
Bill Goad	USA	.2647
Ed Adams	USA	.2665
Steve Williams	SAF	.2665

Two Gun
Jari Raudaskoski	FIN	.2480
Bill Goad	USA	.2545
Billy Stevens	USA	.2588
Larry Scharnhorst	USA	.2599
Mike Ratigan	USA	.2603
Jean Louis Espinet	FRA	.2610
Ed Adams	USA	.2618
Lester Bruno	USA	.2620
Allie Euber	USA	.2654
Charles Decanini	FRA	.2668
Jyrki Vuorjoki	FIN	.2678
Robert Persson	SWE	.2706
Jack Neary	USA	.2708
Vlad Lobaev	RUS	.2718
Bill Gammon	CAN	.2788
Steve Williams	SAF	.2837
Dale Boop	USA	.2854
Dwight Scott	USA	.2871
Vince Bottomly	UK	.2903
Paul Sullivan	AUS	.2922

Heavy Varmint 10-200
Larry Scharnhorst	USA	.2987
Alberto Lenzi	ITA	.3075
Steve Brown	AUS	.3076

Small Group   Bill Gammon .371

Back Row, from left. Billy Stevens, Bill Goad, Rex Reneau, Ed Adams, Cecil Tucker, Don Powell.
Front, Dale Boop, Mike Ratigan, Larry Scharnhorst, Lester Bruno, Allie Euber, Jack Neary, Ken Hottenstein, Dwight Scott.

Rex Reneau & Mike Ratigan

Bengt Nilsson, Sweden

Ed Adams

Jack Neary, Jacques Badenhorst, Phil Sammons

World Benchrest Championships VIII

Every two years the best Benchrest shooters from around the world gather for the World Benchrest Championships. Don Powell, the US Delegate to the World Benchrest Shooting Federation, successfully bid for the 2005 World Championships for the USA while in New Zealand in 2001. The Eighth World Benchrest Championships were held in the United States at Kelbly's Range September 11 thru 17, 2005.

Hosting the World Championships is a monumental undertaking requiring years of planning and sweat, 50 times that of a weekend match. Preparations include qualifying to pick our team, wardrobe, fund raisers and helping with our teams issues. Our host provides information for international teams though contact with international team delegates. Teams need help with travel arrangements, area maps, car rental information, currency exchange rates, hotel recommendations, invitations in order to obtain rifle permits, help dealing with US Dept of the Treasury for rifle import permits, and help with Visas for countries required to have them to visit.

Our host makes arrangements for a formal awards banquet, they fly flags for each country that participates, and we provide a place to receive equipment shipped in advance, plan to provide powder, primers, solvent, and many more things which are not part of normal match planning. I hope this helps explain how monumental an undertaking this is. Don drafted George Kelbly, family and staff, along with slave Hobie Bond who spent countless hours to help with the list of details in preparation.

Qualifying for the United States World Benchrest Team is among the toughest things to accomplish in Benchrest. Making a World Team and representing the United States is an honor almost impossible to put into words. Our qualifying takes place the year preceding the Championships, we earn points at each of three qualifying matches in 2004, Cactus, Super Shoot and NBRSA Nationals. The highest twelve point's earners were offered a coveted spot on the United States World Benchrest Team. Ed Watson was the only qualifier unable to make the tournament due to health issues. The World Benchrest Championships is a four person team event, held every other year. Each participating country can field three teams of four. We had 145 shooters from twenty countries answer the call for the commencement of the 8th World Championships. This World Championships had the largest participation ever, since the first Championship held in France in 1991.

Ed Adams and I arrived Monday, September 4, to find the grounds in immaculate condition, buildings painted, beautiful flowers, new lights in the loading barn, flags from every participating country hanging from the ceiling, and attention to every detail. After a lengthy search for the USA loading area we ran into the groundskeeper who took a break from mowing behind George's house, it was George Kelbly Sr. After our initial greeting we received a speech from our host about how we should have had no trouble finding our loading area, since we were loading underneath our flag. I felt compelled to explain to George how we are Benchrest shooters and as such could never make the connection of the flags flying over our respective loading area and felt no competitor would make the connection. I am still waiting for George to pay our wager.

Jack Neary provided early entertainment by parking 50 yards away from the loading area and walking back and forth between his vehicle and the loading barn with stuff...... LOTS of stuff. I suggested early on he move his vehicle to the doorway to unload since it was just the three of us. After thirty minutes I felt sorry for Jack. I moved his vehicle in front of the door of the loading barn.......I am sure glad I did.

An hour later I returned to the loading area to find Ed Adams standing in the aisle laughing almost uncontrollably. I asked "Ed what's the matter?" He could not speak. Ed extended his arm and pointed toward Jack's vehicle. I turned in the direction of Ed's outstretched arm to see Jack's feet sticking out of the drivers side rear door not touching the ground, Jack was laying in the truck. Looking inside the back of Jack's vehicle, there was a mountain of MTM cartridge boxes. Jack was sorting, looking, rummaging, and throwing cartridge boxes into the air looking for one in particular. I explained to Ed this is how Jack operates. Ed is now in therapy.....you see, Ed thought he had the most stuff when arriving with six rifles.

Chapter 26: 8th World Benchrest Championships

Each new World Championship brings new United States shooters without previous World Championship experience. Repeat members explain feelings of putting on your uniform, but words don't go far enough. When you dress in the uniform the first time and walk onto the range, you realize others are dependent on your performance and your help, and as if this were not enough pressure, United States Shooters are under the microscope and everything we do is being watched. For some, this atmosphere requires a whole new attitude to make sure you don't do or say something inappropriate. Just try sitting down on your shootin stool knowing 12 other USA World Team members are watching your performance, now that's pressure.

Saturday preceding the first official practice day brings the arrival of all international competitors. The atmosphere turns more serious; with unpacking gear, finding powder, primers, solvent, filling sand bags, and catching up will old friends.

On lookers while your author shoots – No Pressure!

Benchrest shooters living outside of the USA express how coming to the WBC in the United States, the Home of Benchrest, is like visiting Benchrest heaven, and this week provided a special treat by having many legends of Benchrest in attendance during the WBC................. "it's like Benchrest Mecca" as quoted from a couple of foreign shooters.

George and Don tell of times where the atmosphere at local matches was one of friends and fellowship unlike so many small matches today where many competitors don't take time to get to know each other. Part of the spirit of World Benchrest is to bridge distance and cultures and spend time with people from around the world with the same passion. Anyone involved will tell the uninformed we do not take part for financial gain; these Championships are for the love of the sport on a world stage.

Official practice started Sunday Sept 11th. Smiley flags with white tails covered the range which was an awe inspiring sight. If only all of the US shooters could have seen how consistent things looked across the range. You could see a condition coming, going, and any whirl wind.........what a sight. How nice it would be to have this type of flag setup at our nationals, oh I forgot, we know not how to cooperate.

Practice Day 1 was used by foreign shooters testing rifles with unfamiliar powder and primers. I spent the day helping any way I could, from tuning, flag reading, and strategy. The evening of practice day 1 brought team meetings following the day's activity. We talk about every aspect of this Championship from equipment, flags, powder, conditions, strategy; everything.

All United States competitors were willing to help the foreign competitors, answer questions concerning any part of Benchrest. Lets face it we love this sport, it certainly doesn't pay.

Official Practice day 2 with temp's in the high 80's and 5-10 mph winds gave an opportunity to try equipment in conditions and enough time to fix equipment problems.

The World Benchrest Championships are a team event. USA teams have not always acted the part, this time would be different. I scheduled our first Official US team event early in day two. With our past team history, Don and I planned to get things started off right and early. We asked every US World Team shooter for 10 minutes of their time in the morning, and all agreed. I organized a small event to help identify any non-team players and correct any misconceptions before the event starts, instead of half way into the tournament. Visiting teams were given time to prepare for a photo opportunity. At 10:00am sharp, the US team members performed their first Official Team Event.......the target change.

Chapter 26: 8th World Benchrest Championships

The US Team following "The Target Change"

The US competitors changed practice targets without one complaint about the process, what a treat indeed! After changing targets Lester Bruno commented about one competitor's practice targets saying, "Look here, we won't have to worry about this competitor," Cecil Tucker was quick to respond with "Yes, you do.......those are my groups," The whole US team broke into laughter. The United States competitors changed targets the rest of the day for everyone. This type of teamwork lasted all week. From Lester helping solve a bag problem of Jack's, Dwight shooting one of Bart's rifles, Rex shooting one of mine, Jack eventually shot a rifle of Allie's which led to a grand aggregate win. Every US World Team member acted together with a singular goal, to win every team medal. What a pleasure to be a part of all this.

Towards the end of the day's practice session was the technical meeting. Every country participates and all questions are addressed. Also late in the practice day we had the rifle check in. Competitors are required to have all rifles checked to make sure they fit within the rules; checked for weight and stock forend width. Several were over weight and width. Each rifle is required to have an equipment inspection sticker while on the firing line. Thanks to all who helped with the tech inspection; Walt Berger, Hobie Bond, Stan Buchtel, Charlie Dalesandro, Terry Donaldson, Don Gentner, John Inman, Perry Morton, and Paul Schmid.

After closing the range at 6:00pm on our second practice day we had a chicken dinner courtesy of Lester Bruno of Bruno's Shooters Supply. Thanks again Lester, we enjoyed the food and fellowship. Following dinner we had our last team meeting before the start of the tournament. We discussed the next day's event and about everything needed come the following morning. Team duties include looking & acting like a team, a 12 man team, working together with flags, equipment, watch through the spotting scopes when not shooting or loading, attend all functions and meetings, share loading information, share info on which conditions to shoot, help with team equipment evaluation, be a gracious host and help international competitors, and many other things too lengthy to mention. We would meet every night after the competition to discuss the day's event and address any troubles we had during the day.

Herve du Plessis, George Kelbly, Skip Gordan

Competition Day 1 brought opening ceremonies with introduction of the Shooters who conceived the idea of the World Championships. Of those, Walt Berger and Carlos Pacheco are not pictured. Jim Kelbly gave the famous call of shooters to the start of our event, "relay 1 to the line".

"Relay 1 to the Line!"

We started with Light Varmint 100 yard warm-up and format like the Super Shoot; four relays, Nationals bench rotation, six targets a day. Conditions on day one were hot with light wind and a bit of mirage. Charles Decanini from France captured the individual honors for the day with a nice agg of .1892. As a matter of fact, the top three shooters today are all from France; Paul Jung was second with a nice. 1982 and Jean-Louis Espinet, also known as "The Pig Man," finished third in the yardage. Chris Vanzijl from South Africa was the only competitor to shoot a zero, Chris's .077 would hold up for small group.

Team standings after the LV 100 yard stage of shooting are as follows. Twelve teams had aggregates in the twos on day one.

LV 100 Yard Team Standing

1. USA B   .2316
2. USA C   .2456
3. Canada C   .2658
4. AUS B   .2691
5. SAF A   .2772

Competition Day 2 brought Heavy Varmint 100 yards. David Holmes from Canada started with a very nice .080 which would hold up for small group of the day.

Steve Williams from South Africa started with a low three, then shot very well to better the field with a nice agg of .2150 and the yardage win. Steve was overcome with excitement after his performance; he wore a smile from ear to ear for the rest of the afternoon, congratulations Steve!

After the Heavy Varmint 100, the two US teams leading from yesterday changed places, USA C leading the way through the Heavy 100 with a very nice team agg. Seven teams had aggregates in the twos.

HV 100 Yard Team Standing

1. USA C   .2323
2. USA B   .2456
3. FRA B   .2713
4. NZL A   .2827
5. USA A   .2852

Running totals after two days of shooting were unbelievable. USA team C and B were almost tied with running totals that represent 8 aggs with an average of .23. This is a pretty good average for any four man team any time. Two USA teams were on course to better the previous world team 2 gun record, but as everyone knows, there is still much shooting to be done before this could be realized.

Team Standings after Day 2
1.	USA C	.2386
2.	USA B	.2389
3.	FRA B	.2789
4.	USA A	.2827
5.	NZL A	.2915

Jim and Cheryl Kelbly welcomed shooters to their home Wednesday for a barbeque cookout sponsored by Sinclair International, and we were treated to a band which was sponsored by Kathi at Cyro Plus. Again the food and fellowship were wonderful. Cheryl Kelbly will have to trust me, by the time Cheryl made it to the line she found all the meat had been eaten. Jim Kelbly wanted to convey how much of an honor it was to have everyone at their home.

Our Hosts Jim & Cheryl Kelbly

Jack Neary is Co-dependent and needs someone to watch him constantly when not on his medication. Ed Adams was to watch him during the barbeque. During dinner with Ed and I, Jack indicated a desire to dance with Ken Hottenstein and as any sane person would do, Ed and I advised against. Jack found his way to Ken and asked for a dance. About midway through the dance Jack dropped Kenny while performing a twirling and broke the rebar reinforced concrete pavilion in Jim's back yard. Yes sports fans, Jack had Kenny on his shoulders.

Jack & Kenny in "The Dance"

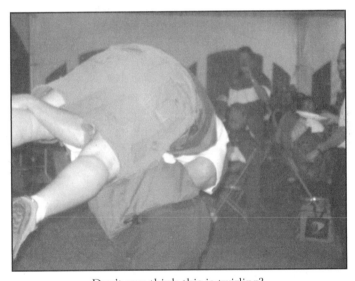

Don't you think this is twirling?

I believe twirling is the correct term. Jack insisted he tripped over a pebble in the pavilion concrete......so there is some issue over fault. Litigation Kelbly's vs. Neary - Hottenstein has yet to be resolved. No competitor was fatally injured as a result of the incident, most everyone found this to be a life changing event.

We wished Annie Elliott from Australia a Happy 29th birthday for the 21st time. For Benchrest shooters that's .290 + .210 = .50 in the add up. Happy Birthday! Ask Annie about her birthday gifts. I would tell you but I'm afraid young children might be reading this.......or I just can't remember, you decide. Thanks for the drink from your cup.

Competition Day 3 brought LV 200 yards with morning fog, slightly cooler conditions with almost no wind. Fog delayed starting relay 4 warm up about 40 minutes, which gave us another opportunity to socialize. After the fog lifted we had light wind and a little mirage which would prevail throughout the rest of the day, with temps back up into the middle 80's by the day's end. Relay 2 match 5, Ivaldo Gabasio from Italy shot a nice .184 which captured small group honors. Nice shooting!

Paul Jung from France wins the Light Varmint 200 with a nice aggregate of .2277. I first met Paul in Italy during the World Championships in 1999. For those who don't know Paul he is a very good shooter from France and no stranger to winning and good aggregates. Paul wins the individual Light Varmint Grand with his 2nd at 100 yards and 1st at 200. Paul's .2129 grand was a great grand aggregate any day. Good Shooting my Friend! Rumor has it you're learning English; I am looking forward to visiting with you about strategy and shootin stuff when we meet again.

USA team C wins the team yardage and their second in a row, team USA B and Australia B round out the top three.

LV 200 Yard Team Standing

1.	USA C	.2811
2.	USA B	.2909
3.	AUS B	.3078
4.	USA A	.3297
5.	FRA A	.3309

Team USA B wins the Light Varmint Grand World Team Championship. USA team B consists of Ed Adams, Cecil Tucker, Bill Goad and Lester Bruno. USA Team C finishes second in the grand consisting of Billy Stevens, Jack Neary, Larry Scharnhorst and Allie Euber. Third was Australia B which was David Kerr, Graham Keppie, Barry Edgley and Paul Sullivan.

LV Grand Team Standing
1. USA B   .2612
2. USA C   .2633
3. AUS B   .2884
4. FRA A   .3046
5. USA A   .3048
6. SWE A   .3107
7. CAN C   .3181
8. AUS C   .3185
9. AUS A   .3205
10. SAF A   .3282

After three days of shooting two, USA teams are still at the level of the current world record for the team 2 gun. USA A, Australia B and France A are all within reach of the bronze medal.

2 Gun Team Standings after Day 3
1. USA C   .2530
2. USA B   .2560
3. USA A   .2983
4. AUS B   .3012
5. FRA A   .3056

World Championship day 4 started off with heavy rain which started about 7:00 am but by match time the rain ceased and clouds were breaking with sun trying to shine through. Jim Kelbly took credit for the shower, which I quote "How did you like the dust control I ordered for this morning?" By the time we started the Heavy Varmint 200 yard stage, we had tougher conditions, switching winds, cooler temps and just a bit of mirage for the final day of the 2-gun. Rex Reneau from USA team A took individual honors with a nice .2218 which included two two's of which Rex had small group until Jyrki Vuorjoki from Finland shot a .209 in match number 5 to capture small group honors, and move into the second spot in the yardage. Nice shooting!

Ratigan "better than getting sun burnt on head"

After the last group was fired, team standings were unclear but it looked like Jari Raudaskoski from Finland would win the individual two gun.

Jack Neary from USA team C wins the individual Heavy Varmint Grand aggregate with a .2434 and in a close second was Andrey Komkov from Russia team A with .2467. Andrey was all smiles after finding out how he finished. Jack sure was happy to shoot Allie Euber's rifle. It's unclear if Jack was able to purchase the rifle. Top five in the individual Heavy were USA, Russia, Finland, Finland and France congrats to all.

After the protest period expired, it was official, Jari Raudaskoski wins the individual 2-Gun. Jari ran a couple very emotional laps through the loading area waving Finland's flag.

Jari Raudaskoski, Individual 2 - Gun Champion.

Jari landed back on earth to congratulations from all for his fine performance in the individual 2-Gun, besting the field with a nice aggregate of .2480. I loaded across from Jari all week and can assure you there wasn't a happier shooter to be found. I can tell you from experience how it feels to represent your country knowing you couldn't have done better. Congratulations again, my friend, and thanks for the Finland sticker on my loading box.

WOW what a day for my four man team, I started out with a nice group and watched my team shoot well all day. My team had only one group over an inch all day, and it was barely over an inch. I was proud of our performance and glad to be able to participate and watch this day. USA Team A in the HV 200 was the only run away finish of the Championships.

HV 200 Yard Team Standing
1. USA A   .2496
2. USA C   .3011
3. CAN C   .3339
4. SWE A   .3388
5. FRA B   .3441

When the scores were combined for the Grand, USA team C captures the top spot in the Heavy Varmint Grand, just besting USA team A and their strong finishing performance of day 4 by .0007 of an inch. Team USA C was Billy Stevens, Jack Neary, Larry Scharnhorst and Allie Euber.

HV Grand Team Standing
1. USA C   .2667
2. USA A   .2674
3. USA B   .2977
4. FRA B   .3077
5. AUS A   .3205
6. RUS A   .3303
7. NZL A   .3350
8. SWE A   .3376
9. CAN C   .3418
10. FRA C   .3581

World Benchrest Championship 2 Gun Team standings were official with the USA sweeping the top spots on the podium. Team C shooters were all in the top 13 of the individual 2 gun, a very good performance by all. Team B had three shooters in the top 10, Team A had three in the top 20, overall a very good performance by all. There is no feeling quite like standing on the podium while your national anthem is played. We looked nice, dressed in our blue blazers thanks to Shilen Rifle Barrels.

2 Gun Team Standing

1. USA C   .2649
2. USA B   .2794
3. USA A   .2860
4. FRA B   .3189
5. AUS A   .3204
6. SWE A   .3241
7. AUS B   .3265
8. CAN C   .3298
9. FRA A   .3323
10. RUS A   .3335

Gold Medal Team   USA C
Allie Euber, Jack Neary, Larry Scharnhorst, Billy Stevens

All week we had an ongoing discussion that centered on the pond behind George's house and if Larry Scharnhorst would float, 6 were for and 6 were against Larry floating. Jack felt the only way to resolve the matter was to throw Larry in the pond, but we were unable to find Larry come time to test the theory. Rex and I agree that the only thing about Larry that would float is his picture.

Silver Medal Team   USA B
Ed Adams, Bill Goad, Cecil Tucker, Lester Bruno

Bronze Medal Team   USA A
Dwight Scott, Rex Reneau, Mike Ratigan, Dale Boop

Day 5 is a fun day where we shoot Heavy Varmint 10 shot at 200 yards. There is no pressure this day, the team event has ended and the final day is all about the fun of shooting and socializing. This day leads up to the crowning event of the Championship, the Awards Banquet.

Two USA team members got things started by helping break the tension with a wager on the first target. Rules were defined before the shooting would start. Rule one was you could not tell anyone about what was to happen, not even your neighbors at the bench. Independent judging of the final product would determine a winner. I normally ignore shooters talking behind the line but this target I would listen intently to my neighbors and spectators. My neighbors watched in disbelief when my first shot hit way high and left, then the second landed 1.5 inches to the right. I did what any shooter would do, I pounded the bench then took careful aim and fired my third shot which hit the ten ring on the right side, I was OK, the group looked bad but did not get any bigger.

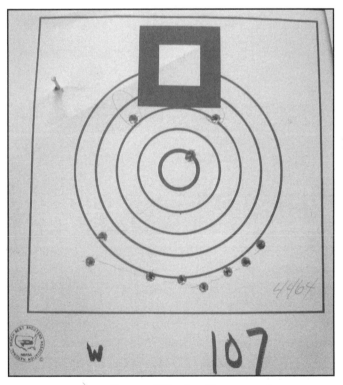

Quarter Winning Target

After reloading, I took careful aim then fired the fourth shot hitting the six ring low and left. This is when the comments really started. After a couple more shots my neighbors were not sold on my gun trouble. I then proceeded to shoot all my remaining required shots around the bottom of the six ring.

I sat quietly at the bench waiting for the end of the relay so I could find out about Billy's target. What the wager was, was 25 cents for whoever shot the best <u>looking</u> happy face on the record target during relay one. After seeing Billy's target hanging, I asked for my 25 cents, which he was reluctant to give up. About the time I asked for payment, Bart happened by and Billy enlisted Bart for his opinion. Bart looked at both targets and said "I'm sorry Billy, I just can't back you on this one, pay up."

Bill Gammon from Canada was the talk of the day after shooting a .371, a new World Benchrest Championship Record for the 10 shot Heavy 200, Good Job Ea.

Bill Gammon "Did I cross fire 7 shots ?"

During relay three I waited until thirty seconds left to start shooting. Paul Jung seemed to enjoy watching. While walking to the line for our last group Paul Jung asked about waiting to shoot till 20 seconds left on the last target, now that's the spirit. Paul decided against just before the start of relay five. I still took the opportunity to convey my pleasure of being able to shoot with my neighbors all week and about how much fun I have had and wished everyone a safe trip home.

Larry Scharnhorst took top honors, someone forgot to tell Larry the serious part was over. After the event, we found out Larry had sold this rifle before the start of the match and was just trying to get the good out before going to its new home after the Nationals at St. Louis, sorry Tom.

10 shot Heavy 200 Yards		
Larry Scharnhorst	USA	.2987
Alberto Lenzi	ITA	.3075
Steve Brown	AUS	.3076
Cecil Tucker	USA	.3100
Allie Euber	USA	.3306

On the evening of the last day of competition, we gathered at the Pines Golf Club in Orrville to socialize, eat dinner which was sponsored by Leupold and Krieger barrels, and present the awards. Don and George selected a nice venue for our awards ceremony.

Pines Golf Course Banquet Room

Two of the Four Fire trucks that responded to the alarm.

Just before our awards ceremony was to begin, we were interrupted by the fire alarm. Apparently so many hot shooters gathered together was enough to trip the alarm, after about 20 minutes the fire dept arrived to reset the alarm. In Ohio they must respond to every alarm of this type. It was a good thing the medics came with the four fire trucks because George's blood pressure was through the roof. Jack Neary explained, "The situation had deteriorated quickly which required action. After three attempts, I was able to talk the Fire Chief, yes it was the Chief, out of his hat, then immediately proceeded to a microphone."

Jim "I hope he's not going to sing"

Jack apologized for any inconvenience caused by alarm and explained, apparently Bill's truck had caught fire and all of Smiley's T powder was lost, fire had completely destroyed the evidence. It looked like there was never any T powder at all.

The Fire Chief thought arson might explain the fire, but after meeting Stan Buchtel (main suspect) and finding out Stan was celebrating his 95th birthday on the very evening of the awards banquet, the Fire Chief dismissed this theory, Happy 95 Stanley! It wasn't really Stan's 95th, just having a bit of fun.

Stuart and Annie Elliott from Australia presented appreciation plaques for their hard work to Don Powell and George Kelbly Sr. Herve du Plessis also presented a nice gift to Jim Kelbly, who acted as our range officer all week long, among many other duties.

Don receiving appreciation from Stuart and Australia

Chapter 26: 8th World Benchrest Championships

We composed ourselves after the fire department's exit of the banquet room, then proceeded with the formal awards presentation. We gave away top twenty patches and beautiful medals which were sponsored by MTM molded products. We had Top twenty patches for the Grands and 2-Gun. We gave medals to the top three using the format of the Olympics of Gold, Silver and Bronze. Medals and top twenty patches were designed by George Kelbly Jr. and Don Powell. All the awards lay out on the awards table was an impressive sight indeed.

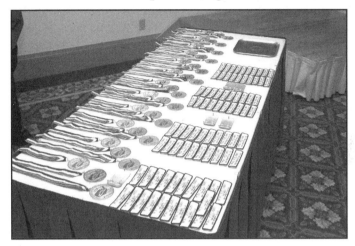

It's hard to say goodbye. After the evenings festivities, we spent the better part of the early morning hours visiting and thanks to the Aussie's and the Swede's for keeping us up all night before our hour trip home. We enjoy every minute of our time with our friends from around the world.

George Kelbly Jr. Scoring

On behalf of Don, George, Jim, and all United States World Benchrest Team members, I wish to thank everyone who helped and worked to make all of this a great success. Thanks to George Jr. for scoring, Mike Kelbly and target crew, Jim for taking care of the firing line, guys in the shop for all their help. Smiley and Bart, thanks for your help and flags. Sorry for anyone I have missed.

I received an emergency phone call last evening from the gentleman who's been helping proof this report about an important missing paragraph. After a short phone conversation, I was embarrassed about my oversight. Something everyone remembers about Kelbly's is the pie. One of the most important jobs all week are attended to by the Kitchen Staff. Everyone from the Shooters and Spouses, traveling companions, spectators, workers and everyone in attendance enjoys the food and local homemade pies. Thanks to Karen Kelbly, Ruthie Kelbly and Arlene Inman. And special thanks for all who donated their time to help with all the other things needed to make this the World event it was.

Mike Ratigan

"I can't explain how proud we were to have everyone to visit our home, thanks for a week of a lifetime."

George Kelbly Sr.

United States
Benchrest Hall of Fame

The year was 1970; the idea was to recognize those few shooters who consistently excel by repeatedly winning the biggest events. Dave Wolfe and Neil Knox, two benchrest shooters who worked for Rifle Magazine, started the ball rolling. Dave and Neil convinced Rifle Magazine, the official publication of the NBRSA, to entertain the idea of starting a Benchrest Hall of Fame and sponsoring the affair. They assembled an anonymous panel to decide on the qualifications for entry into the Hall of Fame.

**Patches given to the Early Rifle Magazine
Bench Rest Hall of Fame Members**

After deciding on the preliminary qualifications they poured over records for the NBRSA Nationals going back about 17 years. Only six shooters had earned enough points to gain induction into the Hall of Fame. Three shooters were within a few points for entry into the Hall of Fame.

Today, induction into the United States Benchrest Hall of Fame is a dream of many who strive to excel in Benchrest.

In 1972, Rifle Magazine announced the start of the Benchrest Hall of Fame.

The first six inductees of the United States Benchrest Hall of Fame were:

L.E. "Red" Cornelison
Tom Gillman
Paul Gottschall
Dave Hall
Warren Page
Ed Shilen

Points System

Since the beginning of the Hall of Fame, points were awarded for performance at the two NBRSA National Championships, the group Championships at 100 and 200 yards. At that time, the Unlimited Nationals and Varmint Sporter Nationals were held separately. One point is awarded to any shooter who wins any 100 or 200 yardage National Championship in any of the four classes, Unlimited, Heavy Varmint, Light Varmint and Sporter Class. A competitor who wins any Grand Aggregate (combined 100 and 200) is awarded 2 points. The winner of the 3-Gun at the Varmint Sporter Nationals is awarded 2 points.

Win a Range Aggregate (100 or 200 yards*)..............1 Point
Win a Grand Aggregate*......................................2 Points
Win a 3-Gun Championships**.............................2 Points

*Points awarded in all four classes.
**Points awarded for winner of multi gun Sporter, Light and Heavy Varmint at the Nationals.

The basic idea is to have everyone chasing Hall of Fame points gathered together at one place and shoot it out. This theme is identical to qualifying for the United States World Benchrest Championships.

It was originally intended to be extremely difficult to qualify for induction into the United States Benchrest Hall of Fame. It took approximately two years to hash out the qualifying criteria. An anonymous committee made an early decision that if they would make an error in the entry requirements it would be to make the entry requirements too difficult, the decision was unanimous. The committee took into account every consideration of the day, finishing 2nd and 3rd at the Nationals, setting world records and other major tournaments of the day.

Often new shooters have questions about why some of the current multi guns contested at the Nationals receive no points. With a short history lesson, the reasons will become evident. At the time of the inception of the Hall of Fame, the NBRSA Unlimited Nationals and the Varmint Sporter Nationals were held at different times and venues. The only multi gun aggregate contested at the Varmint and Sporter Nationals was a 3-Gun. There was no 2-Gun, as in the present day, and there was no 4-Gun for the obvious reason; the two Nationals were shot at different times, not everyone would shoot both.

Many shooters would like to relax the qualifications for entry into the Hall of Fame. Rex Reneau (current curator of the Hall of Fame) gets many requests to consider second and third place. "You wouldn't believe how many times I've been asked about second and third places getting ½ and ¼ points," Rex has said. This type of thinking is like the qualifying requirements for the United States World Benchrest Team, many shooters wanting in without working for it.

Caution is necessary when deciding on making any changes to the process. Any changes in the Hall of Fame are not taken lightly. The safest way to not irreversibly damage the credibility of the Hall of Fame is to leave the status unchanged, like it or not!

Records

Points for the setting of records was considered. After much thought about the matter, it was decided to award no points for the setting of records. Some of the thinking about records was the ability to set up a range with controlled conditions with the sole purpose of bettering records to gain Hall of Fame points. Many places around the country don't have prime real estate for the setting of records and even to this day a group record does not make you a consistently good performer or "Top Gun". The continuing idea is to have everyone at the same range, at the same time, when competing for the Hall of Fame points. Any Range constructed with the sole intent of besting records would not give everyone an equal opportunity for those Hall of Fame points.

Major Tournaments

Even today, attendance at major shoots change with the times. The Speer matches of years ago were considered a Major, today it's not even contested. Current history of the Cactus Classic is a good example; 6-8 years ago you must get your registration in early for the Cactus, which was sold out at four relays and 265 competitors. In 2005, attendance at the Cactus was 134. The Crawfish used to be considered a major (but with limited attendance), one hell of a lot of fun, food and fellowship. Today the Crawfish match is no more.

The Super Shoot is the only major which has stabilized in attendance. The Super Shoot often almost doubles the shooters of the NBRSA Nationals and often more than doubles the attendance of the IBS Nationals. Unlike some of the past tournaments which were considered to be "majors," the NBRSA and IBS Nationals are required to allow anyone wanting to shoot to participate. Many of the major tournaments limited the number of entrants due to the number of benches and time constraints.

It's more difficult than ever to obtain entry into the Benchrest Hall of Fame. Today having great shooting ability isn't enough, it must be coupled with a great shooting rifle and Superman bullets. Hot shooting equipment can make a professional out of a rookie, at least until the equipment or bullets dry up. The best of the best are the ones who consistently perform over a long period of time, but with only first place points it is becoming harder to earn the recognition and become a member of ...

the

"United States Benchrest Hall of Fame"

Relevant History

In 1980 Kelbly's held the two Nationals back to back, first came the Varmint and Sporter Nationals then the Unlimited Nationals. During that era the Unlimited Nationals was contested over four days. To listen to George Kelbly tell the story about the match, it was an overwhelming amount of work. George vowed to never run this eight day format every again, some wishes do come true.

In late 1980, Rifle Magazine decided they would no longer handle the administration of the Benchrest Hall of Fame. Skip Gordon (originator of the Super Shoot) was selected to take charge of the Benchrest Hall of Fame.

In 1981, the two Nationals were again at different venues, the Varmint and Sporter Nationals were contested at Austin, TX; the Unlimited was held in New Braunfells, TX. This would be the last time the two NBRSA Nationals were separate.

The NBRSA Nationals were combined for the first time in 1982. This format is still used today. The Varmint and Sporter Nationals are held over four days from Wednesday thru Saturday. The Unlimited Nationals was changed from 4 to 2 days, with 8-10 shot groups at 100 and 8-10 shot groups at 200. Previously the Unlimited Nationals course of fire was 5-10 shot groups each day for four days. The first two days were shot at 100 yards, the last two were shot at 200.

Chapter 27: United States Benchrest Hall of Fame

Today the Unlimited Nationals would be contested before the Sporter and Varmint Nationals and starts on Sunday or Monday, preceding the Sporter and Varmint Nationals.

In 1984 the administration of the Benchrest Hall of Fame would be independent of the NBRSA. In the United States, there are two organizations which were formed after the eastern region of the NBRSA withdrew from the NBRSA and formed the IBS in 1970. Instead of having two independent Hall of Fames which would take away from both organizations, the IBS was added to the Hall of Fame in 1984.

In the words of Skip Gordon, "There are two shooting organizations but only one sport." Under the watchful eye of Skip Gordon the IBS Nationals were included and points were awarded retroactively back to their first Nationals in 1970. Any shooter now could earn points toward the Hall of Fame from either or both the NBRSA or IBS nationals.

Boars Head, a marketing and communication company from New Jersey, with help from Al Angerman, integrated the information from the IBS National Championships into the data from the NBRSA Nationals. There was no change to the points system except points were awarded at both the NBRSA and IBS Nationals. During the integration of the two US Benchrest organizations into the Hall of Fame, the name was changed from "Rifle Magazine Bench Rest Hall of Fame" to the name still used today, the "United States Benchrest Hall of Fame".

In 1985 seven shooters were inducted into United States Benchrest Hall of Fame after the consideration of the IBS nationals was integrated to the points system. They were in alphabetical order;

Lester Bruno
Jack Demming
Allie Euber
P.J. Hart
Myles Hollister
Gary Ocock
Jim Stekl

There was almost no negative reaction to the induction of the shooters from the IBS. They are/were all good shooters and well respected in our sport.

In 1987, Fletcher Williams took over; as Skip would say, "the benevolent dictatorship" from Skip Gordon. During Fletcher's watch over the Hall of Fame, annual ballots concerning honorary membership were changed to every five years. This reduced the time, effort and cost of the mailings. Any person or shooter worth honorary membership would be remembered over the five year term between polls for honorary membership.

Shortly after Rex Reneau's induction into the Hall of Fame in 1994 Fletcher Williams asked Rex of Oklahoma City to take over the helm of the US Benchrest Hall of Fame. Fletcher passed away not long after the transition of the duties to Rex.

In 1997, Skip Gordon wrote another opinion on the Hall of Fame. Skip's thoughts were about the relative disparity in the numbers of shooters in the matches between the two nationals and a couple of the bigger tournaments of the day. Skip wrote, "It's not supposed to be easy to shoot your way into the Hall of Fame." Skip's contention was which would be more meaningful beating up on 350 shooters at the Super Shoot or 140 at a lesser venue. Food for thought.

Independence

The United States Benchrest Hall of Fame is an independent entity. It's not associated with either of the National group shooting organizations of the United States, NBRSA or IBS. At the helm of the United States Benchrest Hall of Fame is Rex Reneau. Make no mistake, it's a one man band (or dictatorship in a good way) and it needs to be. Rex does all of the work; record keeping, administration, fund raising, ordering plaques and jackets, and basically runs the show. Good Job Rex!

Currently the United States Hall of Fame is funded by donations, mostly by the members themselves and the occasional raffle of past years. Many thanks to everyone who has helped keep this program ongoing.

Honorary Membership

From the inception of the Hall of Fame, it was possible to be inducted as an honorary member. Honorary membership was intended to honor those individuals who have made extraordinary contributions to our sport of Benchrest. Originally to gain honorary induction you must be nominated by a Hall of Fame member and then the nomination must be approved by 100% of the members of the Hall of Fame, a high mark indeed.

As more members earned induction into the Hall of Fame, honorary induction would become more difficult. To remove any one member's personal bias towards any one honorary nominee the qualifications for honorary induction needed to be changed. Under the watchful eye of Skip Gordon, the honorary program requirements where changed in 1984.

Today, to gain honorary membership into the Hall of Fame, you must be nominated by a member of the Hall of Fame or a shooter who has earned at least 6 Hall of Fame points. Then you must be ratified by 75% or more of the current living members of the United States Benchrest Hall of Fame. To date, the honorary members are Harvey Donaldson and L. E. "Sam" Wilson who were inducted in 1973, Robert W. Hart and Raymond Speer who were inducted in 1975, Clyde Hart in 1981 and Homer Culver who was inducted in 1984. Mike Walker, Skip Gordon, Nate Boop and Ross Sherman are Honorary members; I'm not sure when they were inducted.

Chapter 27: United States Benchrest Hall of Fame

After 54 years and counting, and as of this writing, this is the short list of inductees into the Untied States Benchrest Hall of Fame (10 Honorary Members).

Tony Boyer	105
Allie Euber	45
Lester Bruno	42
Gary Ocock	33
Ed Watson	28
Don Geraci	26
Ron Hoehn	25
Tom Gillman	25
Lowell Frei	24
Perry Morton	22
Walt Berger	19
Jef Fowler	18
Don Powell	17
Lee Euber	17
Jim Stekl	16
Paul Gotschall (D)	16
Jack Demming	16
Russell Boop	16
Smiley Hensley	15
L. E. (Red) Cornelison (D)	15
Ferris Pindell	14
Warren Page (D)	14
Richard Maretzo	14
P.J. Hart	14
Bill Forrester	14
Jim Borden	14
Allen Arnette	14
Wayne Campbell	14
Ed Shilen	13
Myles Hollister	13
Dave Hall (D)	13
Speedy Gonzales	13
Rex Reneau	12
Charles Huckeba	12
Fred Hasecuster	12
Pat Byrne	12
Gerald Masker	11
Dwight Scott	10
John Brown Jr.	10
Faye Boyer	10
Richard Baker	10

(as of September 2006)

The most prized trophies in Benchrest, a United States Benchrest Hall of Fame jacket.

Rex Reneau, caretaker of the Hall, displaying his coat.

Three more Hall of Fame Members, Allie Euber, Lee Euber and Tony Boyer.

Pat Byrne's Trophy for induction into the Hall of Fame.

Gary Ocock, Hall of Famer and one of the best shooters on the planet earth.

Walt Berger, Hall of Famer, Originator of World Benchrest Championships, 2006 photo.

Ed Watson at the 1997 Nationals, Phoenix, AZ.
Ed is one of the winningest Benchrest shooters of all times,
Ed's won matches in about every state in the US which holds tournaments.

Lowell Frei

Lester Bruno

Pat Byrne

Allie Euber

Ron Hoehn

Faye Boyer

PJ Hart

Tony Boyer

Charles Huckeba

Don Geraci

Smiley

Allen Arnette

Gerald Masker

Russell Boop

Doc Maretzo

Wayne Campbell

Rex Reneau

Don Powell

Jim Borden

Bench and Range Design

Before starting to build a rifle range, I wanted to try to learn what to do, and what not to do. After talking to many match directors around the United States, I began looking for someplace to build a range. The intention, from the start, was to build a range which would be used to hold registered Benchrest tournaments at 100 and 200 yards. I also wanted to be able to use the facility for many other rifle disciplines with little or no extra effort.

I asked many questions about their home range construction. Specifically about top shapes and material, pedestal types and materials, roof or awning construction and materials, target frames, backers, etc. I had spent hundreds of hours talking about what they liked and disliked. I asked everyone if given the opportunity what would be done differently next time.

Whether planning to build a single bench or 100 you will benefit from the information in this chapter.

Figure 1. Mooreland Public Range firing line.

Bench Tops

Most all modern bench tops are built of concrete. There are several ranges which have tops made of wood; I discourage using wood in new construction unless it's the only choice.

Wood tops are typically nailed or screwed together and eventually rot and loosen, causing instability problems. The wood top surface is good to set your front rest feet onto (it's only good point). But the negative aspects of constructing a bench top out of wood outweigh the only good point. Wood tops typically cost more in materials and labor, need ongoing maintenance, become rotten and are flammable.

Concrete bench tops require forming, but after the forms are made you will be able to make multiple tops from each form. Concrete will stand the test of time better than wood and will add stability just by its sheer weight. The tops at my home range weigh approximately 550 pounds.

Shape
After choosing what material to use, the shape must be considered before the construction can start. Concrete allows the use of more shapes than could be easily built from wood. Concrete can very easily be formed into curved shapes. Top shape is one area I highly recommend you "Do Not Reinvent the Wheel".

After more than 50 years of formal Benchrest shooting, three slightly different bench types have survived. The most popular bench design is the T shape, then the benches with the tapered sides (toughest to use), and finally the horseshoe shaped.

There are a few ranges which use the horseshoe style of bench. Horseshoe shaped benches are more fragile to handle and require a more elaborate pedestal. The horseshoe style can cause problems when shooting the rail guns by crowding the center. The horseshoe benches cause problems when using many of the common dual port actions on the market today. When using a dual port action you have virtually no bench to eject the cases onto. One final point, larger shooters can have trouble getting into the cutout.

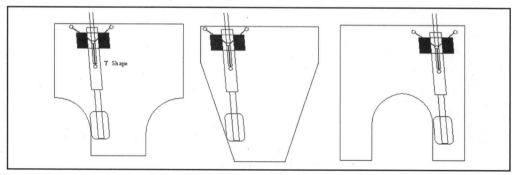

Figure 2. Different bench top design.

The middle bench in figure 2 is the style used at Kelbly's Range in Ohio, where the Super Shoot is held, and at the Benchrest Rifle Club of St. Louis. DO NOT copy this style of bench. Many current bench guns have the loading port on the same side the shooter sits. Forgive my drawing, but you can see the shooter's side of the bench is very small. Often, there is less room than shown in my drawing. You literally have little to no room for your loading block or loaded rounds on the shooter side of the bench.

Okie Shooters northeast of Oklahoma City, OK, and Midland, TX, use the following true "T" shape. With this style of bench there is plenty of room on both sides of the rifle. Another good quality of the true T type shape is the ease to build the concrete forms.

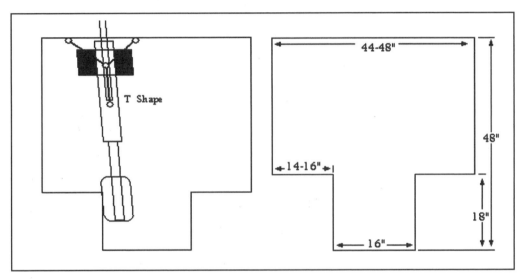

Figure 3. Top style used at Okie Shooters and Midland, TX.

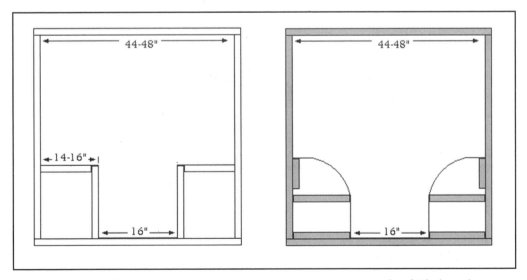

Figure 4. Form ideas using 2x4 construction, curve is made of tile board.

Where to Pour Tops

If human power will be used to lift the bench tops onto the pedestals save yourself some work. Pour the bench tops directly behind the pedestal on which they will ultimately rest as shown in figure 5. I first poured the tops for Mooreland, OK. too far away from the pedestals, we had to lift them up and place them on the back of a truck then lift again to place onto the pedestal. Hey, if you're using a tractor or lifting device, this will not apply.

Figure 5. Pedestals made of concrete blocks. Mooreland, OK.

St. Louis, MO.   Raton, NM.
Figure 6. St. Louis pedestals make of concrete formed in Sonotube.

Figure 7. Tops poured behind the pedestals on which they will rest.

Pedestal

The purpose of the Pedestal is to hold the bench top, hopefully without moving when the shooter leans against the side. Bench height is important and the top of the bench should be at a height of 32 inches. This is 3.5 concrete blocks high plus the mortar joints. When omitting the mortar, the height will be 4 blocks tall. Most shooters have adjustable chairs, shorter folks are used to having their chair a bit higher. Taller shooters are used to having their chair a bit shorter. Make your bench the standard height and you'll be comfortable most everywhere. One good "bad example" of bench height is Raton, NM. The tops are too high. The average height shooter, after setting their chair height, will have trouble reaching the ground.

After going through all of the trouble to make a good bench top it wouldn't make sense to put it onto a pedestal that moves. Two basic types of pedestals have become standard, one is the concrete block pedestal and the second is to make the legs from columns of concrete poured inside a cardboard tube called a Sonotube. Both can make a stable end product.

Common bench spacing is 6 foot center to center; 5'6" (Super Shoot) center to center is ok when trying to get the most benches for your firing line. Raton, New Mexico has benches which are 8 feet center to center. Raton's benches are too far apart. There are 75 benches at Raton. This makes the firing line 200 yards long. It's not much fun rotating benches at major tournaments, moving equipment from bench to bench. Raton could have 100 benches in the same firing line length if they would have used 6 foot spacing. Raton also has converging targets, five on one 12 foot frame, which leaves a rather large open space between the frames with no flags. You can see, sometimes more is not better, it's just MORE.

The numbers painted on the front of the benches, as seen in figure 1, are to aid when setting flags. When you get farther down range, it can be difficult to see who you are looking, for especially when they are in the shade.

Sonotube

Most lumber yards sell the hollow cardboard concrete forms called sonotube. They take a bit more time to layout where the holes will be drilled, but require less over-all construction labor. After digging the holes, you build a frame to hold the tubes at the correct spacing, cut them to the correct height and install your stabilizing frame, fill with rebar, then concrete, and remove tubes after the concrete dries.

When filled with concrete, the block "T" shaped pedestal is the most stable. But this pedestal is more labor intensive and harder to build, requiring special block cutting tools, block laying skill, and is more expensive. The decision to build the "T" shaped pedestals at the Mooreland Public Range was easy. I felt, since this was a Public Park, and open all year to the public, it was necessary to build the most indestructible pedestal possible. After building the pedestals, I poured them full of concrete to tie them together.

Several years later I would come to realize how good my decision really was. First, there was bit of vandalism. Some friendly visitors felt it would be nice to relocate several of the bench tops to the ground. I am certain if the pedestals were hollow they would have also been destroyed.

I had a front seat to witness a shooter lose control of his vehicle. I just happened to be looking at the right place at the right time to see a car drive onto the firing line and strike a pedestal dead center. The pedestal stopped the car dead in its tracks. There was no damage to the pedestal or bench top. The car was not so lucky. As it turned out, the vehicle's neutral safety switch had been bypassed. This allowed the car to be started while in gear. The shooter had been interrupted when arriving at the range and not put the vehicle in park (range is flat as a pool table). The shooter reached into the window and started the car. The car took off, driving up onto the firing line. What a sight.

Angled Pedestal

If you will be shooting up-hill or down-hill, consider building your tops at an angle. Level the tops from side to side but with the range from back to front. Now your thinking, "what the heck for," shouldn't it be level? Ranges where we shoot up or down hill with level benches can get you into trouble with your front rest being too tall or short, rear bag too tall or short. By angling the bench top front to back with the range, your equipment heights will be just as shooting on a level range, think about it. At my favorite range, Okie Shooters, we shoot down to 100 yards and up to 200 yards. Of course you take the middle ground and make the benches level in this situation. At Okie Shooters, the front rest is all of the way down shooting 100 and is way up when shooting 200. Just some food for thought, against the grain.

Pipe or wood pillars can also be used to support your bench top; wood has the obvious drawbacks when in contact with the ground, it WILL NOT stand the test of time. When using wood, you have done all the required work by locating and digging the holes. Find another area to save money.

Steel is flexible. Hollow steel legs should be filled with concrete to help dampen their movement.

Firing Line

The following picture is of the Benchrest Rifle Club of St. Louis and is one of the most luxurious and roomy in the United States. Most firing lines have less room to move equipment and provide less shelter during rain storms. You can see from the picture there is plenty of room behind the benches AND in front to move equipment when rotating benches.

Figure 8. St. Louis firing line.

In figure 8 you can see how the shooter when seated at the bench will be centered under the roof. The roof is low enough to protect the shooters from about any driving rain. This picture was taken at the 2005 NBRSA Nationals. You can clearly see the sidewalk in front of the benches. There is also plenty of room behind the benches for the equipment while still leaving the walkway free of obstructions. Most ranges are not so well protected.

At many of the smaller ranges you will have a small place to load right behind the benches on 2x12 boards between some of the roof supports. This gives shooters a chance to load right behind their bench. Figure 9 shows a portion of the Mooreland Public Range and shows the 2 x 12's between for reloading at the smaller local tournaments. I would estimate 20-25% of shooters load behind their bench.

Figure 9.
Mooreland firing line, tops poured behind pedestals where they go and loading boards.

What materials are used to construct your awning or roof over the firing line should be considered carefully. Every side of this structure will be exposed to the elements and, if in a high humidity environment, you should carefully consider using steel uprights, roof trusses, and a metal roof. Treated lumber has a finite life expectancy. You should expect to replace wooden truss construction about every thirty years. Initial installation costs are lower, but wood will most certainly be more expensive in the long run. Somewhere toward the middle of the firing line should be a range officer's station. During NBRSA group tournaments you will have moving backers that might be controlled from the range officers position in the middle of the firing line. Also, the public address or PA system will be needed at the range officer's station regardless of the type of tournament.

Down Range Warning Systems

There are a couple of ranges which have down range warning systems. Caution is the name of the game when shooting on one of these ranges, especially during open practice sessions. During practice sessions before tournaments you will have many shooters visiting for the tournament. They will not be familiar with the systems and are likely to go down range without first activating them. The trouble arises when a club member happens to the range while a visitor is downrange without activating the warning system. Club members might assume no-one is downrange, because the warning system is inactive, and will sit down and shoot. These nice gadgets have no idea if someone is downrange or not, they simple alarm or light when they are turned on. Be careful, look down range before shooting.

Figure 9A.
This light will not stop someone from dying! Can you find one in the photo below?

Figure 9B. Right half of the firing line at Raton, NM.
This roof is for looks only! It's so high it almost never keeps the rain off the shooters.

Target Frames

Having a stable target frame is essential when shooting accurate rifles of any type. It's impossible to evaluate your rifle and your ability when your target is moving. Benchrest tournaments use targets with an unusual feature called a moving backer. It is used to record number of record shots. This is unique to Benchrest for two reasons. First is because multiple shot groups at the same target and, secondly, because of the extreme accuracy of the equipment being used. A card, unseen by the shooter, moves back and forth behind the target which records the number of shots through the "Record Portion" of each target. Your target may only appear to have one hole, which is the goal, but you must have the required number of holes in the moving backer card. Backers systems eliminate cheating caused by shooting one shot and claiming you've fired more (five). Benchrest group tournaments are held to an extremely high standard. I personally will not shoot any group competition without a moving backer system. No fun matches for me, I don't want to be accused of shooting less than the required number of shots, EVER.

Scoring is very simple; shot your group, targets are changed, backers changed and inspected. Any which appear to have less than the required number of shots will be brought to the scorer's attention. Then the target is inspected. If five shots can be identified on the target, the backer is not needed, if the target is unclear and the scorer is experienced, the backer will be inspected for any holes which clearly have had more than one bullet pass through. If there is still a question, the competitor number is covered to promote impartiality and the refs are called to inspect the backer and target. Referees are experienced competitors who have seen thousands of small groups. They determine whether or not there are enough holes in backer and/or target. If they cannot tell, the competitor is only credited for the shots which can be seen. In my experience I have only heard of four times where a competitor was penalized for missing shots. I have just tried to give you an idea of how many things have to happen to have a problem reading the target and backer system. There is no such thing as a system which would be 100%. With the number of years I have participated, there's been almost no trouble.

Frame Design Considerations

One of the first things to consider about designing targets is whether or not you will have five targets per frame (converging) or one target in front of each bench. If you have an unlimited budget and work force, one target in front of every bench might be your choice. A target for every bench and having the 200 and 300 yard targets lined up right behind the 100 yard target make shooting a rail gun more convenient. The shooter can use the same position on the bench for every yardage. When selecting this type of target system you will have many more parts to build and frame anchors to bury. I will give you an example of the differences in poles, frames, frame anchors, backers etc between the different systems, one which has bench spacing of 6 foot and a target in front of each bench and the same range with converging targets. With 6 foot spacing or smaller, you can have two targets on an 8 foot wide board, as does St. Louis.

60 benches	Boards	backers	poles	frame anchors
Non-converging	30	30	60	180
Converging	12	12	24	48

After carefully considering every option, I, just like many match directors, decided to build converging targets or 5 on a single 8-12 foot wide frame. If you use a smaller 8 foot wide board, the flags will be crowded close to the targets.

At home, I move the targets between yardages, and the less work the better. Many match directors who build and design the ranges will also have to move targets. Even after the substantial difference in the initial construction and material costs, the targets take longer to move during match time. The maintenance requirements of money and time are also greater with a target in front of every bench.

Frame Anchors and Poles

The foundation will determine how stable your target frame will be. Your support poles must be firmly affixed to the ground and not move. Whether you have dedicated support poles or buried frame anchors, both can cause problems. Any movement in the anchors will allow the target to move in the wind. Furthermore, the frame can be influenced by the pushing/pulling of the moving backer system. Depending on where the range is located, you might have special circumstances which require special construction considerations such as having a shallow water table (water close to ground level, swamp), or when building on solid rock.

Figure 10. Photo of CS pipe joint, this joint is straight threaded or not tapered.

Extreme Rifle Accuracy

Most rifle ranges use removable poles. The poles will be shot at if left standing by the members and the general public. When considering buried anchors, stability or movement should be carefully considered. It was common years ago to find two different pole sizes which slip into one another. I would advise against this. With current accuracy levels of the rifles, any movement of the frames will add significantly to the aggregates. Even if all of the frames move the same amount, it would not affect everyone's targets or aggregates the same.

I carefully considered the problem of frame movement after talking to many match directors from around the country. I paid more attention to the special needs of extremely windy places like the Prairie Dog Target Club, Don Dickers' place in South Dakota. After visiting with all of the match directors, I decided on a buried female 2 3/8 CS pipe. This type of thread joint is non-tapered and tightens on three shoulder areas. The photo in figure 10 shows this pipe joint, the right female box end is buried at ground level. By being level with the ground, there is nothing exposed to be shot at, less damage from stray bullets and lawn mowers. This type of thread joint has two different diameters of threads, the left male joint you can see I have turned off the upper portion or larger diameter thread. This was done in case the upper portion of the buried female end would receive some minor damage the anchor would still be useable.

I have had some intentional damage from a 22 caliber rifle or pistol. The damage was only to the top buried thread section which did not matter. The smaller thread was too deep inside the joint to be damaged, even with direct fire into the joints.

This type of straight threaded joint can be completely tightened with no tools, you turn it down until the shoulders contact and they are tight. When selecting a tapered pipe thread you are required to use a pipe wrench to tighten them. If you don't, they will wobble, allowing the frame to move.

Anything above ground WILL be shot. If you extend your anchors above ground level, they can be seen from the firing line, they will attract bullets as if by magic. I leave mine open and exposed to the weather all year. After ten years there has been no measurable damage from rust. I have had trouble when a friend, who thought was helping, installed bright red thread protector caps which extended about ½ inch into the air. I discovered the caps about one week later. Three anchors where damaged from shooters shooting the nice red caps. Again, anything which can be seen from the firing line will be shot, it's just a fact of life at the range.

The only drawback of installing the frame anchors at ground level is they can fill with grass, water, dirt and sand. After more than ten years of experience at the Mooreland Public Range using this anchor type I would rebuild with exactly the same frame and anchor arrangement. The simplicity to move, more than outweighs the maintenance. I made a small auger to clean out the buried frame anchors as needed, not too much trouble.

Figure 10A. Auger

Figure 11 C-clamps to secure boards to poles

Frame Anchor Spacing

If you choose buried anchors, bury them 8 feet center to center. By using an 8 foot spacing you will be able to use the anchor system with about any score shooting targets by hanging a half sheet of plywood (2 foot by 8 foot) from the poles with a very simple strap which has a hook bent in the top. Score targets of different sizes can be stapled to the board. Score targets which receive one bullet per target do not require moving backers. These brackets hook over the top of the pipe, gravity does half the work. Use a C-clamp to secure the bottom of the board to the pipe, as shown in figure 11. This gives you a very solid connection and is quick to change yardages.

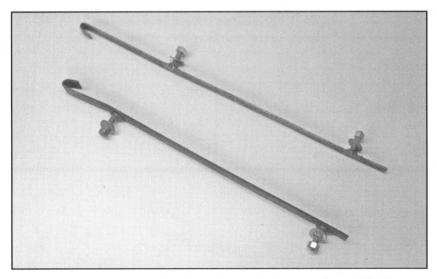

Figure 11A. Hangers for 8 foot boards, used when staples will hold targets.

Coors Range at Raton, NM

Figure 11B. Raton firing line and loading building.

Practice Boards

You will need something for the general membership and/or the public to shoot at. Build something which does not use your below ground anchors. I have learned much when making practice target boards. The 100 yard targets must be able to be laid down. As a matter of fact, every distance but the longest must be removable. I buried 3 inch pipe stubs to hold 2 3/8 inch pipes. I welded two bolts onto the pipes and bolted a 2 foot by 8 foot piece of plywood to the back of the pipes. Make sure the bolts are <u>on the back</u> where the shooters cannot see them. They make good targets if they can be seen. After more than ten years, not one bolt has been shot off while on the back.

I recommend installing the practice boards between the locations of the tournament target frame anchors and behind the line a yard or so. The practice board height should be below the height of the backer cable. This will allow the use of the practice boards for sight in boards come match time. If your range only has 200 yards, you can install permanent 200 yard practice boards, just like the 100 yard frames, place them between the tournament frame anchors and behind so as not to interfere with the backer cabling. I thought the 200 yard practice boards could be behind the tournament frame location. Wow they really get shot up come tournament time.

Benchrest Target Frames

There are many schools of thought on building target frames for use in registered benchrest tournaments. The frames need to be stable without moving in the wind, hold the target without the target moving or blowing away, be easy to change targets, and have a moving backer. The easier to move from one yardage to another, the better. No one wants a workout come match day during the summer heat. Light weight frames are nice, but need to be strong enough so they do not move or buffet in the wind. In this section, I will describe the target frames used at the Mooreland Public Range at Mooreland, OK.

My primary considerations were to have a non-moving stable frames, and backer system which are easy to move. I talked to many match directors, from ranges around the country, before deciding what to do. Being lazy by nature, I definitely wanted the frames which would be easy to move. I believe I have designed one of the best systems to date.

The targets are twelve feet wide. There is a single piece of angle iron at the top of the frames that run the length of the frame. This angle iron holds the frame up and connects the two pieces of plywood. Two pins extend down through the angle. These pins go down into the pipe to locate the frame, gravity holds the frame down. The bottom is clamped to the pipe with a c-clamp as was used in figure 13. Simple.

A garage door roller goes into a small piece of pipe welded to the angle on the back of the frame, as shown on the right side of figure 13B. This roller extends to the rear of the target frame. The backer frame hangs on the rollers. The pipe legs help hold the spacing between the backer and the target frame, so the backer doesn't lean into the frame or get caught on it.

Figure 12. Target frames at Raton, NM.

Figure 13. Benchrest target frames at Mooreland, OK.

Figure 13B.

Raton   Mooreland

Figure 14. Backer frame from Raton, NM.

Electricity

When hosting tournaments you will, at the very least, need power on the firing line for the public address system. If hosting group tournaments, you will need electricity for the moving backer system.

The most important electrical design decision you will make, and one of the most difficult to change, will be where to run the power downrange. Don't make the same mistake almost all ranges have made.

Run power for the backer system down the middle of the range!

It seems that, for some reason, most all ranges bury the downrange power to one end of the targets. I am guilty as charged. Before I ever turned on the power, I stood on the firing line at Mooreland wondering why I had made more expense and work for myself. Not to mention, the backer system would work better if the motor was in the middle. In order to get the power to the side of the targets I had to run the conduit and cabling from the center of the firing line (range officers position) to the side of the firing line, then bury the conduit and cable. If I would have went down the center, my cable would have been 25% shorter and cheaper.

Control

You must also consider some way to turn the backer system on and off. A simple way is to have a circuit breaker and box at the range officers station. Motor remote controls are more complicated and can be the cause of more trouble.

Below Ground Enclosures

The electrical enclosures must be at or below ground level. If they are not they will also attract bullets. This will become more important if the power points are in the middle of the range which will have more traffic. You may have to make a lockable enclosure to keep the curious folks from opening the man hole cover. When the power point is to one side, few shooters will notice the enclosures. The lids of my enclosures have never been shot.

Figure 15. Breaker box behind benches, and downrange buried outlets, Mooreland, OK.

Moving Backers

When shooting groups, there is a need, and a rule, that you must use a moving backer. This is agian to count the shots fired through the target. Many groups are shot at every registered tournament where it can be hard to tell by looking at the target how many shots were fired. The moving backer system moves a card back and forth behind the record portion of the target to confirm that the required number of shots has been fired. At no time should the card be exposed to the shooter.

The challenge is to build a moving backer system which is easy to build, easy to set up, and is easy to take down and move, and reliably records the number of shots fired at the record target.

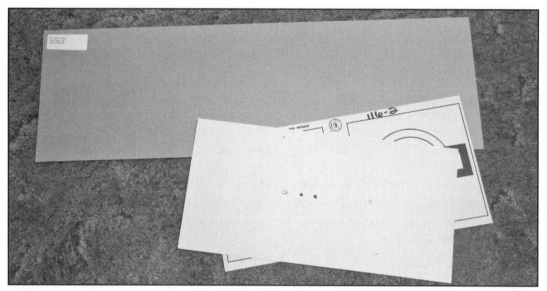

Figure 16. Backer cards, larger card from Raton, NM., small card from Mooreland, OK.

Card Size and Material

Backer cards material and size can pose some unique challenges when designing the system. The cards must record the shots through the record and be easy to change. About the best material to use in order to see the hole is target paper. I use actual targets at Mooreland for backers. The unprinted side is placed forward in the backer frames so that the bullets leave clean holes. Target paper used as backers are more difficult to change and handle than the card board or "chip board."

The larger cards used at Raton are made of chip board. They are easier for the target crew to handle when changing targets but make seeing any overlapping holes more difficult.

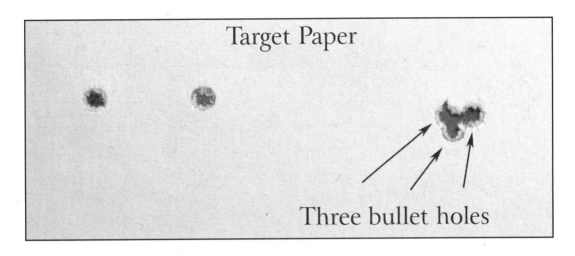

Target Paper

Three bullet holes

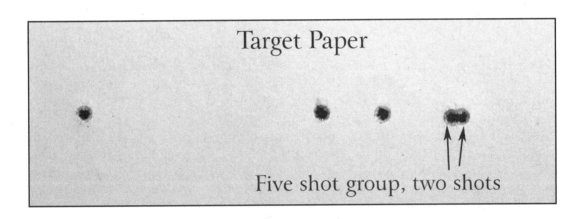

Target Paper

Five shot group, two shots

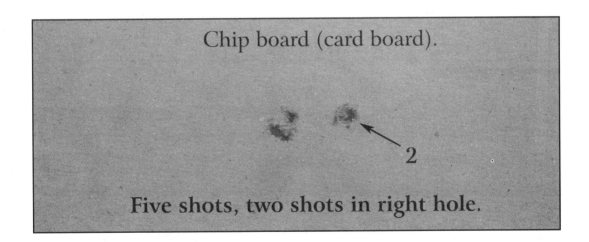

Chip board (card board).

2

Five shots, two shots in right hole.

Figure 17. Firing line at Canastota, NY

Figure 18, NY target holder

How They Move

The backer frame needs to move back and forth behind the target without moving the target frame. This means there needs to be some sort of low friction connection between the target frame and backer frame. The backer frame is held up by the target frame. The backer frame moves by riding along with the moving backer cable. A gear motor moves the cable back and forth, simple.

A garage door roller with bearing (not friction plastic) is used as the roller, as seen in figure 13B. The garage door roller is attached to the target frame. Garage door track is attached to the backer frame. The backer frame hangs on the rollers. This type of setup provides an almost friction free movement of the backer frame behind the target. This also reduces the chance of the backer frame movement causing the target frame to move back and forth. A moving target is a definite distraction when trying to shoot a one hole group.

Design

Every backer system uses a motor to move the backer frames and cards or paper. The minimum movement should be 1 inch per minute. Some systems use a continuous pull in one direction, others oscillate back and forth, and yet some others moved around in a circle. The circular backer systems used a drive motor for every target, and were hardware intensive, and are all but gone.

Simple is the name of the game when designing a new backer system. There are two basic types of drive motor systems used to build moving backer systems. Linear actuators and rotary oscillating gear motors.

Braided cables are used to connect the backer motors to a counter weight or weights. In years past, many different types of connectors were used; solid rods, flat steel, and many others. At Kelbly's, where the Super Shoot is held, they use steel connectors. They use one small board for every target and use clips to hold the backer cards.

Connection Schemes, Cables or Solid Connectors

Most new backer systems use a cable to connect the motor to the backer frames and ultimately to a counter weight. Many ranges use individual cables between the backer frames. This requires some way to vary the length of the cables to set the timing or the relationship between the backer frame and the target frame. The backer card must stay behind the target frame at all times. Target frames are rarely the exact same distance apart.

Many of the systems in the mid-west part of the United States used pieces of cable which ran between the backer frames. These systems used turnbuckles and elaborate systems to vary the cable lengths to properly time the backer frames. This type of system transmitted the preload of the counter weight through the wooden backer frame. I've been at several matches where the wooden backer frame broke, disabling the system at best. Many times the backer frames would fall to the ground when a frame would break under the stress.

I decided to use a continuous cable system after talking to many range operators about their systems. One cable spans the distance from the motor to the counter weight. With this type of cable system, you simply clamp the backer frame to the cable. The backer frame goes along for the ride with the cable. There are no more turnbuckles or broken backer frames. Timing by varying the cable length is no longer an issue. During the set up, simply put the backer frames in time where they should be and then clamp the cable to the frame.

Figure 19. Picture of cable clamped to the backer frame at Mooreland, OK.

Figure 20. Backer cable clamps, Raton, NM.

Continuous Cable, continued...

Also, when using a continuous cable from one end to the other, you are not required to put up all of the targets. A great time saver if you have 20 shooters and 75 benches. Nowhere was this more apparent than Raton, NM, which has 75 benches. With the old backer system of aluminum connector rods it was necessary to start with target frames on the motor side (left) and work across the range with targets and backer frames.

This made it very inconvenient to use the middle of the range when having a small number of shooters. By using one continuous cable, targets can be set up anywhere and can be omitted where not needed. Now we can shoot in the middle without extra work.

Unsupported Cable

If, for example, we use the four middle frames at Raton, there is a long expanse of cable that is unsupported. This cable will sag. To help hold up the cable when spanning large empty spaces you only need something minor to help eliminate the sag. I suggest using a wooden dowel with a metal loop or small c-clamp. Not near as much work as putting up the targets and backer frames, easy. Whatever you might decide to help hold the cable from sagging, choose something simple. All that's required is to hold the cable up, doesn't even have to be rigid, just needs to hold the cable up off of the ground.

Cable Reel

About the only challenge to using one continuous cable is how to handle the cable when changing yardages or storing. I have a wire roller which is used to roll up the cable. I store a spare cable on the reel, as seen in figure 21. This type of cable cannot be rolled up like an extension cord, it will become tangled. When needed for the next use, it will be very difficult to untangle.

Figure 21. Photo of cable reel from Mooreland, holds two cables.

Solid Connectors in lu of Cable

One of the most labor intensive backer systems I have seen to date was the previous design used at Raton, NM. The original design at Raton used 1/2 inch conduit between the backer frames with no counter weight. It's 26 feet between the target frames. The conduit would sag between the targets almost touching the ground. This system needed two supports between the targets to hold up the conduit. And, as if the sag wasn't bad enough, the conduit would bow up in the middle when the backer motor would push on the conduit. To stop the bow, the two supports needed a loop in order to contain the conduit. What a nightmare to set up and to move. The target crew had to thread the long pieces of conduit into the holes in the supports. Just when you thought it couldn't get any worse, they needed some way to vary the length. Just like many ranges, the targets were not exactly the same distance apart and needed connectors of different lengths. Figure 22 shows the variable end attached to the conduit connector.

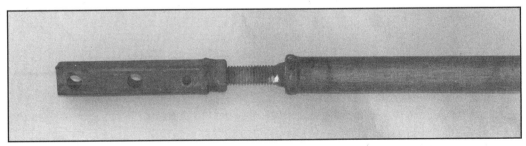

Figure 22. Rod end used to vary the length of the connector, Raton, NM.

One final thought, if you choose solid connectors. They should be solidly connected to the frames. Just like a train, the backer system would not react instantly to the movement of the motor. The far end would not move at all until all of the slack had been taken up. If this type of system reverses direction, there will be substantial delay between the motor's change of direction and the last frame movement. In order to reduce the lag time, the solid connectors should be rigidly mounted to the frame. The bad news, this increases the complexity, set up, and tear down time. When starting from scratch, build something else.

Umea, Sweden, hosts for the seventh World Benchrest Championships, had a unique backer system. They used a single continuous paper which spanned the entire range from right to left. After every target the target crew would roll up the backer paper from the previous relay which would roll out another sheet from a giant roll of paper on the right side of the range. This system had a couple of shortcomings. First, since the paper ran from one side of the range to the other, the target frame needed to span the whole range from right to left. There was enough space for a couple extra targets in the space. Secondly, the system was very sensitive to water and wind. This required a roof over the whole target system to keep the rain off the paper. If the paper would get wet, it would tear. I guess this system could also fail if the paper where to tear when being pulled by the motor.

Figure 23. Continuous target frames in Umea Sweden.

Motors
The linear actuator type is a straight pull. The more popular type drive is the rotating gear motor. After talking to range owners and operators from around the country about their likes and dislikes about their backer systems, I decided to use a rotating gear motor system. The minimum movement is 1 inch per minute, no matter which drive motor type you choose. The rotating type systems generally run between 6 to 12 rpm, plenty fast. The only drawback about a oscillating system is when the frame stops, then reverses.

Figure 24. Motor used at Mooreland, OK.

Figure 25. Motor used at Raton, NM.

Block and Tackle

On the end, or ends, where the weight will be attached, make a simple triangle shape to hold a roller. Figure 26 shows the simple holder I made for Mooreland; need nothing special to attach it. Just slip it over the pole and gravity does the rest.

Do not hang the weight on the end frame as in figure 25A. Attaching the block and tackle to the last target frame can cause movement of the last target toward the backer motor when the backer motor pulls on the cable. The frame might also move away from the backer motor when the motor lets down on the weight. Use a stand-alone holder so as to isolate the push and pull of the backer motor from the target frames that hold the targets.

Figure 26. Block and tackle for counter weight at Mooreland, OK.

Counter Weight

The counter weight holds tension on the cable and is used to pull the backer frames away from the backer motor when the motor arm moves away from the motor. Figures 27 and 28 are of the weights from Mooreland and Raton and clearly show a metal arm welded to the side of the weight. This is to keep the weight from unraveling the twisted cable. Without the anti-rotate bar the weight would spin until it has straightened out much of the twisted cable, at least up to the first clamp on the closest target frame.

Raton's Weight

After picking up the weight at Mooreland too many times, I realized there was a better way. For Raton, I made a simple double hook with the anti-rotate bar attached. The weight holder in figure 28 can be attached to the cable and ran over the pulley on the block and tackle, then, smaller weights can be added. Barbell weights work just fine. They slide over the J hooks one at a time. This is quite nice for those with sore backs and muscles.

Figure 27. Weight used at Mooreland,
notice anti-rotate rod.

Figure 28.
Counter weight used at Raton, N.M..

Figure 28A. Counter weight used at Canastota, N.Y..

Dead Man, for Motor and Counter Weight

When using a backer motor with a counter weight connected by a cable there is tension between the weight and motor. This tension is attempting to pull the motor and the weight support together. The natural tendency is for the motor and weight to move closer together. Unless you have a very large foundation for the motor and weight you will need a diagonal member connected to a dead man in the ground. If you use a small foundation, or post hole, eventually the motor or weight foundation will fail. Either the weight pole or the motor will fall over. Figure 29 shows the connection between the top of the weight end and the ground. This connection will stop the eventual movement of the backer motor foundation or weight foundation.

All that's needed is a come-along to connect the motor and weight poles to a dead man. I have used both a chain with load binder and come-along. This system is as easy as can be designed.

Figure 29. Block and Tackle, Weight and dead man, Raton, NM.

Sound System

Every range hosting tournaments will need a public address (PA) sound system. The PA system will be needed by the range officer at the range officers station or the middle of the range. Wiring will be installed to speakers strategically placed on the firing line so the competitors will be able to hear emergency commands, time warnings, and any other necessary announcements.

Stationary Backers

Its a requirement when hosting Nationals and World Championship matches that a stationary backer be used. This backer is used to identify cross-fires. Stationary backers are located 3 feet behind the 100 yard target, 6 feet at 200, and 9 feet at 300. If there has been no cross-fire, the group on the stationary backer and the record target look the same. If there is a shot which was fired from another bench, the groups will look different. Any bullet from you neighbor will be offset from the group. The farther away the shooter is who shot the shot, the more displacement there is in the shot in the stationary backer.

Stationary backers are recommended at smaller local tournaments, but not required. Almost no-one uses a stationary backer unless they are hosting a Major tournament, National or World Championship events.

Design Considerations

One important consideration when thinking of building a stationary backer system is "Who will be changing targets". Historically, stationary backers are constructed as a separate set of targets, with frame anchors and uprights. When designing a new system DO NOT hang the stationary backer on the frame as pictured in figure 30.

Figure 30. Raton target frame with stationary backer attached.

Figure 31. Stationary backer at New York.

Notice in Figure 31, there is a walk way between the targets on the left and the stationary backers. This is great to give you a walk way between the back of the targets and the stationary backers. Look back to the photo in figure 30. You might imagine having to duck under the stationary backer frame to tape the stationary backer and change the moving backers behind the main target frame. This makes changing targets more difficult. Hanging the stationary backer on the main frame also makes holding the target still more difficult. The anchors must be very strong to resist the extra wind loading from the addition of the extra area supported by the main frame anchors.

While visiting with the maintenance supervisor before the 2006 NBRSA Nationals at Raton, we talked in depth about the stationary backers and the several shortcomings of the design at this range. I was worried about a couple things as previously discussed. I didn't see how any adult would be able to duck under the stationary holder every time we needed to change targets. We would need a target change in about 6 minutes and with 15 frames this would really slow the process down. Further, I was worried about the relative weakness and instability of the stationary holder in high winds.

It just so happened my worries were well founded. We had a very strong wind and rain storm which damaged several of the stationary backer holders. The wind picked up the holders and folded them up and over the front of many of the target frames. These stationary backer holders are connected by a pin at the top and gravity holds them down against the frame. The wind damaged several of them to the point they needed to be rebuilt before use. Thanks to the work of the Whittington Center Crew, they were able to repair the frames with only a two hour delay. This type of damage at any other range would have required at least over night repairs at a minimum. When deciding on a design, build something else.

St. Louis firing line, 2004 NBRSA Nationals.

St. Louis target frame, note 2 targets per 8 foot board.

Kelbly's targets, N. Lawrence, Ohio.

Kelbly's firing line 2005.

Kelbly's loading shed, before World Benchrest Championships 2005.

Firing Ling at Phoenix, Paul Jung from France is pictured on right. (1997).

Kelbly's loading barn during the World Benchrest Championships 2005.

Raton, NM loading building. Building is 60 feet wide and 300 feet long, yep 100 yards.

Stat house at Mooreland, OK.

Firing line at Phoenix range which hosts the Cactus Classic. Note there are no roof supports in front of the firing line.

Frequently Asked Questions

How Do I Get Started?

Join the NBRSA, IBS or, if you live outside of the United States, join Benchrest shooting organizations of your country. If you live in a country without active participation, the World Benchrest Shooting Federation can help you get started. Read all you can about the sport of precision and accuracy shooting. If you have access to a computer, you can read about the sport at the forums on Benchrest.com. Contact a tournament director in your area, they can get you in touch with someone from your area that will be able to answer many questions you might have. Attend a tournament in your area, it's the easiest way to get exposure to extreme rifle accuracy. To find a tournament, contact the NBRSA or IBS secretary.

Can I Use My Factory Rifle to Get Started?

Certainly. You can use any bolt action rifle that has a removable bolt. The action and barrel must be two separate pieces. You can get your feet wet with a factory rifle, but it will take a minute or two to lust after a purebread Benchrest rifle. Many shooters are happy to loan spare equipment and rifles. Many established shooters will have stories about borrowed equipment when they were getting started. I shot a borrowed rifle at my first Nationals while waiting for mine to be built.

What Type Rifle Should I Buy?

Sporter, Light Varmint, Heavy Varmint or Unlimited? Buy a 6PPC in a 10.5 pound rifle or "Sporter." This will allow you to shoot any class of tournament. Many shooters are talked into purchasing a Heavy for their first rifle. This is a mistake. It only takes one weekend tournament to figure out why you need a 10.5 pound 6mm. When you're forced to borrow a rifle because your Heavy will not meet the weight restrictions, the need for the lighter rifle becomes obvious. Although a Heavy is easier to shoot because of the added weight, you'll need a Sporter if you have plans to shoot a tournament.

Should I Buy a Used Rifle?

There are many used rifles for sale at any time, many of which are competitive. The best chance of buying a good used rifle is from a non-competitor. Most all of the competitors will tell you why they are selling the rifles and if they're competitive or not. If a good competitor tells you his forsale piece should be used as a prairie dog rifle, believe it! I've sold many good shooting rifles, most of which had one or two mechanical things that just irritated me, bolt handle too short, harder than normal bolt lift, etc. Many things I insist on are non-issues to others. Just don't be afraid to ask about how the rifle performs.

What's it Cost to Get Started?

Wind flags can be homemade or purchased and can cost as much as 100 dollars a piece for the flag and pole or stand. Standard used rifles are about $1600 - $2400, depending on the action and stock. Scopes cost from about $350 for a new Sightron to $1000 for a new Leupold, and more for the newer March scope. You'll need a rest and rear bag. A used Hart front rest runs under $200 with no fancy tops. A new Farley front rest will set you back about 775 plus shipping. Rear bags cost anywhere from $30 to $200 dollars. You'll need a few loading tools, seater, sizer and a couple other odds and ends. Most everyone thinking of Extreme Rifle Accuracy will already have some loading tools, some of which can be used. There are many fancy tools used by Benchrest shooters, many are just smaller and lighter than some of the tools you already own. Many are not necessary. Flags always seem to get forgotten about or left off of the wish list of things to buy to get started. Of all the fancy gadgets in my repertoire, my flags are my MOST IMPORTANT equipment. Without flags, you are relegated to luck. Shooting without flags is like driving down the highway without being able to see.

Are Shooters Classified?

No. This is part of the lure of the game. You're thrown right into the mix and everyone competes as equals. It would be almost impossible to administer some sort of system of segregation or classification. New shooters are invited into the mix as equals. If shooters were classified, it would be just wrong if a new shooter would shoot a aggregate that would have won a particular tournament but was excluded because they weren't in that class. From time to time, new shooters are blessed with early success, gotcha.

What is an Aggregate?

A yardage aggregate for any varmint class is the average of 5 groups at each distance converted to an approximate minute of angle (MOA). An MOA is 1.047 inches at 100 yards, but the sport uses 1.000 inch at 100 yards. This eliminates the extra math that's involved to convert to the exact MOA. At 100 yards, you add the group sizes together, then divide by the number of groups. A 200 yard average is divided by two in order to convert to MOA. A 300 yard average is divided by three and so on.

A Grand aggregate is two yardage aggregates added together then divided by two. 2 – Gun aggregate is two grand aggregates added together then divided by two. In the United States, groups are measured in inches and aggregates are calculated to four decimal places. In many countries, targets are measured in millimeters and aggregates are calculated to three places. Many tournaments shot at metric distances are then converted to MOA. There is no comparison between identical aggregates at the different distances, because the longer metric distances are harder to shoot. In other words, two aggregate of .2500, one shot at 100 yards and the other at 100 meters, the one shot in meters would be better, or more difficult to shoot. This is why there are normally two sets of records, imperial and metric.

Can I learn with a non-competitive rifle.

No. Worse, you'll never be able to learn what the wind flags are trying to tell you without using a rifle that will shoot every shot in about the same hole at 200 yards (in good conditions, of course). You won't know why the shots hit where they do. The rifle will be part of the problem.

Records

NBRSA - Sporter Class

Single Groups	Size	Shooter	Date
5-100	.041	Jerry Thornbrugh	10-21-1978
5-200	.110	Tom Minder	7-4-1981
5-300	.247	Bob Dodd	7-17-2004
Yardage Aggregates	*Size*	*Shooter*	*Date*
5-5 at 100	.1573	Dick Katchmar	4-14-1985
5-5 at 200	.1523	Larry Cohen	10-26-2003
5-5 at 300	.2203	Jim Carstensen	6-13-1999
Grand Aggregates	*Size*	*Shooter*	*Date*
100, 200	.1936	Smiley Hensley	7-27-1998
200, 300	.2496	Tony Boyer	9-3-1983
1,2 & 300	.2425	Tony Boyer	9-3-1983

NBRSA - Light Varmint Class

Single Groups	Size	Shooter	Date
5-100	.009	Mac McMillan	9-23-1973
5-200	.099	Skip Otto	4-7-2002
5-300	.291	Brady Knight	8-27-2005
Yardage Aggregates	*Size*	*Shooter*	*Date*
5-5 at 100	.1500	Jeff Fowler	6-11-1994
5-5 at 200	.1605	Dick Howell	2-21-1998
5-5 at 300	.1518	Bart Sauter	9-20-2003
Grand Aggregates	*Size*	*Shooter*	*Date*
100, 200	.1786	Dick Howell	2-21-1998
200, 300	.2621	James Jarrett	9-4-1982
1,2 & 300	.2732	James Jarrett	9-4-1982

NBRSA - Heavy Varmint Class

Single Groups	Size	Shooter	Date
5-100	.027	Ralph Landon	9-13-1975
5-200	.102	Wayne Blackketter	5-6-2006
5-300	.149	Gary Ocock	4-5-1998

Yardage Aggregates	Size	Shooter	Date
5-5 at 100	.1399	Rex Reneau	9-6-1982
5-5 at 200	.1485	Dennis Thornberry	3-3-1996
5-5 at 300	.1844	Pat Byrne	7-17-2005

Grand Aggregates	Size	Shooter	Date
100, 200	.1773	Clarence Hammonds	7-2-1995
200, 300	.2497	Jeff Summers	9-1-1984
1,2 & 300	.2572	Tony Boyer	9-1-1984

NBRSA - Unlimited Class

Single Groups	Size	Shooter	Date
5-100	.050	Ed Watson	3-9-1985
5-200	.120	Dennis Thornberry	10-27-1985
5-300	.373	Art Freund	7-11-1981
10-100	.097	Tom Libby	4-1-2004
10-200	.202	Fred Hasecuster	9-15-1989
10-300	.516	Wayne Campbell	8-27-2005

Yardage Aggregates	Size	Shooter	Date
5-5 at 100	.1283	Steve Kostanich	8-10-2003
5-5 at 200	.1396	Bart Sauter	7-4-2003
5-5 at 300	.1801	Lee Andrews	5-23-1983
5-10 at 100	.1945	Tony Boyer	9-2-2000
5-10 at 200	.2079	Wayne Campbell	9-10-2005
5-10 at 300	.2660	Jeff Graves	9-20-2003
8-10 at 100	.2165	Lester Bruno	9-17-2001
8-10 at 200	.1928	Lester Bruno	9-27-2005

Grand Aggregates	Size	Shooter	Date
5-5 at 100,200	.1496	Bill Forrester	8-12-1989
5-5 at 200,300	.2578	Art Freund	7-11-1981
5-5 at 1,2 300	.2515	Lee Andrews	5-28-1983
5-10 at 100,200	.2148	Tony Boyer	9-2-2000
5-10 at 200,300	.3567	Ed Watson	7-14-1984
5-10 at 1,2,300	.3555	Walt Berger	6-26-1982
8-10 at 100,200	.2096	Lester Bruno	9-27-2005

IBS - Sporter Class - yards

Single Groups	Size	Shooter	Date
5-100	.060	Jack Neary	8-10-2005
5-200	.140	Lester Bruno	8-23-1990
5-300	.329	J. Cowles	6-8-1991

Yardage Aggregates	Size	Shooter	Date
5-5 at 100	.1696	Allie Euber	8-22-2003
5-5 at 200	.1919	Russ Boop	8-20-1998
5-5 at 300	.2835	Allie Euber	6-8-1991

Grand Aggregates	Size	Shooter	Date
100, 200	.1977	Tony Boyer	8-21-1996
200, 300	.2811	Allie Euber	6-1-1991
1,2 & 300	N/A		

IBS - Light Varmint Class - yards

Single Groups	Size	Shooter	Date
5-100	.054	H. Hoffer	7-2-1983
5-200	.134	Glenn Newick	8-16-1985
5-300	.240	Dale Boop	7-30-2000

Yardage Aggregates	Size	Shooter	Date
5-5 at 100	.1605	Pat McMillan	8-4-1977
5-5 at 200	.1652	Wayne Campbell	8-20-2004
5-5 at 300	.1937	Bill Sutton	7-30-2000

Grand Aggregates	Size	Shooter	Date
100, 200	.1998	Lee Euber	8-23-1990
200, 300	.2253	Dave Bruno	7-17-2005
1,2 & 300	.2272	Dave Bruno	7-17-2005

IBS - Heavy Varmint - yards

Single Groups	Size	Shooter	Date
5-100	.052	J. Ventriglia	8-16-1980
5-200	.109	J. Greene	7-10-1994
5-300	.259	T. Horenburg	6-20-1987

Yardage Aggregates	Size	Shooter	Date
5-5 at 100	.1582	R. Czarnota	9-9-2000
5-5 at 200	.1602	Tony Boyer	8-22-1992
5-5 at 300	.1828	T. Horenburg	6-20-1987

Grand Aggregates	Size	Shooter	Date
100, 200	.1675	Tony Boyer	8-22-1992
200, 300	.2269	D. Collins	6-21-1987
1,2 & 300	.2429	Dave Bruno	7-17-2005

IBS - Heavy Bench (Unlimited) - yards

Single Groups	Size	Shooter	Date
5-100	.063	H. Zeiser	8-30-1958
5-200	.152	A. Snyder	12-6-2003
5-300	.739	W. Miller	9-19-1982
10-100	.119	Dick Maretzo	9-10-1983
10-200	.245	Ed Watson	7-26-1999
10-300	.669	Bob Adamowicz	6-13-1992

Yardage Aggregates	Size	Shooter	Date
5-5 at 100	.1386	R. Howell	12-3-2004
5-5 at 200	.1616	Lester Bruno	12-6-2004
5-5 at 300	.4095	W. Miller	9-19-1982
5-10 at 100	.1898	Lester Bruno	8-16-2004
5-10 at 200	.2234	Ed Watson	8-21-1990
5-10 at 300	.3495	Dale Boop	6-18-1988

Grand Aggregates	Size	Shooter	Date
5-5 at 100,200	.1575	Lester Bruno	12-3-2004
5-10 at 100,200	.2298	Smiley Hensley	8-18-1992
5-10 at 200,300	.3524	Dale Boop	6-18-1988
5-10 at 1,2,300	.6386	A. King	9-5-1976

IBS - Multi Gun - yards

Grand Aggregates	Size	Shooter	Date
LV-HV at 100	.1867	Jim Prettie	9-28-1996
LV-HV at 200	.2273	A. Skiver	9-30-1995
LV-SP at 100-200	.2586	Lee Euber	8-19-1987
LV-HV at 100-200	.1966	Tony Boyer	8-22-1992
LV-HV at 200-300	.2264	B. Weider	6-22-1986
SP-LV-HB 1,2	.1970	Tony Boyer	8-22-1992
LV-HV-HB 1,2	.2949	Dick Maretzo	8-21-1983
SP-LV-HV-HB 1,2	.2204	Tony Boyer	8-22-1992

IBS - Sporter Class - meters

Single Groups	Size	Shooter	Date
5-100	.090	J. Oliver	8-31-1985
5-200	.245	Mike Gamble	8-29-2002
5-300	.817	D. Kiel	5-30-1969

Yardage Aggregates	Size	Shooter	Date
5-5 at 100	.2100	Wayne Campbell (moa.1919)	8-28-2002
5-5 at 200	.2198	Mike Gamble (moa.2009)	8-29-2002
5-5 at 300	.4989	W. Dunn (moa .4562)	5-30-1969

Grand Aggregates	Size	Shooter	Date
100, 200	.2308	Clay Spencer (moa .2170)	8-29-2002

IBS - Light Varmint Class - meters

Single Groups	Size	Shooter	Date
5-100	.085	B. Weider	9-3-1984
5-200	.197	Dave Pessall	8-29-2002
5-300	.887	D. Hall	5-30-1969

Yardage Aggregates	Size	Shooter	Date
5-5 at 100	.1898	John Brown (moa .1735)	8-28-2002
5-5 at 200	.2053	Jack Neary (moa .1876)	8-29-2002
5-5 at 300	.5527	T. Seitz (moa .5054)	6-22-1968

Grand Aggregates	Size	Shooter	Date
100, 200	.2047	Jack Neary (moa .1871)	8-29-2002

IBS - Heavy Varmint Class - meters

Single Groups	Size	Shooter	Date
5-100	.061	Allie Euber	9-6-1981
5-200	.133	G. Manfredini	4-27-1986
5-300	.787	Bassett	10-6-1968

Yardage Aggregates	Size	Shooter	Date
5-5 at 100	.1812	R. Maretzo (moa .1657)	2-13-1983
5-5 at 200	.2183	F. Obrachta (moa .1996)	6-27-1982
5-5 at 300	.4646	Mick (moa .4243)	5-7-1967

Grand Aggregates	Size	Shooter	Date
100, 200	.2391	Nate Boop (moa .2186)	9-4-1983

IBS - Heavy Bench (Unlimited) - meters

Single Groups	Size	Shooter	Date
5-300	.605	Paul Gottschall	5-9-1965
10-100	.183	M. Bennett	8-26-2002
10-200	.291	Butch Wahl	8-27-2002
10-300	.918	Rhinehart	8-30-1957

Yardage Aggregates	Size	Shooter	Date
5-5 at 300	.3547	Demoise (moa .3243)	5-14-1966
5-10 at 100	.2692	Allie Euber (moa .2462)	9-6-1981
5-10 at 200	.3242	Bart Sauter (moa .2963)	8-27-2002
5-10 at 300	.5105	A. Angerman (moa .4668)	6-1-1969

Grand Aggregates	Size	Shooter	Date
5-10 at 100,200	.2973	Allie Euber (moa .2719)	9-7-1981

IBS - Multi Gun - meters

Grand Aggregates	Size	Shooter	Date
LV-HV at 100-200	.2540	Pat Byrne (moa .2321)	8-31-2002

World Benchrest Shooting Federation
World Benchrest Championship Records

Team Two Gun Aggregate Record

USA2 (Skip Otto, Bob White, Mike Ratigan, Glenn Newick)   Italy 1999   .2552

Individual Records

Two Gun

LV & HV 100, 200 yards   Mike Ratigan   USA   Italy 1999   .2317

Light Varmint

Single Groups	Shooter	Country	Where	Year	Size
5-100	Giuliano Turine	ITA	Italy	1999	.073
5-200	Tony Boyer	USA	New Zealand	2001	.214

Yardage Aggs	Shooter	Country	Where	Year	Size
5-5 at 100	Brendan Atkinson	AUS	New Zealand	2001	.1588
5-5 at 200	Mike Ratigan	USA	Italy	1999	.2180

Grand Agg	Shooter	Country	Where	Yeat	Size
100, 200	Mike Ratigan	USA	Italy	1999	.2090

Heavy Varmint

Single Groups	Shooter	Country	Where	Year	Size
5-100	Joachim Schaefer	GER	Italy	1999	.049
5-200	Giuliano Turini	ITA	Italy	1999	.170
10-200	Bill Gammon	CAN	Ohio USA	2005	.371
5-300	Enrico Arenzi	ITA	Phoenix	1997	.482

Yardage Aggs	Shooter	Country	Where	Year	Size
5-5 at 100	Paul Jung	FRA	Italy	1999	.1860
5-5 at 200	Enrico Arenzi	ITA	Italy	1999	.2161
5-10 at 200	Karl Dieter Kochendorfer	GER	Italy	1999	.2924
5-5 at 300	Enrico Arenzi	ITA	Phoenix USA	1997	.2767

Grand Agg	Shooter	Country	Where	Yeat	Size
100, 200	Paul Jung	FRA	Italy	1999	.2193

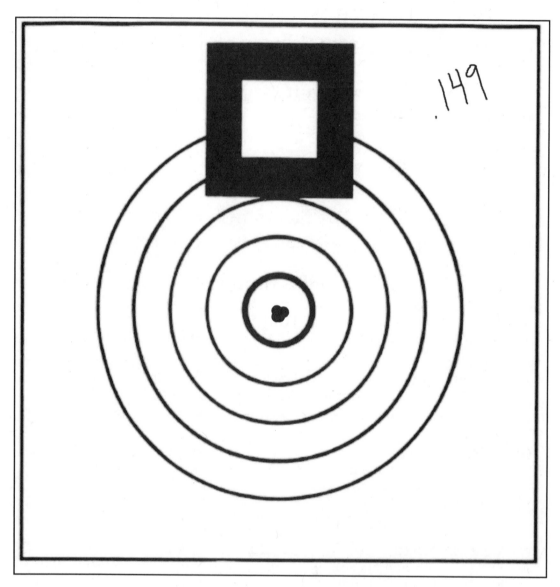

149

NBRSA 300 yard Heavy Varmint Group Record.
Shot by Gary Ocock on April 5 1998.

In the words of another well known shooter, after noticing Gary was cleaning his rifle,

"You CAN'T be Done!"

Glossary

220 Russian	The parent case for forming into a PPC
Accurized	Reworking of an action, or rifle, for improved grouping ability. Normally a production (factory) action.
Accuracy	The ability of the rifle to place a bullet on a specific spot.
Action	The heart of the rifle. Where the barrel is threaded into, where the trigger and scope are attached, and where the bolt fits into.
Action Wrench	A tool used to provide leverage for unscrewing the barrel. The barrel is clamped into a barrel vise.
Aggregate	Average group size at 100 yards, in minute of angle (MOA). Average group size at 200 yards divided by 2. Average of group size at 300 yards divided by 3.
Anvil	The portion of the primer on which the primer mixture is crushed when the firing pin strikes the primer thus; causing ignition.
Arbor Press	Small press used for mechanical advantage for the purpose of neck sizing or bullet seating.
Backers	See Moving Backers and Stationary Backers

Bag Gun	Rifle used in Benchrest competition shot off a front rest and rear sand bag.
Bag Squeezer	A shooter who aims a bag gun by squeezing the rear bag.
Bag Stabilizer	See Prairie Dog Life Raft. A raft shaped bag, or piece of rubber, used to help stabilize the rear sand bag.
Ballistic Coefficient	The ratio of the bullet mass to a function of the aerodynamic drag force.
Barrel Tenon	The threaded portion of a barrel which screws into the action.
Barrel Vise	When clamped to the barrel, is used with an action wrench for the removal of a rifle barrel. Many barrel vises are mobile tools for use at the range.
Bedding	Part of the rifle stock that the action fits onto. Typically the action is set onto epoxy and removed when dried. When the epoxy dries, the action fits perfectly onto the dried bed of epoxy. Benchrest actions are then glued to the bedding.
Blacken the Hole	How to describe what happens when shooting at your previous bullet hole. When firing subsequent shots that do not enlarge the hole, just blacken one side of the hole. "After the first shot my next three shots just blackened the right side of the hole".
Blow	Benchrest slang term for a strong or heavy wind.
Blown Primer	Hole in the primer caused by chamber overpressure. This hole in the primer is caused by the pressure pushing the firing pin to the rear, then pushing the primer into the hole.
Boat Tail	Style of bullet with a taper on the back end.
Boil	Mirage that appears to travel straight vertical.
Bolt	Heart of the action, containing the firing pin, bolt handle, firing pin sear, bolt lugs, bolt face, extractor claw, and ejector pin(if equipped).

Bolt Holster   A leather or nylon carrier for a rifle bolt. Bolt Holsters are typically carried on a belt or clipped onto a waist line or pocket.

Bolt Shroud   The portion of the rear of the bolt which helps align the firing pin and sear for engagement with the trigger sear.

Bore   Center of the barrel.

Bore Cleaning   Use of patches and brushes to clean the inside of the rifle barrel. Always patch out the solvent before firing a shot.

Bore Guide   A rod inserted into the action to prevent the cleaning rod from rubbing against the rifling in the throat. The bore guide also prevents solvent from running into the action or trigger and bedding.

Bore Scope   A tool for inspecting inside small spaces like the inside of a rifle barrel.

Bug Hole   Benchrest Slang for a tiny group. Not necessarily a finished group. "I had a bug hole until I fired the last shot".

Bull Barrel   Term used to describe a heavier than standard barrel.

Bullet Launcher   Slang term used to describe a rifle.

Bullet Seating Depth   The depth that the bullet is seated into the case neck. Also refers to the relationship of the bullet to the throat of the barrel.

Burning Rate   Description of the speed at which powder burns. Faster and slower are typical approximations.

Bushing   See Neck Bushing or Firing Pin Bushing

Button   Carbide tool used to form the rifling lands and grooves when pulled through a barrel.

Calling the Shot   Knowing where the bullet should go before you fire it.

Cant   Any deviation in the sight to bore axis from vertical.

Case   Piece of brass that holds the powder, primer, and bullet.

Case Trimming	To remove metal from the open end of the case. This is done to provide clearance to the end of the chamber and to obtain case to case uniformity.
Cash Option	A optional program at some tournaments to shoot for money.
CG	Center of gravity.
Chamber	The cavity in a rifle barrel that contains a cartridge up to the start of the throat or leade.
Chase	What is done when the first shot did not hit where it should. "I had to chase the first shot, it was high and left".
Chronograph	A measuring tool for measuring the speed of a bullet, normally expressed in feet per second (fps) or meters per second.
Cleaning Rod	A thin rod used to clean barrels. Many of these rods are coated in plastic to protect the barrel from the metal interior of the rod. Almost 100% of shooters use two rods, one equipped with a jag, one with a brush. It takes only minutes to become tired of changing back and forth between the two.
Click(s)	Benchrest slang for a unit of measurement on many powder measures used in Benchrest. "I went up two clicks on the measure".
Comparator	Tool used to measure the a relative seating depth.
Concentricity	When the centerline of two concentric circles are parallel they are concentric. If the wall thickness of a case is exactly the same around the circumference, then the outside diameter and inside diameter are concentric. If the centerline of the bullet is the same as the centerline of the body of the case, then they are concentric.
Concentricity Checker	A specialty tool used to measure concentricity.
Condition	Benchrest slang term for atmospheric and light conditions. "I am afraid of that condition" or "I didn't see the condition change, it cost me the grand".
Coned Bolt Face	Where an angle is cut onto the front of a bolt. A matching angle is cut onto the barrel making feeding the case easier. The most common cone angle is 30 degrees.

Copper Fouling	Bullet jacket material stripped from the bullet jacket during the act of firing. This fouling can be detrimental to accuracy.
Creep	When the trigger moves without breaking. What you think of the guy that beats you for small group at the Super Shoot.
Crown	The metal work done to the end of the barrel where the bullet exits. The crown should let go of the bullet all the way around at the same time.
Cruiser	Heavy rifle that does not qualify to shoot in any class of competition except the Unlimited or Heavy Bench, but is not a conventional rail gun. Most cruisers look like a regular bench gun only larger, bigger barrel, stock, etc.
Daisy	A plastic pin wheel used as a decoration, adapted for use on the front of many popular wind flags. This daisy on a flag is commonly used to aid in the determination of the angle.
De-Capping Pin	A hand tool or pin used to remove fired primers.
Die Wax	Lube applied to a fired case to ease the full length sizing operation, so the case does not stick in the die.
Die Shims	Great invention, used in conjunction with sizing and seating dies. Shims of different thicknesses are removed and added to make predictable changes to seater top and die adjustment.
Doping	Holding in different spots on the target. Many of the Top Guns in Benchrest change their hold as the conditions change and hit in the same spot.
Double	When you and a neighbor shoot at the exactly the same time.Many times, whomever goes second will be adversely affected on the target. "I doubled with the guy on my left".
Drop Port	Action with a hole in the bottom for the fired case to drop through onto the bench. This is to help speed up the rate of fire.
Dual Port	Action with a small hole on the opposite side of the loading port to eject the fired case. If it's a left port action, there will be a right ejection port.
Elevation	Vertical sight adjustment (up and down).

Ejector	Part of the bolt or action responsible for ejecting the empty or fired case.
Ejection Port	Small hole in the action where the fired case comes out. Most actions with dedicated ejection ports are referred to as "dual port" or "drop port" actions.
Erosion	Hot combustion gases that wear away small pieces of metal out of the inside of the barrel. Through a bore scope the surface of the barrel showing erosion looks like an alligator hide.
Excuse	Long list of reasons why you messed up your group.
Extreme Spread	The difference between the lowest and highest muzzle velocities of a group of bullets and the dimension between the centers of the widest bullet holes in a group.
Farley Rest	Jim Farley, the developer of the coaxial front rest. A single joystick is used to adjust the windage and elevation at the same time.
Fire Forming	The process of forming a case to a bigger chamber by firing it with the bullet firmly jammed into the lands.
Fire Forming Bullet	A bullet of below average quality used when fire forming cases, instead of using good quality bullets.
Firing Line	Usually assumed to be the front edge of the bench. If the firing line is a point other than the front edge of the bench, it should be clearly marked. During a tournament, the front of the barrel must be forward of the firing line, the shooter must stay behind the line.
Firing Pin Bushing	The firing pin hole in the front of the bolt is bored out and bushed to a smaller size to reduce the pin diameter. This is done to eliminate primer piercing.
Firing Pin Protrusion	How far the firing pin extends past the bolt face when the firing pin is let down in the fired position.
First Shot Trouble	This is when you fire the first shot on the record target (top portion) and the shot does not hit where it was supposed to.
Flat Base	A style of bullet with a flat bottom or base. This type of bullet is used by the majority of Benchrest shooters.

Flyer	A bullet that goes someplace unexpected for no reason.
Four Gun	Combination of four grand aggregates divided by four.
Fouled	A term used to describe when a rifle barrel no longer shoots to it's potential because of continued firing without cleaning.
Fouling	Copper and carbon inside of the barrel after firing.
Fouling Shot	A shot or shots to foul the barrel after cleaning. Many times the fouling shot or shots will impact at a different point on the target.
fps	Abbreviation for "feet per second". Common reference to describe the speed of a bullet.
Free Floating	Used to describe a barrel which does not contact the stock at any point. In Benchrest, the clearance between the stock and barrel will exceed 1/8 of an inch or .125.
Free Recoil	Describes the act of shooting a rifle while it rests on a front rest and rear bag without holding the rifle. The only part of the shooter to touch the rifle is the trigger finger. The rifle is aimed by moving the front rest top or the rear sand bag.
Full Length Die	Resizing die that reduces the length of case while also slightly reducing the body diameter.
Glue-in	When the action is glued to the stock, it's referred to as a glue-in. The most common glue used to glue an action and stock is slow dry JB Weld.
Grain	Unit of weight. There are 7000 grains in one pound.
Grand Aggregate	The average of two yardage aggregates. For example, you have a .2013 100 yard aggregate and a .3208 200 yard aggregate. Your Grand would be .26105,
Groove	The large portion of the rifling, or major diameter. This is also the barrel diameter, .243 for a 6mm or .224 for a 22 caliber.
Group Size	The distance between the centers of bullet holes that have the largest spread in a group. Also Precision.
H322	Common powder from Hodgen for the PPC.

Headspace	The distance between the bolt face and the shoulder of the chamber. Excessive headspace can be very dangerous.
Handloading	Process of loading to increase accuracy with hand tools.
Heavy Bench	Unrestricted class of rifle competition used in the IBS. There are no weight limits, stock or barrel size limits, rest restrictions, or configuration limitations.
Heavy Varmint (HV)	Bag gun of any caliber limited to 13 1/2 pounds, still the most popular class in competition, and the easiest bag gun class to shoot.
Hold Over	Changing the position of the crosshairs based on the current flag readings. "I held two inches on the other side of the target for the last shot, and I hit the first four shots".
Hollow Point	The only bullet type used in Benchrest. It's safe to say "The most accurate type of bullet ever". The hollow point bullet has very little lead in the area of the front of the bullet where the jacket folds in to create the point. This keeps the majority of the mass in the unaltered area of the bullet.
Hunter Class	Score shooting rifle class. Hunter rifles are limited to 10 pounds, have case capacity minimums, 6 power maximum scope magnification, and shot at 100, 200 and 300 yards.
IBS	Abbreviation for the International Benchrest Shooters, mainly in the northeast region of the United States.
Jag	The removable tip of the cleaning rod used to push a patch through the barrel.
Jam	A point where the bullet is pushed back to by the rifling. This point is dependent on the neck tension. The more tension the farther out the bullet jam distance will be. The lighter the neck tension, the farther back the bullet will be pushed by the rifling.
Kentucy Windage	A method of correcting for windage by aiming to one side of the target instead of adjusting the sighting system.
Keyhole	An out-of-round hole in the target caused by a bullet that is not completely stable.

Knockout Pin	The punch used to eject a bullet after being pushed into the point up die. Pull the handle to form the point on the bullet, then return the handle until the knockout pin ejects the finished bullet from the point up die.
Lands	The raised ribs separating the groves in a rifle barrel.
Lap	Soft metal slug coated with a mild abrasive and stroked through the barrel to remove minor tooling marks and help make the bore and land height more uniform.
Leade	The throat portion of the chamber. It's the beginning of the rifling in the barrel. The lands are cut away at this angle to ease the engagement of the bullet into the rifling.
Let-up	Decrease in wind velocity. "I got caught by the let-up."
Light Varmint (LV)	Benchrest rifle class, limited to 10.5 pounds, of any caliber.
Loading Area	Where competitors gather to assemble their reloads. Some ranges have buildings to reload, some have outdoor loading pavilions.
Loading Block	A container used to hold cases while loading and transporting the loaded rounds to and from the firing line. Some loading blocks are completely enclosed to help protect from dirt and rain.
Loading Density	When a case is filled with powder to the bottom of the bullet, you have 100% loading density.
Loading Port	Opening on the side of the action for placing the loaded cartridges into the action (also see ejection port).
Lock Time	Time for the firing pin to strike the primer after the trigger sear disengages.
Lot Number	Used to identify specific powder, bullets, and primers. When an accurate component is discovered, many shooters will buy large quantities of the exact same lot numbered components.
Machine Rest	Also known as an Unlimited Rest or Return to battery rest. These rests eliminate any holding error by guiding the rifle to exactly the same aiming point shot after shot. These rests will not eliminate the need for wind flags.

Make Weight	At nearly every registered Benchrest tournament, rifles are weighed to ensure they are not over the maximum allowable weight. You must "make weight."
Match	Used interchangeably for either an individual group or an entire event. "I just shot the second record match", or "I've been to five matches this year".
Micrometer Top	Adjustable top for a bullet seater graduated around the circumference of the top. This allows the user to make predictable adjustments to the seater top.
mil	One thousandth of an inch.
Minute of Angle (MOA)	1/60th of a degree. At 100 yards this is 1.047 inches, generally acknowledged as one inch at 100 yards, 2 inches at 200 yards, 3 inches at 300 yards and so on.
Mirage	The bending or reflection of light rays by layers of heated air of varying density. The end result is the target is not where you see it.
Mirage Board	Black and white stripes oriented horizontally used as an aid to help read the mirage.
Mirage Shield	A thin piece of material attached to the barrel that deflects the heat generated by the barrel around where you look through with the rifle scope.
mm	Millimeter, 1/1000 of a meter, 1/25.4 of an inch.
Moly	Short for molybdenum disulfide (MoS2). A dry lubricant that's been used as a bullet coating to extend accuracy life between cleanings.
Moving Backer	A card that moves horizontally back and fourth behind the record portion of the target to record the number of shots fired at the record target. In a five shot match there must be five shots in the backer, ten for a ten shot match.
N133	Gun powder manufactured by VihtaVuori Oy of VihtaVuori, Finland, widely used in the 6PPC and short 22's.
NBRSA	National Benchrest Shooters Association. The organization which first organized the sport of Benchrest shooting and who sanctions tournaments in the whole of the USA. The

NBRSA currently represents the USA to the World Benchrest Shooting Federation.

Neck Bushing — Small pieces of metal tubing that have very accurately sized holes used for precisely sizing the neck of a case. Bushings are used in neck sizing and full length dies and are made of car bide in increments to .0005, coated and uncoated steel in increments of .001, and give about any desired neck tension.

Neck Sizing — The type of partial resizing used mostly by Benchrest shoot ers. The body of the case is not sized, it is left unaltered. Only the neck is reduced, just enough to hold a new bullet.

Neck Tension — The amount of "grip" a case neck has on the bullet.

Neck Turning — The process of removing metal from the neck of a case where by reducing the thickness. This also make the neck a uniform thickness around the circumference.

Over-all-length (OAL) — The length of the loaded round measured to the bul let nose. This measurement is of no value to the precision reloader. When the bullets are seated properly, the length will vary slightly because the length of the bullet, base to tip, is the only part of the bullet that varies in dimension. This measurement is of value only to a shooter using a magazine where the loaded round might be longer than the magazine.

Official Screamer — Slang term used to describe a group below .100 at 100 yards, below .200-.250 at 200 yards and .300-.399 at 300 yards. Precision Shooting Magazine gives a patch to any shooter who shoots a group smaller than .100, .250 and .399 in any NBRSA or IBS tournament. "I shot an Official Screamer".

Ogive — Portion of the bullet where the curve starts ahead of the base.

Patch — Small pieces of cloth used to clean a barrel. "I run a couple of wet patches before brushing, then a couple patches to dry out the solvent".

Parallax — An Optical problem in a telescopic sight where the image (target) appears to move when the eye is moved off of the optical axis (center) of the scope. Test by moving eye up and down slightly while looking through scope. If the crosshairs appear to move on the target, you have parallax error.

Paper Puncher — Term for a target shooter or target rifle.

Pedestal	Portion of the front rest which holds up the rest top.

Prairie Dog Life Raft Rear Bag Stabilizer. A sand bag in the shape of a small raft that is used to help stabilize the rear bag and keep it from rocking. The one made of leather was originally conceived by Skip Otto (deceased).

Pillar Bed

A style of bedding for a bolt in rifle action which helps negate the effects of temperature and humidity.

Pin Wheel

1. A term used mainly by score shooters to describe a shot that lands exactly in the center of the target,
2. Plastic wheel used to aid in determination of angle.

Powder Measure

An adjustable device which gives semi repeatable volumetric charges of gunpowder every time it is operated. It's a common misconception that Benchrest powder measures can drop to +/- .1 grains every time, they CANNOT.

PPC

The Palmisano-Pindell Cartridge, which in one form or another is used by about 99.987630% of Benchrest shooters, except Larry Baggett, Larry Engelbrecht and George Kelbly Sr, soon to change his first name to Larry.

Precision

The ability to place every bullet into the same spot on the target. Generally, accuracy is used in place of precision but they mean different things. Accuracy is to hit a specific spot.

Preload

To bring enough loaded ammunition to shoot a tournament with out reloading at the range. Preloading is rarely done in Benchrest, most shooters load at the range between targets.

Pressure Ring

A small oversize ring on the heel of some bullets, produced during their manufacture.

Quit

Something you'll not be able to do once you get hooked on this shooting sport.

Rain Shot

Major impact point change caused normally by water entering the muzzle of the rifle. It is possible to strike a raindrop in flight, it too will result in major impact changes and a non-round hole in the target.

Rail Gun

A rail gun has a barrel and action clamped to a carriage which slides on rails that ride on bearings (can be plastic bearings). They are usually heavy and are used for testing purposes, although they are used in Benchrest Unlimited competition where the idea was born.

Read Used to describe the ability to hold for changes in the wind conditions. "I read that change perfectly, held two rings to the right and put the last shot right into the group".

Rechamber Cutting off the threads and most of the old portion of the chamber and cutting a new chamber. Sometimes used in an attempt to get the last little bit of good from an outstanding barrel, or to change the size of the chamber, say from a full length 22PPC to a .100 short.

Record Match Match that counts toward your aggregate score.

Record Shot An individual bullet fired at the top portion of the target, which will be counted in the measurement of the group size. Bag gun or Varmint classes are five shots, Unlimited and Heavy Bench are 10 shots.

Record Target 1. The top portion of the target. Any shot above the top line of the sighter target is a record shot. Any bullet above the top line of the sighter target and not touching the outline of the record portion of the target is also a penalty.
2. Any target group smaller than the previous small group. "I just shot a new NBRSA record".

Relay Having more shooters than benches requires relays. Each relay will shoot in turn. Each relay will shoot match 1 start ing with relay one. When relay one finishes their first group they remove their equipment, then relay 2 will shoot, etc. At the major tournaments, it's common to have several relays, the Super Shoot normally has 6-7 relays.

Rests The pedestal and sandbags, or machine rest which rifles are shot from.

Reload What happens between record targets by replacing primers, powder, and bullets. Typically a Benchrest shooter will shoot one record target, then head back to the loading area to
reload his fired cases from the previous target.

Reverse Change of conditions from one direction to the opposite.

Ribbon Slang for surveyor's ribbon commonly used for flag tails.

Rimfire | A rimfire is a type of firearm cartridge. It's called a rimfire because, instead of the firing pin striking the primer cap at the center of the base of the cartridge to ignite it (as in a centerfire cartridge), the pin strikes the base's rim. The rim contains the priming compound, used to light the powder. Once the cartridge has been struck and discharged it cannot be reloaded, as the head is deformed by the firing pin impact.

Class of rifle used for score or group shooting at 50 and 100 yards. There are several different governing body's outside of the NBRSA and IBS all which use different targets, most shoot for score.

Run Out (RO) | The measurement taken on the surface of a cylinder with a dial gauge that is rotated about a longitudinal axis, not necessarily on it's centerline.

Sail Tail | Wind flag tail made of material that is starched into a semi circle. These tails are used by shooters who do not want to see the flutter of the standard surveyor ribbon tail.

Sandbags | Mostly leather or cordura bags made in many different styles and sizes which the front and rear of the rifle are supported.

Scharnhorst Maneuver | 1. Most generally used to describe leaving after the first bad group or two, no matter how far you had too travel. 2. Also used to describe planting a rifle, barrel first in the mud after shooting a bad group or two.

Scope | Optical high powered sighting device.

Scope Checker | Special mount to allow the use of two scopes mounted on the same rifle at the same time for the purpose of testing the scopes for impact point shifts.

Scope Screws | External screws added opposite of the turrets to aid in holding the erector tube still when shooting.

Sear | Upper part of the trigger that holds the firing pin back or cocked and is released when the trigger is moved to the rear, allowing the firing pin to fall.

Seater | Bullet seating die, mostly referring to straight line hand seater.

Shooter | Term used to describe an accurate rifle.

Sizer	Either a full length die or neck sizing die.
Shoot Through	A condition your rifle should be able to shoot through with out looking at a flag, and shoot a good group.
Shoulder Gage	A simple piece of metal that fits over the case neck to measure the amount of shoulder set back when seating up a full length or shoulder bump die.
Shoulder Mirage	Slang term for shooting a shot out of the bottom of group by mis-using shoulder pressure. "Your last shot looked like some shoulder mirage to me".
Sighter	1. Bottom portion of the target. Usually designated by two small letters "s" on the target. 2. A shot taken at the sighter portion of the target to gage the current conditions.
Sighter Cam	An attachment to a pedestal rest to travel quickly between the record and sighter portion of the target.
Single Shot	Style of action without a magazine, able to hold only one loaded round at a time. Stiffer solid bottom action with more bedding and gluing surface area.
Sissy Bag	A sand bag placed between your shoulder and the butt stock for heavy recoiling rifles.
Slack Grabber	Slang term for a really good group. "That slack grabber will pull me way up in the stats".
Sleeve	An aluminum or steel tube epoxied or glued over the outside of an action to help make the action stiffer and increase the bedding area. I haven't seen a sleeved action for a long time in a Benchrest tournament. This procedure has fallen out of favor, most actions today are custom's.
Sporter (SP)	A 10.5 pound rifle class where you must shoot a .243 caliber or larger. Originally developed to promote experimentation.
Stationary Backer	A target behind the target used to identify crossfires.
Steering	Pressure to the stock, rear bag, or joy stick to influence aim.
Stock.	1. A better investment than shooting. 2. Part of the rifle which the action is glued or bolted to.

Stool Shootin	What we do in Benchrest.
Surveyor's Ribbon	Most common material used for wind flag tails. The most commonly used width is about 1 3/8, most common colors are safety orange, pink, and white.
Swage, bullet	Process of making custom bullets. Jacket and core are forced together into the core seating die, then ran into the swage die to close the point.
Switch	Same as a reverse. Change in wind or mirage from one direction to another.
Switch Barrel	A rifle with multiple barrels, sometimes in different calibers.
T-Powder	A gun powder packaged by Thunderbird. This powder has not been packaged since the early 1980's and is hard to find.
Tack Driver	Slang term for an accurate rifle, mainly used outside of the sport of Benchrest.
Tail	Wind flag velocity indicator.
Three Gun	Combination of three grand aggregates divided by three.
Throat	The tapered entrance just ahead of the chamber where the bullet enters the barrel. Also, "Leade".
Time Limit	How long to shoot your group. In the bag gun or Varmint classes you are allowed 7 minutes to complete your firing. Unlimited or Heavy Bench you are allowed 12 minutes. You are allowed an unlimited number of sighter shots during your time.
Tong Tool	A nutcracker type resizing tool, mainly used for neck sizing and de-priming.
Top Gun	Slang for a very good Benchrest Shooter, (long term).
True	Process of correcting misalignments commonly found in factory actions, a definite accuracy enhancer.
Turret	Scope adjustment knob. Turret adjustments are typically for windage, elevation, and sometimes parallax.
Twist	The length of the barrel the bullet must pass through to rotate 360 degrees, normally expressed in inches. Most bar-

rels for a 6PPC are a 14 twist. This means the bullet makes a complete rotation in 14 inches.

Two Gun	Combination of two grand aggregates divided by two.
Two Ounce Trigger	A trigger with a pull weight that can be set from about 1.5 ounces to about 4 ounces. Most all bench guns use two ounce triggers of some sort.

Ultimate Strength (stress) The stress where a piece of metal breaks.

Unobtainium	Things which some shooters believe is the secret to Benchrest that has not been produced for many years, sometimes decades. Things such as T-powder or a Sinclair powder measure.
Varmint	Creatures like coyotes, prairie dogs, or wood chucks. These animals started many on their search for a more accurate rifle and started the founders of Benchrest on their endless search to improve rifle accuracy. This word is used in the earliest classes of Benchrest competition; the Heavy Varmint and later the Light Varmint class.
Varmint for Score	A rifle class in the IBS where the group guns (SP, LV & HV) are used to shoot score targets. This is popular in the eastern US and allows the range owner or operator to run tournaments without the need for a moving backer system.
Wailing Wall	The area where the targets are displayed after being shot and scored. Targets must be left hanging on the wailing wall until after the aggregate has been posted and made official.
Waldog	22PPC shortened by 1/8 inch (.125) first done by Dan Dowling in 1980.
Warm-up	An optional match fired before the start of the first record match.
WBC	World Benchrest Championships
WBSF	World Benchrest Shooting Federation. World organization and sanctioning body for the WBC.
Weather Report	Bad target showing all of deflection possible from the conditions. This is the type of target you will get by aiming in the same place for every shot and not watching the flags.

Weight System   Removable weights added to the stock of a rifle for two rea-
                  sons. First would be to bring the rifle up to the class weight
                  limit. Second would be to add weight to a specific area of the
                  rifle to affect the recoil characteristics.

Wildcat   A cartridge for which there is no factory loaded ammunition.
                  Usually designed by someone looking for something better.

Wind Flag   An indicator designed to give the shooter quantifiable infor-
                  mation about the direction and intensity of the wind.

Windage   Horizontal adjustment of the sights.

Windage Top   A rest top that has the ability to adjust right and left to
                  change the aiming point for changes in the wind intensity.

Wind Drift   The absolute value of the wind affect on the bullet.

Wipe-Out   When shooting for score and you completely shoot out the
                  center dot or the "x".

Yield Strength (stress) The stress level where a piece of metal starts failing and will
                  no longer return to its original shape when the load (pres-
                  sure) is removed.